Software Design by Example

The best way to learn design in any field is to study examples, and some of the best examples of software design come from the tools programmers use in their own work. **Software Design by Example: A Tool-Based Introduction with Python** therefore builds small versions of the things programmers use in order to demystify them and give some insights into how experienced programmers think. From a file backup system and a testing framework to a regular expression matcher, a browser layout engine, and a very small compiler, we explore common design patterns, show how making code easier to test also makes it easier to re-use, and help readers understand how debuggers, profilers, package managers, and version control systems work so that they can use them more effectively.

This material can be used for self-paced study, in an undergraduate course on software design, or as the core of an intensive weeklong workshop for working programmers. Each chapter has a set of exercises ranging in size and difficulty from half a dozen lines to a full day's work. Readers should be familiar with the basics of modern Python, but the more advanced features of the language are explained and illustrated as they are introduced.

All the written material in this project can be freely re-used under the terms of the Creative Commons - Attribution license, while all of the software is made available under the terms of the Hippocratic License. All proceeds from the sale of this book will go to support the Red Door Family Shelter in Toronto.

Features:

- Teaches software design by showing programmers how to build the tools they use every day
- Each chapter includes exercises to help readers check and deepen their understanding
- All the example code can be downloaded, re-used, and modified under an open license

Dr. Greg Wilson is a programmer, author, and educator based in Toronto. He co-founded and was the first Executive Director of Software Carpentry, which has taught basic software skills to tens of thousands of researchers worldwide, and he has authored or edited over a dozen books (including two for children). Greg is a member of the Python Software Foundation and a recipient of ACM SIGSOFT's Influential Educator of the Year Award.

Software Design by Example

A Tool-Based Introduction with Python

Greg Wilson

CRC Press
Taylor & Francis Group
Boca Raton London New York

CRC Press is an imprint of the
Taylor & Francis Group, an **informa** business

A CHAPMAN & HALL BOOK

First edition published 2024
by CRC Press
2385 NW Executive Center Drive, Suite 320, Boca Raton FL 33431

and by CRC Press
4 Park Square, Milton Park, Abingdon, Oxon, OX14 4RN

CRC Press is an imprint of Taylor & Francis Group, LLC

ISBN: 978-1-032-72525-3 (hbk)
ISBN: 978-1-032-72521-5 (pbk)
ISBN: 978-1-032-72523-9 (ebk)

DOI: 10.1201/9781032725239

Typeset in Arial
by KnowledgeWorks Global Ltd.

Publisher's note: This book has been prepared from camera-ready copy provided by the authors.

Dedication

_____

This one's for Mike and Jon:
I'm glad you always found time to chat.

Contents

1

Introduction

- The complexity of a system increases more rapidly than its size.

- The best way to learn design is to study examples, and the best programs to use as examples are the ones programmers use every day.

- These lessons assume readers can write small programs and want to write larger ones, or are looking for material to use in software design classes that they teach.

- All of the content is free to read and re-use under open licenses, and all royalties from sales of this book will go to charity.

Terms defined: **cognitive load**

The best way to learn design in any field is to study examples [Schon1984; Petre2016], and the most approachable examples are ones that readers are already familiar with. These lessons therefore build small versions of tools that programmers use every day[1] to show how experienced software designers think. Along the way, they introduce some fundamental ideas in computer science that many self-taught programmers haven't encountered. We hope these lessons will help you design better software yourself, and that if you know how programming tools work, you'll be more likely to use them and better able to use them well.

1.1 Audience

This learner persona [Wilson2019] describes who this book is for:

> Maya has a master's degree in genomics. She knows enough Python to analyze data from her experiments, but struggles to write code other people can use. These lessons will show her how to design, build, and test large programs in less time and with less pain.

Like Maya, you should be able to:

- Write Python programs using lists, loops, conditionals, dictionaries, and functions.

- Puzzle your way through Python programs that use classes and exceptions.

- Run basic Unix shell commands like `ls` and `mkdir`.

- Read and write a little bit of HTML.

- Use Git[2] to save and share files. (It's OK not to know the more obscure commands[3].)

---

[1] https://en.wikipedia.org/wiki/Programming_tool
[2] https://git-scm.com/
[3] https://git-man-page-generator.lokaltog.net/

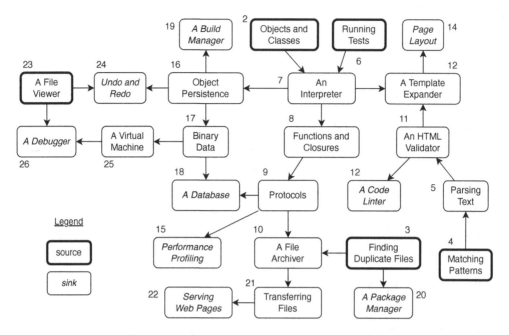

Figure 1.1: Lesson topics and dependencies.

These chapters (Figure 1.1) are also designed to help another persona:

Yim teaches two college courses on software development. They are frustrated that so many books talk about details but not about design and use examples that their students can't relate to. This book will give them material they can use in class and starting points for course projects.

1.2   The Big Ideas

Our approach to design is based on three big ideas. First, as the number of components in a system grows, the complexity of the system increases rapidly (Figure 1.2). However, the number of things we can hold in working memory at any time is fixed and fairly small [Hermans2021]. If we want to build large programs that we can understand, we therefore need to construct them out of pieces that interact in a small number of ways. Figuring out what those pieces and interactions should be is the core of what we call "design".

Second, "making sense" depends on who we are. When we use a low-level language, we incur the **cognitive load** of assembling micro-steps into something more meaningful. When we use a high-level language, on the other hand, we incur a similar load translating functions of functions into actual operations on actual data.

More experienced programmers are more capable at both ends of the curve, but that's not the only thing that changes. If a novice's comprehension curve looks like the lower one in Figure 1.3, then an expert's looks like the upper one. Experts don't just understand more at all levels of abstraction; their *preferred* level has also shifted so they find $\sqrt{x^2 + y^2}$ easier to read than the Medieval equivalent "the side of the square whose area is the sum of the areas of the two squares whose sides are given by the first part and the second part". This

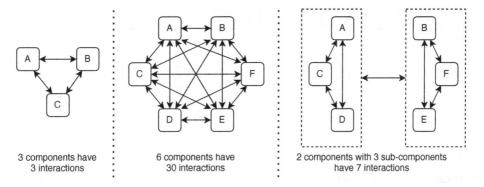

3 components have
3 interactions

6 components have
30 interactions

2 components with 3 sub-components
have 7 interactions

Figure 1.2: How complexity grows with size.

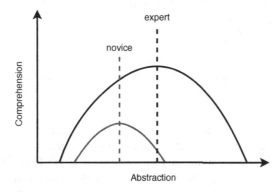

Figure 1.3: Novice and expert comprehension curves.

curve means that for any given task, the code that is quickest for a novice to comprehend will almost certainly be different from the code that an expert can understand most quickly.

Our third big idea is that programs are just another kind of data. Source code is just text, which we can process like other text files. Likewise, a program in memory is just a data structure that we can inspect and modify like any other. Treating code like data enables us to solve hard problems in elegant ways, but at the cost of increasing the level of abstraction in our programs. Once again, finding the balance is what we mean by "design".

1.3 Formatting

We display Python source code like this:

```
for ch in "example":
    print(ch)
```

and Unix shell commands like this:

```
for filename in *.dat
do
    cut -d , -f 10 $filename
done
```

Data files and program output are shown like this:

```
- name: read
  params:
  - sample_data.csv
```

```
alpha
beta
gamma
delta
```

We use ... to show where lines have been omitted, and occasionally break lines in unnatural ways to make them fit on the page. Where we do this, we end all but the last line with a single backslash \. Finally, we show glossary entries in **bold text** and write functions as `function_name` rather than `function_name()`. The latter is more common, but the empty parentheses makes it hard to tell whether we're talking about the function itself or a call to the function with no parameters.

1.4 Usage

The source for this book is available in our Git repository[4] and all of it can be read on our website[5]. All of the written material in this book is licensed under the Creative Commons - Attribution - NonCommercial 4.0 International license[6] (CC-BY-NC-4.0), while the software is covered by the Hippocratic License[7]. The first license allows you to use and remix this material for noncommercial purposes, as-is or in adapted form, provided you cite its original source; if you want to sell copies or make money from this material in any other way, you must contact us[8] and obtain permission first. The second license allows you to use and remix the software on this site provided you do not violate international agreements governing human rights; please see Appendix D for details.

If you would like to improve what we have, add new material, or ask questions, please file an issue in our GitHub repository[9] or send an email[10]. All contributors are required to abide by our Code of Conduct (Appendix E).

1.5 What People Are Saying

Here's what people said about the JavaScript version of this book [Wilson2022a]:

- Jessica Kerr[11]: "*Software Design by Example* is the book I'll recommend to every new dev... It is nice to you. It wants you to succeed... It's a bridge from 'learn to program' to working programmer."

---

[4]https://github.com/gvwilson/sdxpy/
[5]https://third-bit.com/sdxpy/
[6]https://creativecommons.org/licenses/by-nc/4.0/
[7]https://firstdonoharm.dev/
[8]mailto:gvwilson@third-bit.com
[9]https://github.com/gvwilson/sdxpy/
[10]mailto:gvwilson@third-bit.com
[11]https://jessitron.com/2023/02/20/book-review-software-design-by-example/

- Jenn Schiffer[12]: "I am v much enjoying gvwilson's book *Software Design by Example*. It makes me miss teaching, it would be such a fun text to use!"

- Emily Gorcenski[13]: "There's a lot of books on programming but fewer books that couple software development with effective and practical use of tools, presenting a language not as a main course but as a part of an engineering ecosystem. Greg Wilson's book hits all the right notes in bringing together theory, pragmatism, and best practices."

- Danielle Navarro[14]: "The book is really bloody lovely."

1.6   Acknowledgments

Like [Wilson2022a], this book was inspired by [Kamin1990; Kernighan1979; Kernighan1981; Kernighan1983; Kernighan1988; Oram2007; Wirth1976] and by:

- *The Architecture of Open Source Applications*[15] series [Brown2011; Brown2012; Armstrong2013; Brown2016];

- Mary Rose Cook's[16] Gitlet[17];

- Matt Brubeck's[18] browser engine tutorial[19];

- *Web Browser Engineering*[20] by Pavel Panchekha[21] and Chris Harrelson[22];

- Connor Stack's[23] database tutorial[24];

- Maël Nison's[25] package manager tutorial[26];

- Paige Ruten's[27] kilo text editor[28] and Wasim Lorgat's[29] editor tutorial[30];

- Bob Nystrom's[31] *Crafting Interpreters*[32] [Nystrom2021]; and

- the posts and zines[33] created by Julia Evans[34].

---

[12]https://mastodon.social/@jenn@pixel.kitchen/109985276835264400
[13]https://emilygorcenski.com/post/book-report-software-design-by-example-by-greg-wilson/
[14]https://blog.djnavarro.net/posts/2023-05-31_software-design-by-example/
[15]https://aosabook.org/
[16]https://maryrosecook.com/
[17]http://gitlet.maryrosecook.com/
[18]https://limpet.net/mbrubeck/
[19]https://limpet.net/mbrubeck/2014/08/08/toy-layout-engine-1.html
[20]https://browser.engineering/
[21]https://pavpanchekha.com/
[22]https://twitter.com/chrishtr
[23]https://connorstack.com/
[24]https://cstack.github.io/db_tutorial/
[25]https://arcanis.github.io/
[26]https://classic.yarnpkg.com/blog/2017/07/11/lets-dev-a-package-manager/
[27]https://viewsourcecode.org/
[28]https://viewsourcecode.org/snaptoken/kilo/index.html
[29]https://wasimlorgat.com/
[30]https://github.com/seem/editor
[31]http://journal.stuffwithstuff.com/
[32]https://craftinginterpreters.com/
[33]https://wizardzines.com/
[34]https://jvns.ca/

I am grateful to Miras Adilov, Alvee Akand, Rohan Alexander, Alexey Alexapolsky, Lina Andrén, Alberto Bacchelli, Yanina Bellini Saibene, Matthew Bluteau, Adrienne Canino, Marc Chéhab, Stephen Childs, Hector Correa, Socorro Dominguez, Christian Drumm, Christian Epple, Julia Evans, Davide Fucci, Thomas Fritz, Francisco Gabriel, Florian Gaudin-Delrieu, Craig Gross, Jonathan Guyer, McKenzie Hagen, Han Qi, Fraser Hay, Alexandru Hurjui, Bahman Karimi, Carolyn Kim, Kitsios Konstantinos, Jenna Landy, Peter Lin, Zihan Liu, Becca Love, Dan McCloy, Ramiro Mejia, Michael Miller, Firas Moosvi, Joe Nash, Sheena Ng, Reiko Okamoto, Juanan Pereira, Mahmoodur Rahman, Arpan Sarkar, Silvan Schlegel, Rosan Shanmuganathan, Dave W. Smith, Stephen M. Sturdevant, Diyar Taskiran, Ece Turnator, and Yao Yundong for feedback on early drafts of this material.

I am also grateful to Shashi Kumar for help with LaTeX, to Odin Beuchat[35] for help with JavaScript, and to the creators of Black[36], flake8[37], Glosario[38], GNU Make[39], isort[40], ark[41], LaTeX[42], pip[43], Python[44], Remark[45], WAVE[46], and many other open source tools: if we all give a little, we all get a lot.

All royalties from this book will go to the Red Door Family Shelter[47] in Toronto.

1.7 Exercises

Setting Up

1. Use pip[48] to install Black[49], flake8[50], and isort[51] on your computer.

2. Run them on a few programs you have already written. (The file `setup.cfg` in the root directory of this book's GitHub repository[52] has the settings we use for these tools.) What problems do they report? Which of these reports do you disagree with?

Avoiding Potholes

Go to the GitHub repository[53] for this book and look at the open issues. Which of them can you understand? What makes the others hard to understand? What could you add, leave out, or write differently when you report a problem that you have found?

---

[35]https://www.drafolin.ch/
[36]https://black.readthedocs.io/
[37]https://flake8.pycqa.org/
[38]https://glosario.carpentries.org/
[39]https://www.gnu.org/software/make/
[40]https://pycqa.github.io/isort/
[41]https://www.dmulholl.com/docs/ark/main/
[42]https://www.latex-project.org/
[43]https://pip.pypa.io/
[44]https://www.python.org/
[45]https://remarkjs.com/
[46]https://wave.webaim.org/
[47]https://www.reddoorshelter.ca/
[48]https://pip.pypa.io/
[49]https://black.readthedocs.io/
[50]https://flake8.pycqa.org/
[51]https://pycqa.github.io/isort/
[52]https://github.com/gvwilson/sdxpy/
[53]https://github.com/gvwilson/sdxpy/

2

Objects and Classes

- Objects are useful without classes, but classes make them easier to understand.
- A well-designed class defines a contract that code using its instances can rely on.
- Objects that respect the same contract are polymorphic, i.e., they can be used interchangeably even if they do different specific things.
- Objects and classes can be thought of as dictionaries with stereotyped behavior.
- Most languages allow functions and methods to take a variable number of arguments.
- Inheritance can be implemented in several ways that differ in the order in which objects and classes are searched for methods.

Terms defined: **alias**, **argument**, **cache**, **class method**, **constructor**, **derived class**, **design by contract**, **monkey patching**, **multiple inheritance**, **object-oriented programming**, **parameter**, **polymorphism**, **recursion**, **spread**, **static method**, **upcall**, **varargs**

We are going to create a lot of objects and classes in these lessons, and they will be a lot easier to use if we understand how they are implemented. Historically, **object-oriented programming** (OOP) was invented to solve two problems:

1. What is a natural way to represent real-world "things" in code?

2. How can we organize code to make it easier to understand, test, and extend?

2.1 Objects

As a motivating problem, let's define some of the things a generic shape in a drawing package must be able to do:

```
class Shape:
    def __init__(self, name):
        self.name = name

    def perimeter(self):
        raise NotImplementedError("perimeter")

    def area(self):
        raise NotImplementedError("area")
```

A specification like this is sometimes called a **contract** because an object must satisfy it in order to be considered a shape, i.e., must provide methods with these names that do what those names suggest. For example, we can **derive** classes from `Shape` to represent squares and circles.

```python
class Square(Shape):
    def __init__(self, name, side):
        super().__init__(name)
        self.side = side

    def perimeter(self):
        return 4 * self.side

    def area(self):
        return self.side ** 2

class Circle(Shape):
    def __init__(self, name, radius):
        super().__init__(name)
        self.radius = radius

    def perimeter(self):
        return 2 * math.pi * self.radius

    def area(self):
        return math.pi * self.radius ** 2
```

Since squares and circles have the same methods, we can use them interchangeably. This is called **polymorphism**, and it reduces cognitive load by allowing the people using related things to ignore their differences:

```python
examples = [Square("sq", 3), Circle("ci", 2)]
for thing in examples:
    n = thing.name
    p = thing.perimeter()
    a = thing.area()
    print(f"{n} has perimeter {p:.2f} and area {a:.2f}")
```

```
sq has perimeter 12.00 and area 9.00
ci has perimeter 12.57 and area 12.57
```

But how does polymorphism work? The first thing we need to understand is that a function is an object. While the bytes in a string represent characters and the bytes in an image represent pixels, the bytes in a function are instructions (Figure 2.1). When Python executes the code below, it creates an object in memory that contains the instructions to print a string and assigns that object to the variable `example`:

```python
def example():
    print("in example")
```

We can create an **alias** for the function by assigning it to another variable and then call the function by referencing that second variable. Doing this doesn't alter or erase the connection between the function and the original name:

```python
alias = example
alias()
```

```
in example
```

We can also store function objects in data structures like lists and dictionaries. Let's write some functions that do the same things as the methods in our original Python and store them in a dictionary to represent a square (Figure 2.2):

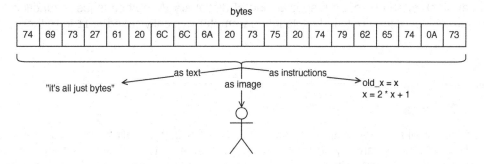

Figure 2.1: Bytes can be interpreted as text, images, instructions, and more.

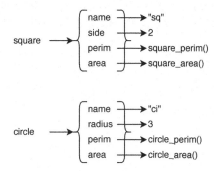

Figure 2.2: Using dictionaries to emulate objects.

```
def square_perimeter(thing):
    return 4 * thing["side"]

def square_area(thing):
    return thing["side"] ** 2

def square_new(name, side):
    return {
        "name": name,
        "side": side,
        "perimeter": square_perimeter,
        "area": square_area
    }
```

If we want to use one of the "methods" in this dictionary, we call it like this:

```
def call(thing, method_name):
    return thing[method_name](thing)

examples = [square_new("sq", 3), circle_new("ci", 2)]
for ex in examples:
    n = ex["name"]
    p = call(ex, "perimeter")
    a = call(ex, "area")
    print(f"{n} {p:.2f} {a:.2f}")
```

The function `call` looks up the function stored in the dictionary, then calls that function with the dictionary as its first object; in other words, instead of using `obj.meth(arg)` we use `obj["meth"](obj, arg)`. Behind the scenes, this is (almost) how objects actually work.

We can think of an object as a special kind of dictionary. A method is just a function that takes an object of the right kind as its first parameter (typically called `self` in Python).

2.2 Classes

One problem with implementing objects as dictionaries is that it allows every single object to behave slightly differently. In practice, we want objects to store different values (e.g., different squares to have different sizes) but the same behaviors (e.g., all squares should have the same methods). We can implement this by storing the methods in a dictionary called `Square` that corresponds to a class and having each individual square contain a reference to that higher-level dictionary (Figure 2.3). In the code below, that special reference uses the key `"_class"`:

```python
def square_perimeter(thing):
    return 4 * thing["side"]

def square_area(thing):
    return thing["side"] ** 2

Square = {
    "perimeter": square_perimeter,
    "area": square_area,
    "_classname": "Square"
}

def square_new(name, side):
    return {
        "name": name,
        "side": side,
        "_class": Square
    }
```

Calling a method now involves one more lookup because we have to go from the object to the class to the method, but once again we call the "method" with the object as the first argument:

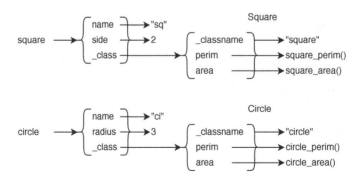

Figure 2.3: Using dictionaries to emulate classes.

```
def call(thing, method_name):
    return thing["_class"][method_name](thing)

examples = [square_new("sq", 3), circle_new("ci", 2)]
for ex in examples:
    n = ex["name"]
    p = call(ex, "perimeter")
    a = call(ex, "area")
    c = ex["_class"]["_classname"]
    print(f"{n} is a {c}: {p:.2f} {a:.2f}")
```

As a bonus, we can now reliably identify objects' classes and ask whether two objects are of the same class or not by checking what their "_class" keys refer to.

Arguments vs. Parameters

Many programmers use the words **argument** and **parameter** interchangeably, but to make our meaning clear, we call the values passed into a function its arguments and the names the function uses to refer to them as its parameters. Put another way, parameters are part of the definition, and arguments are given when the function is called.

2.3 Arguments

The methods we have defined so far operate on the values stored in the object's dictionary, but none of them take any extra arguments as input. Implementing this is a little bit tricky because different methods might need different numbers of arguments. We could define functions call_0, call_1, call_2 and so on to handle each case, but like most modern languages, Python gives us a better way. If we define a parameter in a function with a leading *, it captures any "extra" values passed to the function that don't line up with named parameters. Similarly, if we define a parameter with two leading stars **, it captures any extra named parameters:

```
def show_args(title, *args, **kwargs):
    print(f"{title} args '{args}' and kwargs '{kwargs}'")

show_args("nothing")
show_args("one unnamed argument", 1)
show_args("one named argument", second="2")
show_args("one of each", 3, fourth="4")
```

```
nothing args '()' and kwargs '{}'
one unnamed argument args '(1,)' and kwargs '{}'
one named argument args '()' and kwargs '{'second': '2'}'
one of each args '(3,)' and kwargs '{'fourth': '4'}'
```

This mechanism is sometimes referred to as **varargs** (short for "variable arguments"). A complementary mechanism called **spreading** allows us to take a list or dictionary full of arguments and spread them out in a call to match a function's parameters:

```
def show_spread(left, middle, right):
    print(f"left {left} middle {middle} right {right}")

all_in_list = [1, 2, 3]
show_spread(*all_in_list)

all_in_dict = {"right": 30, "left": 10, "middle": 20}
show_spread(**all_in_dict)
```

```
left 1 middle 2 right 3
left 10 middle 20 right 30
```

With these tools in hand, let's add a method to our `Square` class to tell us whether a square is larger than a user-specified size:

```
def square_larger(thing, size):
    return call(thing, "area") > size

Square = {
    "perimeter": square_perimeter,
    "area": square_area,
    "larger": square_larger,
    "_classname": "Square"
}
```

The function that implements this check for circles looks exactly the same:

```
def circle_larger(thing, size):
    return call(thing, "area") > size
```

We then modify `call` to capture extra arguments in `*args` and spread them into the function being called:

```
def call(thing, method_name, *args):
    return thing["_class"][method_name](thing, *args)
```

Our tests show that this works:

```
examples = [square_new("sq", 3), circle_new("ci", 2)]
for ex in examples:
    result = call(ex, "larger", 10)
    print(f"is {ex['name']} larger? {result}")
```

```
is sq larger? False
is ci larger? True
```

However, we now have two functions that do exactly the same thing—the only difference between them is their names. Anything in a program that is duplicated in several places will eventually be wrong in at least one, so we need to find some way to share this code.

2.4 Inheritance

The tool we want is inheritance. To see how this works in Python, let's add a method called `density` to our original `Shape` class that uses other methods defined by the class

```
class Shape:
    def __init__(self, name):
        self.name = name

    def perimeter(self):
        raise NotImplementedError("perimeter")

    def area(self):
        raise NotImplementedError("area")

    def density(self, weight):
        return weight / self.area()
```

```
examples = [Square("sq", 3), Circle("ci", 2)]
for ex in examples:
    n = ex.name
    d = ex.density(5)
    print(f"{n}: {d:.2f}")
```

```
sq: 0.56
ci: 0.40
```

To enable our dictionary-based "classes" to do the same thing, we create a dictionary to represent a generic shape and give it a "method" to calculate density:

```
def shape_density(thing, weight):
    return weight / call(thing, "area")

Shape = {
    "density": shape_density,
    "_classname": "Shape",
    "_parent": None
}
```

We then add another specially-named field to the dictionaries for "classes" like Square to keep track of their parents:

```
Square = {
    "perimeter": square_perimeter,
    "area": square_area,
    "_classname": "Square",
    "_parent": Shape
}
```

and modify the call function to search for the requested method (Figure 2.4):

```
def call(thing, method_name, *args):
    method = find(thing["_class"], method_name)
    return method(thing, *args)

def find(cls, method_name):
    while cls is not None:
        if method_name in cls:
            return cls[method_name]
        cls = cls["_parent"]
    raise NotImplementedError("method_name")
```

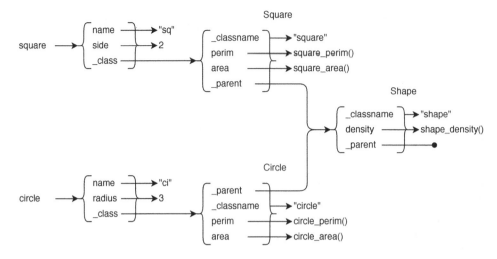

Figure 2.4: Using dictionary search to implement inheritance.

A simple test shows that this is working as intended:

```
examples = [square_new("sq", 3), circle_new("ci", 2)]
for ex in examples:
    n = ex["name"]
    d = call(ex, "density", 5)
    print(f"{n}: {d:.2f}")
```

```
sq: 0.56
ci: 0.40
```

We do have one task left, though: we need to make sure that when a square or circle is made, it is made correctly. In short, we need to implement **constructors**. We do this by giving the dictionaries that implement classes a special key `_new` whose value is the function that builds something of that type:

```
def shape_new(name):
    return {
        "name": name,
        "_class": Shape
    }

Shape = {
    "density": shape_density,
    "_classname": "Shape",
    "_parent": None,
    "_new": shape_new
}
```

In order to make an object, we call the function associated with its `_new` key:

```
def make(cls, *args):
    return cls["_new"](*args)
```

That function is responsible for **upcalling** the constructor of its parent. For example, the constructor for a square calls the constructor for a generic shape and adds square-specific values using | to combine two dictionaries:

```
def square_new(name, side):
    return make(Shape, name) | {
        "side": side,
        "_class": Square
    }

Square = {
    "perimeter": square_perimeter,
    "area": square_area,
    "_classname": "Square",
    "_parent": Shape,
    "_new": square_new
}
```

Of course, we're not done until we test it:

```
examples = [make(Square, "sq", 3), make(Circle, "ci", 2)]
for ex in examples:
    n = ex["name"]
    d = call(ex, "density", 5)
    print(f"{n}: {d:.2f}")
```

```
sq: 0.56
ci: 0.40
```

2.5 Summary

We have only scratched the surface of Python's object system. **Multiple inheritance**, **class methods**, **static methods**, and **monkey patching** are powerful tools, but they can all be understood in terms of dictionaries that contain references to properties, functions, and other dictionaries (Figure 2.5).

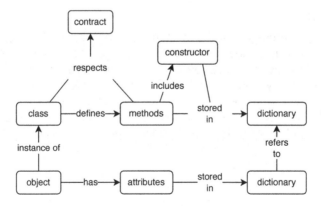

Figure 2.5: Concept map for implementing objects and classes.

2.6 Exercises

Handling Named Arguments

The final version of `call` declares a parameter called `*args` to capture all the positional arguments of the method being called and then spreads them in the actual call. Modify it to capture and spread named arguments as well.

Multiple Inheritance

Implement multiple inheritance using dictionaries. Does your implementation look methods up in the same order as Python would?

Class Methods and Static Methods

1. Explain the differences between class methods and static methods.

2. Implement both using dictionaries.

Reporting Type

Python `type` method reports the most specific type of an object, while `isinstance` determines whether an object inherits from a type either directly or indirectly. Add your own versions of both to dictionary-based objects and classes.

Using Recursion

A **recursive function** is one that calls itself, either directly or indirectly. Modify the `find` function that finds a method to call so that it uses recursion instead of a loop. Which version is easier to understand? Which version is more efficient?

Method Caching

Our implementation searches for the implementation of a method every time that method is called. An alternative is to add a **cache** to each object to save the methods that have been looked up before. For example, each object could have a special key called `_cache` whose value is a dictionary. The keys in that dictionary are the names of methods that have been called in the past, and the values are the functions that were found to implement those methods. Add this feature to our dictionary-based objects. How much more complex does it make the code? How much extra storage space does it need compared to repeated lookup?

3

Finding Duplicate Files

- A hash function creates a fixed-size value from an arbitrary sequence of bytes.

- Use big-oh notation to estimate the running time of algorithms.

- The output of a hash function is deterministic but not easy to predict.

- A good hash function's output is evenly distributed.

- A large cryptographic hash can be used to uniquely identify a file's contents.

Terms defined: **big-oh notation**, **binary mode**, **bucket**, **collision (in hashing)**, **cryptographic hash function**, **hash code**, **hash function**, **hexadecimal**, **SHA-256 (hash function)**, **streaming API**, **time complexity**

Suppose we want to find duplicated files, such as extra copies of photos or data sets. People often rename files, so we must compare their contents, but this will be slow if we have a lot of files.

We can estimate how slow "slow" will be with a simple calculation. N objects can be paired in $N(N-1)$ ways. If we remove duplicate pairings (i.e., if we count A-B and B-A as one pair) then there are $N(N-1)/2 = (N^2 - N)/2$ distinct pairs. As N gets large, this value is approximately proportional to N^2. A computer scientist would say that the **time complexity** of our algorithm is $O(N^2)$, which is pronounced "**big-oh** of N squared". In simpler terms, when the number of files doubles, the running time roughly quadruples, which means the time per file increases as the number of files increases.

Slowdown like this is often unavoidable, but in our case there's a better way. If we generate a shorter identifier for each file that depends only on the bytes it contains, we can group together the files that have the same identifier and only compare the files within a group. This approach is faster because we only do the expensive byte-by-byte comparison on files that *might* be equal. And as we'll see, if we are very clever about how we generate identifiers then we can avoid byte-by-byte comparisons entirely.

3.1 Getting Started

We'll start by implementing the inefficient N^2 approach so that we can compare our later designs to it. The short program below takes a list of filenames from the command line, finds duplicates, and prints the matches:

```python
def find_duplicates(filenames):
    matches = []
    for left in filenames:
        for right in filenames:
            if same_bytes(left, right):
                matches.append((left, right))
    return matches
```

```
if __name__ == "__main__":
    duplicates = find_duplicates(sys.argv[1:])
    for (left, right) in duplicates:
        print(left, right)
```

This program uses a function called `same_bytes` that reads two files and compares them byte by byte:

```
def same_bytes(left_name, right_name):
    left_bytes = open(left_name, "rb").read()
    right_bytes = open(right_name, "rb").read()
    return left_bytes == right_bytes
```

Notice that the files are opened in **binary mode** using `"rb"` instead of the usual `"r"`. As we'll see in Chapter 17, this tells Python to read the bytes exactly as they are rather than trying to convert them to characters.

To test this program and the others we're about to write, we create a `tests` directory with six files:

Filename	a1.txt	a2.txt	a3.txt	b1.txt	b2.txt	c1.txt
Content	aaa	aaa	aaa	bb	bb	c

We expect the three a files and the two b files to be reported as duplicates. There's no particular reason for these tests—we just have to start somewhere. Our first test looks like this:

```
python brute_force_1.py tests/*.txt
```

```
tests/a1.txt tests/a1.txt
tests/a1.txt tests/a2.txt
tests/a1.txt tests/a3.txt
tests/a2.txt tests/a1.txt
tests/a2.txt tests/a2.txt
tests/a2.txt tests/a3.txt
tests/a3.txt tests/a1.txt
tests/a3.txt tests/a2.txt
tests/a3.txt tests/a3.txt
tests/b1.txt tests/b1.txt
tests/b1.txt tests/b2.txt
tests/b2.txt tests/b1.txt
tests/b2.txt tests/b2.txt
tests/c1.txt tests/c1.txt
```

Our program's output is correct but not useful: every file is reported as being identical to itself, and every match of different files is reported twice. Let's fix the nested loop in `find_duplicates` so that we only check potentially differing pairs once (Figure 3.1):

```
def find_duplicates(filenames):
    matches = []
    for i_left in range(len(filenames)):
        left = filenames[i_left]
        for i_right in range(i_left):
            right = filenames[i_right]
            if same_bytes(left, right):
                matches.append((left, right))
    return matches
```

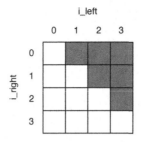

Figure 3.1: Scoping the inner loop to produce unique combinations.

3.2 Hashing Files

Instead of comparing every file against every other, let's process each file once to produce a short identifier that depends only on the file's contents and then only compare files that have the same identifier, i.e., that *might* be equal. If files are evenly divided into g groups then each group will contain roughly N/g files, so the total work will be roughly $O(g(N/g)^2)$ (i.e., g groups times $(N/g)^2$ comparisons within each group). Simplifying, this is N^2/g, so as the number of groups grows, and the overall running time should decrease (Figure 3.2).

filename	contents	hash code	
a1.txt	aaa	6	
a2.txt	aaa	6	
a3.txt	aaa	6	
b1.txt	bb	10	
b2.txt	bb	10	
c1.txt	c	5	

Figure 3.2: Grouping by hash code reduces comparisons from 15 to 4.

We can construct IDs for files using a **hash function** to produce a **hash code**. Since bytes are just numbers, we can create a very simple hash function by adding up the bytes in a file and taking the remainder modulo some number:

```
def naive_hash(data):
    return sum(data) % 13
```

Here's a quick test that calculates the hash code for successively longer substrings of the word "hashing":

```
example = bytes("hashing", "utf-8")
for i in range(1, len(example) + 1):
    substring = example[:i]
    hash = naive_hash(substring)
    print(f"{hash:2} {substring}")
```

```
 0 b'h'
 6 b'ha'
 4 b'has'
 4 b'hash'
 5 b'hashi'
```

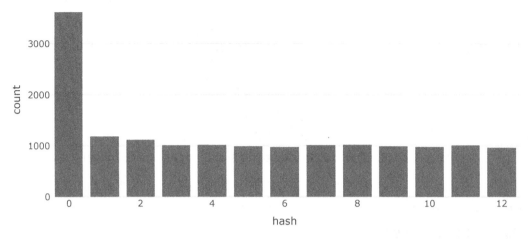

Figure 3.3: Distribution of hash codes per line in *Dracula*.

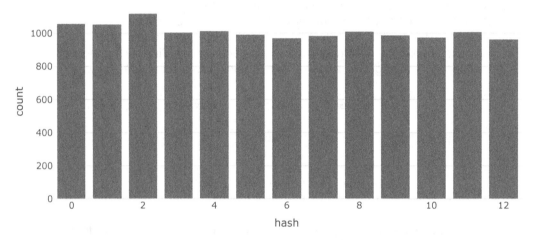

Figure 3.4: Distribution of hash codes per unique line in *Dracula*.

```
11 b'hashin'
10 b'hashing'
```

The output seems random, but is it? As a more stringent test, let's try hashing every line of text in the Project Gutenberg[1] version of the novel *Dracula* and plot the distribution (Figure 3.3).

Most of the **buckets** are approximately the same height, but why is there a peak at zero? Our big-oh estimate of how efficient our algorithm would be depended on files being distributed evenly between groups; if that's not the case, our code won't be as fast as we hoped.

After a bit of digging, it turns out that the text file we're processing uses a blank line to separate paragraphs. These hash to zero, so the peak reflects an unequal distribution in our data. If we plot the distribution of hash codes of *unique* lines, the result is more even (Figure 3.4).

---

[1] https://www.gutenberg.org/

Hashing is a tremendously powerful tool: for example, Python's dictionaries hash their keys to make lookup fast. Now that we can hash files, we can build a dictionary with hash codes as keys and sets of filenames as values. The code that does this is shown below; each time it calculate a hash code, it checks to see if that value has been seen before. If not, it creates a new entry in the groups dictionary with the hash code as its key and an empty set as a value. It can then be sure that there's a set to add the filename to:

```
def find_groups(filenames):
    groups = {}
    for fn in filenames:
        data = open(fn, "rb").read()
        hash_code = naive_hash(data)
        if hash_code not in groups:
            groups[hash_code] = set()
        groups[hash_code].add(fn)
    return groups
```

We can now re-use most of the code we wrote earlier to find duplicates within each group:

```
groups = find_groups(sys.argv[1:])
for filenames in groups.values():
    duplicates = find_duplicates(list(filenames))
    for (left, right) in duplicates:
        print(left, right)
```

```
tests/a2.txt  tests/a1.txt
tests/a3.txt  tests/a1.txt
tests/a3.txt  tests/a2.txt
tests/b1.txt  tests/b2.txt
```

3.3 Better Hashing

Let's go back to the formula $O(N^2/g)$ that tells us how much work we have to do if we have divided N files between g groups. If we have exactly as many groups as files—i.e., if g is equal to N—then the work to process N files would be $O(N^2/N) = O(N)$, which means that the work will be proportional to the number of files. We have to read each file at least once anyway, so we can't possibly do better than this, but how can we ensure that each unique file winds up in its own group?

The answer is to use a **cryptographic hash function**. The output of such a function is completely deterministic: given the same bytes in the same order, it will always produce the same output. However, the output is distributed like a uniform random variable: each possible output is equally likely, which ensures that files will be evenly distributed between groups.

Cryptographic hash functions are hard to write, and it's very hard to prove that a particular algorithm has the properties we require. We will therefore use a function from Python's hashing module[2] that implements the **SHA-256** hashing algorithm. Given some bytes as input, this function produces a 256-bit hash, which is normally written as a 64-character **hexadecimal** string. This uses the letters A-F (or a-f) to represent the digits from 10 to 15, so that (for example) 3D5 is $(3 \times 16^2) + (13 \times 16^1) + (5 \times 16^0)$, or 981 in decimal:

---

[2] https://docs.python.org/3/library/hashlib.html

```
example = bytes("hash", "utf-8")
for i in range(1, len(example) + 1):
    substring = example[:i]
    hash = sha256(substring).hexdigest()
    print(f"{substring}\n{hash}")
```

```
b'h'
aaa9402664f1a41f40ebbc52c9993eb66aeb366602958fdfaa283b71e64db123
b'ha'
8693873cd8f8a2d9c7c596477180f851e525f4eaf55a4f637b445cb442a5e340
b'has'
9150c74c5f92d51a92857f4b9678105ba5a676d308339a353b20bd38cd669ce7
b'hash'
d04b98f48e8f8bcc15c6ae5ac050801cd6dcfd428fb5f9e65c4e16e7807340fa
```

The Birthday Problem

The odds that two people share a birthday are 1/365 (ignoring February 29). The odds that they *don't* are therefore $364/365$. When we add a third person, the odds that they don't share a birthday with either of the preceding two people are $363/365$, so the overall odds that nobody shares a birthday are $(364/365) \times (363/365)$. If we keep going, there's a 50% chance of two people sharing a birthday in a group of just 23 people, and a 99.9% chance with 70 people.

The same math can tell us how many files we need to hash before there's a 50% chance of a **collision** with a 256-bit hash. According to Wikipedia[3], the answer is approximately 4×10^{38} files. We're willing to take that risk.

Using this library function makes our duplicate file finder much shorter:

```
import sys
from hashlib import sha256

def find_groups(filenames):
    groups = {}
    for fn in filenames:
        data = open(fn, "rb").read()
        hash_code = sha256(data).hexdigest()
        if hash_code not in groups:
            groups[hash_code] = set()
        groups[hash_code].add(fn)
    return groups


if __name__ == "__main__":
    groups = find_groups(sys.argv[1:])
    for filenames in groups.values():
        print(", ".join(sorted(filenames)))
```

```
python dup.py tests/*.txt
```

```
tests/a1.txt, tests/a2.txt, tests/a3.txt
tests/b1.txt, tests/b2.txt
tests/c1.txt
```

---

[3]https://en.wikipedia.org/wiki/Birthday_problem

More importantly, our new approach scales to very large sets of files: as explained above, we only have to look at each file once, so the running time is as good as it possibly can be.

3.4 Summary

Figure 3.5 summarizes the key ideas in this chapter, the most important of which is that some algorithms are intrinsically better than others.

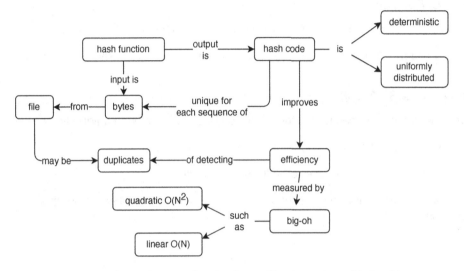

Figure 3.5: Concept map for duplicate file detection with hashing.

3.5 Exercises

Odds of Collision

If hashes were only 2 bits long, then the chances of collision with each successive file assuming no previous collision are:

Number of Files	Odds of Collision
1	0%
2	25%
3	50%
4	75%
5	100%

A colleague of yours says this means that if we hash four files, there's only a 75% chance of any collision occurring. What are the actual odds?

Streaming I/O

A **streaming API** delivers data one piece at a time rather than all at once. Read the documentation for the `update` method of hashing objects in Python's hashing module[4] and rewrite the duplicate finder from this chapter to use it.

Big Oh

Chapter 1 said that as the number of components in a system grows, the complexity of the system increases rapidly. How fast is "rapidly" in big-oh terms?

The `hash` Function

1. Read the documentation for Python's built-in `hash` function.

2. Why do `hash(123)` and `hash("123")` work when `hash([123])` raises an exception?

How Good Is SHA-256?

1. Write a function that calculates the SHA-256 hash code of each unique line of a text file.

2. Convert the hex digests of those hash codes to integers.

3. Plot a histogram of those integer values with 20 bins.

4. How evenly distributed are the hash codes? How does the distribution change as you process larger files?

---

[4]https://docs.python.org/3/library/hashlib.html

4

Matching Patterns

- Use globs and regular expressions to match patterns in text.

- Use inheritance to make matchers composable and extensible.

- Simplify code by having objects delegate work to other objects.

- Use the Null Object pattern to eliminate special cases in code.

- Use standard refactorings to move code from one working state to another.

- Build and check the parts of your code you are least sure of first to find out if your design will work.

Terms defined: **Chain of Responsibility pattern, child class, Extract Parent Class refactoring, globbing, greedy matching, helper method, inheritance, lazy matching, literal (in parsing), Null Object pattern, refactor, regular expression, signature, technical debt, test-driven development**

We used *.txt to tell the duplicate file finder of Chapter 3 which files to compare. Older programmers (like this author) refer to this kind of pattern-matching as **globbing** because early versions of Unix had a tool called glob[1] to do it. Globbing was so useful that it was quickly added to the shell, and the Python standard library includes a module called glob[2] to match filenames in the same way. For example, 2023-*.{pdf,txt} matches 2023-01.txt and 2023-final.pdf but not draft-2023.docx (Figure 4.1).

Globbing patterns are simpler than the **regular expressions** used to scrape data from text files, but the principles are the same. This chapter therefore implements a simple version of globbing to show how pattern-matching works in general. This matcher will only handle the cases in Table 4.1, but as the exercises will show, our design makes it easy to add new kinds of patterns.

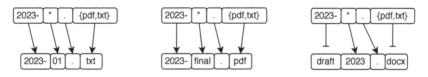

Figure 4.1: Examples of glob matching.

---

[1] https://en.wikipedia.org/wiki/Glob_(programming)
[2] https://docs.python.org/3/library/glob.html

Pattern	Text	Match?	Pattern	Text	Match?
abc	"abc"	true	a*c	"abc"	true
ab	"abc"	false	{a,b}	"a"	true
abc	"ab"	false	{a,b}	"c"	false
*	""	true	{a,b}	"ab"	false
*	"abc"	true	*{x,y}	"abcx"	true

Table 4.1: Pattern-matching cases.

4.1   Simple Patterns

Matching is conceptually simple. If the first element of the pattern matches the target string at the current location, we check if the rest of the pattern matches what's left of the string. If the element doesn't match the front of the string, or if the rest of the pattern can't match the rest of the string, matching fails. (This behavior makes globbing different from regular expressions, which can match parts of strings.)

This design makes use of the **Chain of Responsibility** design pattern. Each matcher matches if it can then asks the next matcher in the chain to try to match the remaining text (Figure 4.2). Crucially, objects don't know how long the chain after them is: they just know whom to ask next.

In some cases we only need to know what kind of matching we're doing: for example, the * pattern matches any characters. In other cases, though, we need some extra information, such as the literal text "abc" or the two alternatives "pdf" and "txt". We therefore decide to create matching objects that can hold this extra information rather than just writing functions.

Our first matcher checks whether a piece of text like "abc" matches a string. We call this class Lit because a fixed string of characters is sometimes called a **literal**, and it has a constructor and a match method:

```
class Lit:
    def __init__(self, chars, rest=None):
        self.chars = chars
        self.rest = rest

    def match(self, text, start=0):
        end = start + len(self.chars)
        if text[start:end] != self.chars:
            return False
        if self.rest:
            return self.rest.match(text, end)
        return end == len(text)
```

chars is the characters to be matched, while rest is responsible for matching the rest of the text. If rest is None, this matcher is the last one in the chain, so it must match to the end of the target string.

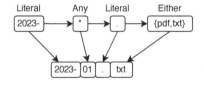

Figure 4.2: Matching with Chain of Responsibility.

The `match` method takes the text to be matched as an input along with an optional `start` parameter that indicates where matching is to start. This parameter has a default value of 0 (meaning "start at the beginning"), but if this `Lit` follows other matchers, they need to tell it where to start looking. To see if this works, let's write and run a few tests:

```
def test_literal_match_entire_string():
    # /abc/ matches "abc"
    assert Lit("abc").match("abc")

def test_literal_substring_alone_no_match():
    # /ab/ doesn't match "abc"
    assert not Lit("ab").match("abc")

def test_literal_superstring_no_match():
    # /abc/ doesn't match "ab"
    assert not Lit("abc").match("ab")
```

Notice that we give tests long, meaningful names to make failure reports from the test runner easier to read.

We could go ahead and build some more matchers right away, but as [Petre2016] explains, good programmers build and check the parts of their code that they are *least* sure of as early as possible to find out if their entire design is going to work or not. We therefore write a test to make sure that chaining works when one literal matcher is followed by another:

```
def test_literal_followed_by_literal_match():
    # /a/+/b/ matches "ab"
    assert Lit("a", Lit("b")).match("ab")

def test_literal_followed_by_literal_no_match():
    # /a/+/b/ doesn't match "ac"
    assert not Lit("a", Lit("b")).match("ac")
```

Chaining two literal matchers together is unnecessary: we could (and probably should) write `Lit("ab")` instead of `Lit("a", Lit("b"))`. However, the fact that these two tests pass reassures us that our design is working.

Test-Driven Development

Some programmers write the tests for a piece of code before writing the code itself. This practice is called **test-driven development**, and its advocates claim that it yields better code in less time because (a) writing tests helps people think about what the code should do before they're committed to a particular implementation and (b) if people write tests first, they'll actually write tests. However, research shows that the order in which the tests are written doesn't actually make a difference [Fucci2016]; what actually matters is alternating short bursts of testing and coding.

These tests for `Lit` pass, so we're ready to move on to wildcards. A * character in our pattern matches zero or more characters, so if there are no more matchers in the chain, then this * matches to the end of the target string and `match` returns `True` right away. If there *are* other matchers, on the other hand, we try matching no characters, one character, two characters, and so on and see if those other matchers can get us to the end of the string if we do so. If none of these possibilities succeeds, the overall match fails (Figure 4.3).

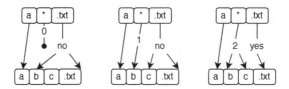

Figure 4.3: How wildcard matching works.

```python
class Any:
    def __init__(self, rest=None):
        self.rest = rest

    def match(self, text, start=0):
        if self.rest is None:
            return True
        for i in range(start, len(text)):
            if self.rest.match(text, i):
                return True
        return False
```

Once again we write a few tests before moving on:

```python
def test_any_matches_empty():
    # /*/ matches ""
    assert Any().match("")

def test_any_matches_entire_string():
    # /*/ matches "abc"
    assert Any().match("abc")

def test_any_matches_as_prefix():
    # /*def/ matches "abcdef"
    assert Any(Lit("def")).match("abcdef")

def test_any_matches_as_suffix():
    # /abc*/ matches "abcdef"
    assert Lit("abc", Any()).match("abcdef")

def test_any_matches_interior():
    # /a*c/ matches "abc"
    assert Lit("a", Any(Lit("c"))).match("abc")
```

Either/or matching works much the same way. If the first alternative matches, we try the rest of the chain. If not, we try the second alternative, and if that doesn't work either, we fail:

```python
class Either:
    def __init__(self, left, right, rest=None):
        self.left = left
        self.right = right
        self.rest = rest

    def match(self, text, start=0):
        return self.left.match(text, start) or \
            self.right.match(text, start)
```

Our first few tests pass:

```
def test_either_two_literals_first():
    # /{a,b}/ matches "a"
    assert Either(Lit("a"), Lit("b")).match("a")

def test_either_two_literals_not_both():
    # /{a,b}/ doesn't match "ab"
    assert not Either(Lit("a"), Lit("b")).match("ab")
```

but further testing uncovers a bug:

```
def test_either_followed_by_literal_match():
    # /{a,b}c/ matches "ac"
    assert Either(Lit("a"), Lit("b"), Lit("c")).match("ac")

def test_either_followed_by_literal_no_match():
    # /{a,b}c/ doesn't match "ax"
    assert not Either(Lit("a"), Lit("b"), Lit("c")).match("ax")
```

```
===================== test session starts =========================

test_glob_problem.py F.                              [100%]

==================== short test summary info ======================
FAILED test_glob_problem.py::test_either_followed_by_literal_match
=================== 1 failed, 1 passed in 0.00s ===================
```

The problem is that `Either.match` isn't using `rest` properly—in fact, it's not using `rest` at all because it doesn't know what to pass it as a starting point. Instead of having `match` methods return `True` or `False`, we need them to return an indication of where the next match should start so that `Either` can pass that information along to `rest`. Before making this change, we will clear up a bit of **technical debt** in our code.

4.2 Rethinking

We now have three matchers with the same interfaces. Before we do any further work, we will **refactor** using a pattern called **Extract Parent Class** to make the relationship between the matchers clear (Figure 4.4). At the same time, each matcher is checking to see if its `rest` is `None`. We can simplify this by creating a class to represent "nothing here", which is known as the **Null Object** pattern.

We Didn't Invent This

We didn't invent any of the patterns or refactorings used in this chapter. Instead, we learned them from books like [Gamma1994; Fowler2018; Kerievsky2004]. And as [Tichy2010] showed, learning these patterns makes people better programmers.

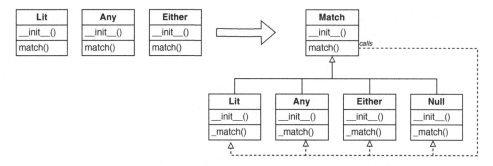

Figure 4.4: Using the Extract Parent Class refactoring.

Our new parent class `Match` looks like this:

```
class Match:
    def __init__(self, rest):
        self.rest = rest if rest is not None else Null()

    def match(self, text):
        result = self._match(text, 0)
        return result == len(text)
```

`Match.rest` requires every **child class** to have a **helper method** called `_match` that returns the location from which searching is to continue. `Match.match` checks whether the entire match reaches the end of the target string and returns `True` or `False` as appropriate.

Our new Null Object class looks like this:

```
class Null(Match):
    def __init__(self):
        self.rest = None

    def _match(self, text, start):
        return start
```

`Null` objects must be at the end of the matching chain, i.e., their `rest` *must* be None, so we remove the `rest` parameter from the class's constructor and pass `None` up to the parent constructor every time. Since `Null` objects don't match anything, `Null._match` immediately returns whatever starting point it was given. Every other matcher can now pass responsibility down the chain without having to test whether it's the last matcher in line or not.

With these changes in place, our literal matcher becomes:

```
class Lit(Match):
    def __init__(self, chars, rest=None):
        super().__init__(rest)
        self.chars = chars

    def _match(self, text, start):
        end = start + len(self.chars)
        if text[start:end] != self.chars:
            return None
        return self.rest._match(text, end)
```

`Lit`'s constructor calls the constructor of its parent class to initialize the things that all classes share, then adds the data specific to this class. It returns `None` for "no match" or whatever `self.rest` returns If this object's `rest` is an instance of `Null`, this result will be the index after the overall match.

As before, the matcher for * checks what happens if it matches an ever-larger part of the target string:

```
class Any(Match):
    def __init__(self, rest=None):
        super().__init__(rest)

    def _match(self, text, start):
        for i in range(start, len(text) + 1):
            end = self.rest._match(text, i)
            if end == len(text):
                return end
        return None
```

(The exercises will ask why loop has to run to len(text) + 1.) Finally, the either/or matcher that prompted this refactoring becomes:

```
class Either(Match):
    def __init__(self, left, right, rest=None):
        super().__init__(rest)
        self.left = left
        self.right = right

    def _match(self, text, start):
        for pat in [self.left, self.right]:
            end = pat._match(text, start)
            if end is not None:
                end = self.rest._match(text, end)
                if end == len(text):
                    return end
        return None
```

Looping over the left and right alternative saves us from repeating code or introducing a helper method. It also simplifies the handling of more than two options, which we explore in the exercises.

Crucially, none of the existing tests change because none of the matching classes' constructors changed and the **signature** of the match method (which they now **inherit** from the generic Match class) stayed the same as well. We should add some tests for Null, but we have now met our original goal, and as the exercises will show we can easily add matchers for other kinds of patterns.

4.3 Summary

Figure 4.5 summarizes the key ideas in this chapter; we will see the Null Object and Chain of Responsibility design patterns again.

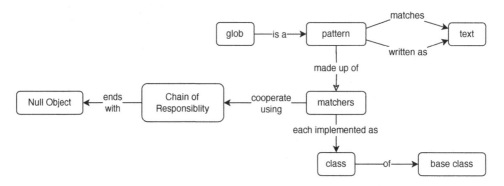

Figure 4.5: Regular expression matching concept map.

4.4   Exercises

Looping

Rewrite the matchers so that a top-level object manages a list of matchers, none of which know about any of the others. Is this design simpler or more complicated than the Chain of Responsibility design?

Length Plus One

Why does the upper bound of the loop in the final version of Any run to len(text) + 1?

Find One or More

Extend the regular expression matcher to support +, meaning "match one or more characters".

Match Sets of Characters

1. Add a new matching class that matches any character from a set, so that Charset('aeiou') matches any lower-case vowel.

2. Create a matcher that matches a range of characters. For example, Range("a", "z") matches any single lower-case Latin alphabetic character. (This is just a convenience matcher: ranges can always be spelled out in full.)

3. Write some tests for your matchers.

Exclusion

1. Create a matcher that *doesn't* match a specified pattern. For example, Not(Lit("abc")) only succeeds if the text isn't "abc".

2. Write some tests for it.

Make Repetition More Efficient

Rewrite `Any` so that it does not repeatedly re-match text.

Multiple Alternatives

1. Modify `Either` so that it can match any number of sub-patterns, not just two.

2. Write some tests for it.

3. What does your implementation do when no sub-patterns are specified?

Returning Matches

Modify the matcher so that it returns the substrings that matched each part of the expression. For example, when `*.txt` matches `name.txt`, the library should return some indication that `*` matched the string `"name"`.

Alternative Matching

The tool we have built implements **lazy matching**, i.e., the `*` character matches the shortest string it can that results in the overall pattern matching. Modify the code to do **greedy matching** instead, and combine it with the solution to the previous exercise for testing.

5

Parsing Text

- Parsing transforms text that's easy for people to read into objects that are easy for computers to work with.

- A grammar defines the textual patterns that a parser recognizes.

- Most parsers tokenize input text and then analyze the tokens.

- Most parsers need to implement some form of precedence to prioritize different patterns.

- Operations like addition and function call work just like user-defined functions.

- Programs can overload built-in operators by defining specially-named methods that are recognized by the compiler or interpreter.

Terms defined: **abstract syntax tree**, **concrete class**, **CSV**, **grammar**, **JSON**, **operator overloading**, **parser**, **token**, **tokenizer**, **YAML**

We constructed objects to match patterns in Chapter 4, but an expression like `"2023-*{pdf,txt}"` is a lot easier to read and write than code like `Lit("2023-", Any(Either("pdf", "txt")))`. If we want to use the former, we need a **parser** to convert those human-readable strings into machine-comprehensible objects.

Table 5.1 shows the **grammar** our parser will handle. When we are done, our parser should be able to recognize that `2023-*.{pdf,txt}` means the literal `2023-`, any characters, a literal `.`, and then either a literal `pdf` or a literal `txt`.

Please Don't Write Parsers

Languages that are comfortable for people to read and write are usually difficult for computers to understand and vice versa, so we need parsers to translate the former into the latter. However, the world doesn't need more file formats: please use **CSV**, **JSON**, **YAML**, or something else that already has an acronym rather than inventing something of your own.

5.1 Tokenizing

Most parsers are written in two parts (Figure 5.1). The first stage groups characters into atoms of text called "**tokens**", which are meaningful pieces of text like the digits making up a number or the letters making up a variable name. Our grammar's tokens are the special characters `,`, `{`, `}`, and `*`. Any sequence of one or more other characters is a single multi-letter token. This classification determines the design of our **tokenizer**:

Meaning	Character
Any literal character *c*	*c*
Zero or more characters	*
Alternatives	{*x*,*y*}

Table 5.1: Glob grammar.

1. If a character is not special, then append it to the current literal (if there is one) or start a new literal (if there isn't).

2. If a character *is* special, then close the existing literal (if there is one) and create a token for the special character. Note that the , character closes a literal but doesn't produce a token.

The result of tokenization is a flat list of tokens. The second stage of parsing assembles tokens to create an **abstract syntax tree** (AST) that represents the structure of what was parsed. We will re-use the classes defined in Chapter 4 for this purpose.

Before we start writing our tokenizer, we have to decide whether to implement it as a set of functions or as one or more classes. Based on previous experience, we choose the latter: this tokenizer is simple enough that we'll only need a handful of functions, but one capable of handling a language like Python would be much larger, and classes are a handy way to group related functions together.

The main method of our tokenizer looks like this:

```
def tok(self, text):
    self._setup()
    for ch in text:
        if ch == "*":
            self._add("Any")
        elif ch == "{":
            self._add("EitherStart")
        elif ch == ",":
            self._add(None)
        elif ch == "}":
            self._add("EitherEnd")
        elif ch in CHARS:
            self.current += ch
        else:
            raise NotImplementedError(f"what is '{ch}'?")
    self._add(None)
    return self.result
```

This method calls `self._setup()` at the start so that the tokenizer can be re-used. It *doesn't* call `self._add()` for regular characters; instead, it creates a `Lit` entry when it

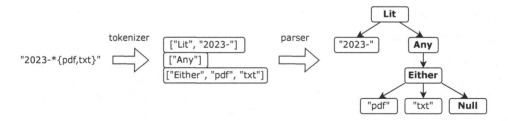

Figure 5.1: Stages in parsing pipeline.

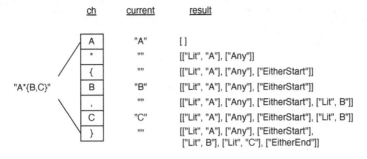

Figure 5.2: Steps in tokenizing a string.

encounters a special character (i.e., when the current literal ends) and after all the input has been parsed (to capture the last literal).

The method self._add adds the current thing to the list of tokens. As a special case, self._add(None) means "add the literal but nothing else" (Figure 5.2):

```
def _add(self, thing):
    if len(self.current) > 0:
        self.result.append(["Lit", self.current])
        self.current = ""
    if thing is not None:
        self.result.append([thing])
```

Finally, we work backward to initialize the tokenizer when we construct it and to define the set of characters that make up literals:

```
CHARS = set(string.ascii_letters + string.digits)

class Tokenizer:
    def __init__(self):
        self._setup()

    def _setup(self):
        self.result = []
        self.current = ""
```

A Simple Constant

The code fragment above defines CHARS to be a set containing ASCII letters and digits. We use a set for speed: if we used a list, Python would have to search through it each time we wanted to check a character, but finding something in a set is much faster. Chapter 17 will explain why the word "ASCII" appears in string library's definition of characters, but using it and string.digits greatly reduces the chances of us typing "abcdeghi...yz" rather than "abcdefghi...yz". (The fact that it took you a moment to spot the missing letter 'f' proves this point.)

We can now write a few tests to check that the tokenizer is producing a list of lists in which each sub-list represents a single token:

```
def test_tok_empty_string():
    assert Tokenizer().tok("") == []


def test_tok_any_either():
    assert Tokenizer().tok("*{abc,def}") == [
        ["Any"],
        ["EitherStart"],
        ["Lit", "abc"],
        ["Lit", "def"],
        ["EitherEnd"],
    ]
```

5.2 Parsing

We now need to turn the list of tokens into a tree. Just as we used a class for tokenizing, we will create one for parsing and give it a `_parse` method to start things off. This method doesn't do any conversion itself. Instead, it takes a token off the front of the list and figures out which method handles tokens of that kind:

```
def _parse(self, tokens):
    if not tokens:
        return Null()

    front, back = tokens[0], tokens[1:]
    if front[0] == "Any": handler = self._parse_Any
    elif front[0] == "EitherStart": handler = self._parse_EitherStart
    elif front[0] == "Lit": handler = self._parse_Lit
    else:
        assert False, f"Unknown token type {front}"

    return handler(front[1:], back)
```

The handlers for `Any` and `Lit` are straightforward:

```
def _parse_Any(self, rest, back):
    return Any(self._parse(back))

def _parse_Lit(self, rest, back):
    return Lit(rest[0], self._parse(back))
```

`Either` is a little messier. We didn't save the commas, so we'll just pull two tokens and store them after checking to make sure that we actually *have* two tokens:

```
def _parse_EitherStart(self, rest, back):
    if (
        len(back) < 3
        or (back[0][0] != "Lit")
        or (back[1][0] != "Lit")
        or (back[2][0] != "EitherEnd")
    ):
        raise ValueError("badly-formatted Either")
    left = Lit(back[0][1])
    right = Lit(back[1][1])
    return Either([left, right], self._parse(back[3:]))
```

An alternative approach is to take tokens from the list until we see an `EitherEnd` marker:

```
def _parse_EitherStart(self, rest, back):
    children = []
    while back and (back[0][0] == "Lit"):
        children.append(Lit(back[0][1]))
        back = back[1:]

    if not children:
        raise ValueError("empty Either")

    if back[0][0] != "EitherEnd":
        raise ValueError("badly-formatted Either")

    return Either(children, self._parse(back[1:]))
```

This achieves the same thing in the two-token case but allows us to write alternatives with more options without changing the code (assuming you solved the "Multiple Alternatives" exercise in Chapter 4). Tests confirm that we're on the right track:

```
def test_parse_either_two_lit():
    assert Parser().parse("{abc,def}") == Either(
        [Lit("abc"), Lit("def")]
    )
```

This test assumes we can compare `Match` objects using `==`, just as we would compare numbers or strings. so we add a `__eq__` method to our classes:

```
class Match:
    def __init__(self, rest):
        self.rest = rest if rest else Null()

    def __eq__(self, other):
        return (other is not None and
                self.__class__ == other.__class__ and
                self.rest == other.rest)

class Lit(Match):
    def __init__(self, chars, rest=None):
        super().__init__(rest)
        self.chars = chars

    def __eq__(self, other):
        return super().__eq__(other) and (
            self.chars == other.chars
        )
```

Since we're using inheritance to implement our matchers, we write the check for equality in two parts. The parent class `Match` performs the checks that all classes need to perform (in this case, that the objects being compared have the same **concrete class**). If the child class needs to do any more checking (for example, that the characters in two `Lit` objects are the same) it calls up to the parent method first, then adds its own tests.

They're Just Methods

Operator overloading relies on the fact that when Python sees `a == b` it calls `a.__eq__(b)`. Similarly, `a + b` is "just" a call to `a.__add__(b)`, so if we create methods with the right names, we can manipulate objects using familiar operations.

5.3 Summary

Figure 5.3 summarizes the key ideas in this chapter. Once again, while it's useful to understand how parsers work, please don't create new data formats that need new parsers if you can possibly avoid it.

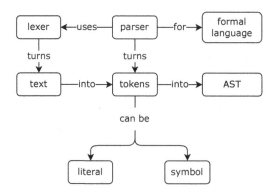

Figure 5.3: Parser concept map.

5.4 Exercises

Escape Characters

Modify the parser to handle escape characters, so that (for example) * is interpreted as a literal '*' character and \\ is interpreted as a literal backslash.

Character Sets

Modify the parser so that expressions like [xyz] are interpreted to mean "match any one of those three characters". (Note that this is a shorthand for {x,y,z}.)

Negation

Modify the parser so that [!abc] is interpreted as "match anything *except* one of those three characters".

Nested Lists

Write a function that accepts a string representing nested lists containing numbers and returns the actual list. For example, the input [1, [2, [3, 4], 5]] should produce the corresponding Python list.

Simple Arithmetic

Write a function that accepts a string consisting of numbers and the basic arithmetic operations +, -, *, and /, and produces a nested structure showing the operations in the correct order. For example, 1 + 2 * 3 should produce ["+", 1, ["*", 2, 3]].

6

Running Tests

> - Functions are objects you can save in data structures or pass to other functions.
>
> - Python stores local and global variables in dictionary-like structures.
>
> - A unit test performs an operation on a fixture and passes, fails, or produces an error.
>
> - A program can use introspection to find functions and other objects at runtime.
>
> Terms defined: **actual result (of test)**, **assertion**, **dynamic typing**, **error (result of test)**, **exception**, **expected result (of test)**, **failure (result of test)**, **fixture**, **global**, **local**, **pass (result of test)**, **pretty print**, **raise (an exception)**, **register (in code)**, **scope**, **unit test**

Not all software needs rigorous testing: for example, it's OK to check a one-off data analysis script by looking at the output of each stage as we add it. But we should all be grateful that 98% of the lines of code in the SQLite[1] database are there to make the other 2% always do the right thing.

The examples in this book lie somewhere between these two extremes. Together, they are over 7000 lines long; to make sure they work correctly, we wrote several hundred **unit tests** using pytest[2]. We used this framework because it makes tests easier to write, and because it runs them in a reliable, repeatable way [Meszaros2007; Aniche2022]. Understanding how tools like this work will help you use them more effectively, and will reinforce one of the big ideas of this book: programs are just another kind of data.

6.1   Storing and Running Tests

As we said in Chapter 2, a function is just an object that we can assign to a variable. We can also store them in lists just like numbers or strings (Figure 6.1):

```
def first():
    print("First")

def second():
    print("Second")

def third():
    print("Third")

everything = [first, second, third]
for func in everything:
    func()
```

---

[1] https://sqlite.org/
[2] https://docs.pytest.org/

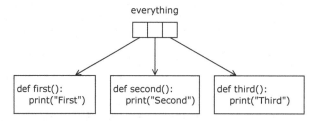

Figure 6.1: A list of functions.

```
First
Second
Third
```

However, we have to be able to call the functions in the same way in order for this trick to work, which means they must have the same signature:

```
def zero():
    print("zero")

def one(value):
    print("one", value)

for func in [zero, one]:
    func()
```

```
zero
Traceback (most recent call last):
  File "/sdx/test/signature.py", line 8, in <module>
    func()
TypeError: one() missing 1 required positional argument: 'value'
```

Now suppose we have a function we want to test:

```
def sign(value):
    if value < 0:
        return -1
    else:
        return 1
```

and some functions that test it (two of which contain deliberate errors):

```
def test_sign_negative():
    assert sign(-3) == -1

def test_sign_positive():
    assert sign(19) == 1

def test_sign_zero():
    assert sign(0) == 0

def test_sign_error():
    assert sgn(1) == 1
```

Each test does something to a **fixture** (such as the number 19) and uses **assertions** to compare the **actual result** against the **expected result**. The outcome of each test can be:

- **Pass**: the test subject works as expected.

- **Fail**: something is wrong with the test subject.

- **Error**: something is wrong in the test itself, which means we don't know if the thing we're testing is working properly or not.

We can implement this classification scheme as follows:

1. If a test function completes without **raising** any kind of **exception**, it passes. (We don't care if it returns something, but by convention tests don't return a value.)

2. If the function raises an `AssertionError` exception, then the test has failed. Python's `assert` statement does this automatically when the condition it is checking is false, so almost all tests use `assert` for checks.

3. If the function raises any other kind of exception, then we assume the test itself is broken and count it as an error.

Translating these rules into code gives us the function `run_tests` that runs every test in a list and counts how many outcomes of each kind it sees:

```python
def run_tests(all_tests):
    results = {"pass": 0, "fail": 0, "error": 0}
    for test in all_tests:
        try:
            test()
            results["pass"] += 1
        except AssertionError:
            results["fail"] += 1
        except Exception:
            results["error"] += 1
    print(f"pass {results['pass']}")
    print(f"fail {results['fail']}")
    print(f"error {results['error']}")
```

We use `run_tests` by putting all of our test functions into a list and passing that to the test runner:

```python
TESTS = [
    test_sign_negative,
    test_sign_positive,
    test_sign_zero,
    test_sign_error
]

run_tests(TESTS)
```

```
pass 2
fail 1
error 1
```

> **Independence**
>
> Our function runs tests in the order they appear in the list. The tests should not rely on that: every unit test should work independently so that an error or failure in an early test doesn't affect other tests' behavior.

6.2   Finding Functions

Making lists of functions is clumsy and error-prone: sooner or later we'll add a function to TESTS twice or forget to add it at all. We'd therefore like our test runner to find tests for itself, which it can do by exploiting the fact that Python stores variables in a structure similar to a dictionary.

Let's run the Python interpreter and call the `globals` function. To make its output easier to read, we will **pretty-print** it using Python's `pprint`[3] module:

```
import pprint
pprint.pprint(globals())
```

```
{'__annotations__': {},
 '__builtins__': <module 'builtins' (built-in)>,
 '__cached__': None,
 '__doc__': None,
 '__file__': '/sdx/test/globals.py',
 '__loader__': <_frozen_importlib_external.SourceFileLoader object \
at 0x109d65290>,
 '__name__': '__main__',
 '__package__': None,
 '__spec__': None,
 'pprint': <module 'pprint' from \
'/sdx/conda/envs/sdxpy/lib/python3.11/pprint.py'>}
```

As the output shows, `globals` is a dictionary containing all the variables in the program's **global scope**. Since we just started the interpreter, all we see are the variables that Python defines automatically. (By convention, Python uses double underscores for names that mean something special to it.)

What happens when we define a variable of our own?

```
import pprint
my_variable = 123
pprint.pprint(globals())
```

```
{'__annotations__': {},
 '__builtins__': <module 'builtins' (built-in)>,
 '__cached__': None,
 '__doc__': None,
 '__file__': '/sdx/test/globals_plus.py',
 '__loader__': <_frozen_importlib_external.SourceFileLoader object \
at 0x108039290>,
 '__name__': '__main__',
 '__package__': None,
```

---

[3]https://docs.python.org/3/library/pprint.html

```
'__spec__': None,
'my_variable': 123,
'pprint': <module 'pprint' from \
'/sdx/conda/envs/sdxpy/lib/python3.11/pprint.py'>}
```

Sure enough, `my_variable` is now in the dictionary.

If function names are just variables and a program's variables are stored in a dictionary, we can loop over that dictionary to find all the functions whose names start with `test_`:

```
def find_tests(prefix):
    for (name, func) in globals().items():
        if name.startswith(prefix):
            print(name, func)

find_tests("test_")
```

```
test_sign_negative <function test_sign_negative at 0x105bcd440>
test_sign_positive <function test_sign_positive at 0x105bcd4e0>
test_sign_zero <function test_sign_zero at 0x105bcd580>
test_sign_error <function test_sign_error at 0x105bcd620>
```

The hexadecimal numbers in the output show where each function object is stored in memory, which isn't particularly useful unless we're extending the language, but at least it doesn't take up much space on the screen.

Having a running program find things in itself like this is called introspection, and is the key to many of the designs in upcoming chapters. Combining introspection with the pass-fail-error pattern of the previous section gives us something that finds test functions, runs them, and summarizes their results:

```
def run_tests():
    results = {"pass": 0, "fail": 0, "error": 0}
    for (name, test) in globals().items():
        if not name.startswith("test_"):
            continue
        try:
            test()
            results["pass"] += 1
        except AssertionError:
            results["fail"] += 1
        except Exception:
            results["error"] += 1
    print(f"pass {results['pass']}")
    print(f"fail {results['fail']}")
    print(f"error {results['error']}")
```

```
pass 2
fail 1
error 1
```

We could add many more features to this (and pytest[4] does), but almost every modern test runner uses this design.

---

[4]https://docs.pytest.org/

6.3 Summary

When reviewing the ideas introduced in this chapter (Figure 6.2), it's worth remembering Clarke's Third Law[5], which states that any sufficiently advanced technology is indistinguishable from magic. The same is true of programming tricks like introspection: the code that finds tests dynamically seems transparent to an expert who understands that code is data, but can be incomprehensible to a novice. As we said in the discussion of comprehension curves in Chapter 1, no piece of software can be optimal for both audiences; the only solution to this problem is education, which is why books like this one exist. Please see Appendix B for extra material related to these ideas.

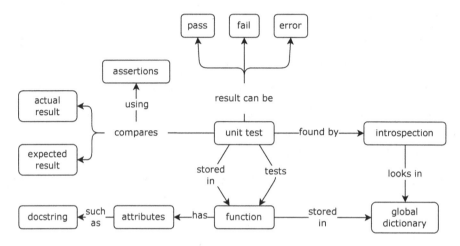

Figure 6.2: Concept map.

6.4 Exercises

Looping Over `globals`

What happens if you run this code?

```
for name in globals():
    print(name)
```

What happens if you run this code instead?

```
name = None
for name in globals():
    print(name)
```

Why are the two different?

---

[5]https://en.wikipedia.org/wiki/Clarke%27s_three_laws

Individual Results

1. Modify the test framework so that it reports which tests passed, failed, or had errors and also reports a summary of how many tests produced each result.

2. Write unit tests to check that your answer works correctly.

Setup and Teardown

Testing frameworks often allow programmers to specify a `setup` function that is to be run before each test and a corresponding `teardown` function that is to be run after each test. (`setup` usually recreates complicated test fixtures, while `teardown` functions are sometimes needed to clean up after tests, e.g., to close database connections or delete temporary files.)

Modify the testing tool in this chapter so that if a file of tests contains a function called `setup` then the tool calls it exactly once before running each test in the file. Add a similar way to **register** a `teardown` function.

Timing Tests

Modify the testing tool so that it records how long it takes to run each test. (The function `time.time` may be useful.)

Selecting Tests

Modify the testing tool so that if a user provides `-s pattern` or `--select pattern` on the command line then the tool only runs tests that contain the string `pattern` in their name.

Finding Functions

Python is **dynamically typed**, which means it checks the types of values as code runs. We can do this ourselves using the `type` function, which shows that 3 is an integer:

```
print(type(3))
```

```
<class 'int'>
```

or that a function is a function:

```
def example():
    pass

print(type(example))
```

```
<class 'function'>
```

However, built-in functions have a different type:

```
print(type(len))
```

```
<class 'builtin_function_or_method'>
```

so it's safer to use `callable` to check if something can be called:

```
def example():
    pass

print(callable(example), callable(len))
```

```
True True
```

1. Modify the test runner in this chapter so that it *doesn't* try to call things whose names start with `test_` but which aren't actually functions.

2. Should the test runner report these cases as errors?

Local Variables

Python has a function called `locals` that returns all the variables defined in the current **local** scope.

1. Predict what the code below will print *before* running it. When does the variable `i` first appear and is it still there in the final line of output?

2. Run the code and compare your prediction with its behavior.

```
def show_locals(low, high):
    print(f"start: {locals()}")
    for i in range(low, high):
        print(f"loop {i}: {locals()}")
    print(f"end: {locals()}")

show_locals(1, 3)
```

7

An Interpreter

- Compilers and interpreters are just programs.

- Basic arithmetic operations are just functions that have special notation.

- Programs can be represented as trees, which can be stored as nested lists.

- Interpreters recursively dispatch operations to functions that implement low-level steps.

- Programs store variables in stacked dictionaries called environments.

- One way to evaluate a program's design is to ask how extensible it is.

Terms defined: **compiler**, **control flow**, **defensive programming**, **dictionary comprehension**, **dynamic dispatch**, **environment**, **expression**, **infix notation**, **interpreter**, **introspection**, **prefix notation**, **runtime**, **statement**, **type hint**

Chapter 2 and Chapter 6 introduced the idea that programs are just data. **Compilers** and **interpreters** are just programs too. Instead of calculating sums or drawing characters on a screen, compilers turn text into instructions for interpreters or hardware to run.

Most real programming languages have two parts: a parser that translates the source code into a data structure, and a **runtime** that executes the instructions in that data structure. Chapter 5 explored parsing; this chapter will build a runtime for a very simple interpreter, while Chapter 25 will look at how we can compile code so that it runs more efficiently.

Two Ways to Run Code

A compiler translates a program into runnable instructions before the program runs, while an interpreter generates instructions on the fly as the program is running. The differences between the two are blurry in practice: for example, Python translates the instructions in a program into instructions as it loads files, but saves those instructions in `.pyc` files to save itself work the next time it runs the program.

7.1 Expressions

Let's start by building something that can evaluate simple **expressions** such as 1+2 or abs(-3.5). We represent each expression as a list with the name of the operation as the first item and the values to be operated on as the other items. If we have multiple operations, we use nested lists:

```
["add", 1, 2]           # 1 + 2
["abs", -3.5]           # abs(-3.5)
["add", ["abs", -5], 9] # abs(-5) + 9
```

Notation

We use **infix notation** like 1+2 for historical reasons in everyday life, but our inter-preter uses **prefix notation**—i.e., always puts the operations' names first—to make the operations easier to find. Similarly, we have special symbols for addition, subtraction, and so on for historical reasons, but our list representation doesn't distinguish between things like + and abs because it doesn't need to. If our program is being compiled into low-level instructions for a particular CPU, it's the compiler's job to decide what can be done directly and what needs multiple instructions. For example, early CPUs didn't have instructions to do division, while modern CPUs may have instructions to do addition or multiplication on multiple values at once.

The function to add two expressions looks like this:

```
def do_add(args):
    assert len(args) == 2
    left = do(args[0])
    right = do(args[1])
    return left + right
```

Its single parameter is a list containing the two sub-expressions to be evaluated and added. After checking that this list contains the required number of values, it calls an as-yet-unwritten function do to evaluate those sub-expressions. (We've called the function do instead of eval because Python already has a function called eval.) Once do_add has two actual values, it adds them and returns the result.

do_abs implements absolute values the same way. The only differences are that it expects one value instead of two and calculates a different return value:

```
def do_abs(args):
    assert len(args) == 1
    val = do(args[0])
    return abs(val)
```

Notice that do_abs and do_add have the same signature. As with the unit testing functions in Chapter 6, this allows us to call them interchangeably.

So how does do work? It starts by checking if its input is an integer. If so, it returns that value right away because integers "evaluate" to themselves. Otherwise, do checks that its parameter is a list and then uses the first value in the list to decide what other function to call.

```
def do(expr):
    # Integers evaluate to themselves.
    if isinstance(expr, int):
        return expr

    # Lists trigger function calls.
    assert isinstance(expr, list)
    if expr[0] == "abs":
        return do_abs(expr[1:])
    if expr[0] == "add":
        return do_add(expr[1:])
    assert False, f"Unknown operation {expr[0]}"
```

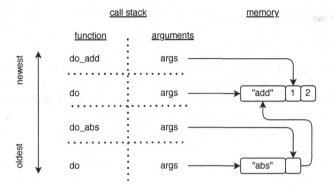

Figure 7.1: Recursively evaluating the expression `['abs',['add',1,2]]`.

This lookup-and-call process is called **dynamic dispatch**, since the program decides who to give work to on the fly. It leads to a situation where `do` calls a function like `do_add`, which in turn calls `do`, which may then call `do_add` (or something other function) and so on (Figure 7.1). Having a function call itself either directly or indirectly is called recursion, which has a reputation for being hard to understand. As our interpreter shows, though, it's a natural way to solve a wide range of problems: each recursive step handles a smaller part of the overall problem until we reach an integer or some other value that doesn't require any further work.

With all of this code in place, the main body of the program can read the file containing the instructions to execute, call `do`, and print the result:

```python
def main():
    assert len(sys.argv) == 2, "Usage: expr.py filename"
    with open(sys.argv[1], "r") as reader:
        program = json.load(reader)
    result = do(program)
    print(f"=> {result}")

if __name__ == "__main__":
    main()
```

The program we want to interpret is a list of lists of lists, so we can read it as JSON using `json.load` rather than writing our own parser. For example, if our program file contains:

```
["add", ["abs", -3], 2]
```

then our little interpreter prints:

```
=> 5
```

This is a lot of code to do something that Python already does, but it shows what Python (and other languages) do themselves. When we run:

```
python expr.py expr.tll
```

Python reads `expr.py`, turns it into a data structure with operation identifiers and constants, and uses those operation identifiers to decide what functions to call. The functions inside Python are written in C and have been compiled to machine instructions, but the cycle of lookup and call is exactly the same as it is in our little interpreter.

7.2 Variables

Doing arithmetic on constants is a start, but our programs will be easier to read if we can define variables that give names to values. We can add variables to our interpreter by passing around a dictionary containing all the variables seen so far. Such a dictionary is sometimes called an **environment** because it is the setting in which expressions are evaluated; the dictionaries returned by the `globals` and `locals` functions introduced in Chapter 6 are both environments.

Let's modify `do_add`, `do_abs`, `do`, and `main` to take an environment as an extra parameter and pass it on as needed:

```
def do_abs(env, args):
    assert len(args) == 1
    val = do(env, args[0])
    return abs(val)
```

Looking up variables when we need their values is straightforward. We check that we have a variable name and that the name is in the environment, then return the stored value:

```
def do_get(env, args):
    assert len(args) == 1
    assert isinstance(args[0], str)
    assert args[0] in env, f"Unknown variable {args[0]}"
    return env[args[0]]
```

To define a new variable or change an existing one, we evaluate an expression and store its value in the environment:

```
def do_set(env, args):
    assert len(args) == 2
    assert isinstance(args[0], str)
    value = do(env, args[1])
    env[args[0]] = value
    return value
```

We need to add one more function to make this all work. Our programs no longer consist of a single expression; instead, we may have several expressions that set variables' values and then use them in calculations. To handle this, we add a function `do_seq` that runs a sequence of expressions one by one. This function is our first piece of **control flow**: rather than calculating a value itself, it controls when and how other expressions are evaluated. Its implementation is:

```
def do_seq(env, args):
    assert len(args) > 0
    for item in args:
        result = do(env, item)
    return result
```

Let's try it out. Our test program is:

```
[
    "seq",
    ["set", "alpha", 1],
    ["set", "beta", 2],
    ["add", ["get", "alpha"], ["get", "beta"]]
]
```

```
=> 3
```

Everything Is An Expression

As we said above, Python distinguishes expressions that produce values from **state-ments** that don't. But it doesn't have to, and many languages don't. For example, Python could have been designed to allow this:

```
# not actually legal Python
result =
    if a > 0:
        1
    elif a == 0:
        0
    else:
        -1
```

7.3   Introspection

Now that we have evaluation, function lookup, and environments, we can write small programs. However, our do function now looks like this:

```
def do(env, expr):
    if isinstance(expr, int):
        return expr
    assert isinstance(expr, list)
    if expr[0] == "abs":
        return do_abs(env, expr[1:])
    if expr[0] == "add":
        return do_add(env, expr[1:])
    if expr[0] == "get":
        return do_get(env, expr[1:])
    if expr[0] == "seq":
        return do_seq(env, expr[1:])
    if expr[0] == "set":
        return do_set(env, expr[1:])
    assert False, f"Unknown operation {expr[0]}"
```

The sequence of if statements that decide what function to call is becoming unwieldy. (Quick: can you see if any of the instruction names are accidentally duplicated?) We can replace this by using **introspection** to create a lookup table that stores every function whose name starts with do_ (Figure 7.2):

```
OPS = {
    name.replace("do_", ""): func
    for (name, func) in globals().items()
    if name.startswith("do_")
}
```

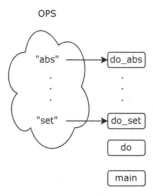

Figure 7.2: Dynamically-generated function lookup table.

Line by line:

1. We use a **dictionary comprehension** to create a dictionary in a single statement.

2. We only add functions whose names start with `do_`.

3. Each key-value pair in the dictionary is the name of an operation and the function that implements the operation. The operation's name is what comes after `do_` in the function's name.

With this lookup table in hand, the code to select and run an operation is:

```python
def do(env, expr):
    # Integers evaluate to themselves.
    if isinstance(expr, int):
        return expr

    # Lists trigger function calls.
    assert isinstance(expr, list)
    assert expr[0] in OPS, f"Unknown operation {expr[0]}"
    func = OPS[expr[0]]
    return func(env, expr[1:])
```

As with unit test functions in Chapter 6, the `do_*` functions must have exactly the same signature so that we can call any of them with an environment and a list of arguments without knowing exactly which function we're calling. And as with finding tests, introspection is more reliable than a hand-written lookup table but is harder to understand. If we write out the lookup table explicitly like this:

```python
OPS = {
    "abs": do_abs,
    "add": do_add,
    "get": do_get,
    "seq": do_seq,
    "set": do_set,
}
```

then we can see exactly what operations are available and what their names are. If we use introspection, we have to search through the source file (or possibly several files) to find all the available operations, but we can write `do` once and never worry about it again.

7.4 Summary

Figure 7.3 summarizes the ideas introduced in this chapter. A lot is going on here, but the central idea is that a program is just another kind of data. Please see Appendix B for extra material related to these ideas.

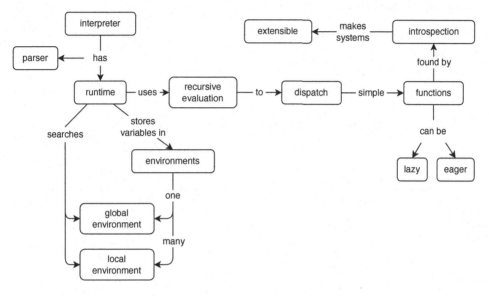

Figure 7.3: Interpreter concept map.

7.5 Exercises

Arrays

Implement fixed-size, one-dimensional arrays: ["array", 10] creates an array of 10 elements, while other instructions that you design get and set particular array elements by index.

Better Error Handling

Several of the instruction functions started with assert statements, which means that users get a stack trace of TLL itself when there's a bug in their program.

1. Define a new exception class called TLLException.

2. Write a utility function called check that raises a TLLException with a useful error message when there's a problem.

3. Add a catch statement to handle these errors.

More Statements

Add `print` and `repeat` commands to the interpreter so that the following program produces the output shown:

```
[
    "seq",
    ["set", "a", 1],
    ["print", "initial", ["get", "a"]],
    [
        "repeat", 4,
        [
            "seq",
            ["set", "a", ["add", ["get", "a"], ["get", "a"]]],
            ["if",
            ["leq", ["get", "a"], 10],
            ["print", "small", ["get", "a"]],
            ["print", "large", ["get", "a"]]
            ]
            ]
    ]
]
```

```
initial 1
small 2
small 4
small 8
large 16
=> None
```

Does your `repeat` command handle "repeat zero times" correctly, i.e., does it handle the program below? If so, what does your `do_repeat` function return as a result in this case?

```
["repeat", 0, ["print", "zero"]]
```

Tracing

Add a `--trace` command-line flag to the interpreter. When enabled, it makes TLL print a message showing each function call and its result.

While Loops

Implement a `while` loop instruction. Your implementation can use either a Python `while` loop or recursion.

Internal Checks

Defensive programming is an approach to software development that starts from the assumption that people make mistakes and should therefore put checks in their code to catch "impossible" situations. These checks are typically implemented as `assert` statements that check the state of the program as it executes, like those in our interpreter that checks the lengths of lists.

1. What other assertions could we add to this code?

2. How many of these checks can be implemented as **type hints** instead?

8

Functions and Closures

- When we define a function, our programming system saves instructions for later use.

- Since functions are just data, we can separate creation from naming.

- Most programming languages use eager evaluation, in which arguments are evaluated before a function is called.

- Programming languages can also use lazy evaluation, in which expressions are passed to functions for just-in-time evaluation.

- Every call to a function creates a new stack frame on the call stack.

- When a function looks up variables it checks its own stack frame and the global frame.

- A closure stores the variables referenced in a particular scope.

Terms defined: **anonymous function, call stack, closure, dynamic scoping, eager evaluation, extensibility, lambda expression, lazy evaluation, lexical scoping, name collision, stack frame, variable capture**

One way to evaluate the design of a piece of software is to ask how **extensible** it is, i.e., how easily we can add or change things [Wilson2022b]. The answer for the interpreter of Chapter 7 is "pretty easily" but the answer for the little language it interprets is "not at all", because users cannot define new operations in the little language itself. We need to give them a way to define and call functions. Doing this will take less than 60 lines of code, and once we understand how definition works, we will be able to understand how an advanced feature of most modern programming languages works as well.

8.1 Definition and Storage

Let's start by defining a function that takes a single parameter and immediately returns it. In Python, this is:

```
def same(num):
    return num
```

It has a name, a (possibly empty) list of parameters, and a body, which in this case is a single statement.

Our little language does things differently. Since a function is just another kind of object, we can define it on its own without naming it:

```
["func", ["num"], ["get", "num"]]
```

To save the function for later use, we simply assign it to a name as we would assign any other value:

```
["set", "same", ["func", ["num"], ["get", "num"]]]
```

Anonymity

A function without a name is called an **anonymous** function. JavaScript makes heavy use of anonymous functions; Python supports a very limited version of them using **lambda expressions**:

```
double = lambda x: 2 * x
double(3)
```

8.2   Calling Functions

In Python, we would call this function as `same(3)`. Our little language requires us to specify an operator explicitly, so we write the call as:

```
["call", "same", 3]
```

To make `"call"` work the way most programmers expect, we need to implement scope so that the parameters and variables used in a function aren't confused with those defined outside it. In other words, we need to prevent **name collision**. When a function is called with one or more expressions as arguments, we will:

1. Evaluate all of these expressions.

2. Look up the function.

3. Create a new environment from the function's parameter names and the expressions' values.

4. Call `do` to run the function's action and capture the result.

5. Discard the environment created in Step 3.

6. Return the function's result.

Eager and Lazy

Evaluating a function's arguments before we run it is called **eager evaluation**. We could instead use **lazy evaluation**, in which case we would pass the argument sublists into the function and let it evaluate them when it needed their values. Python and most other languages are eager, but a handful of languages, such as R, are lazy. It's a bit more work, but it allows the function to inspect the expressions it has been called with and to decide how to handle them.

To make this work, the environment must be a list of dictionaries instead of a single dictionary. This list is the **call stack** of our program, and each dictionary in it is usually called a **stack frame**. When a function wants the value associated with a name, we look through the list from the most recent dictionary to the oldest.

Scoping Rules

Searching through all active stack frames for a variable is called **dynamic scoping**. In contrast, most programming languages used **lexical scoping**, which figures out what a variable name refers to based on the structure of the program text. The former is easier to implement (which is why we've chosen it); the latter is easier to understand, particularly in large programs. [Nystrom2021] has an excellent step-by-step explanation of how to build lexical scoping.

The completed implementation of function definition is:

```
def do_func(env, args):
    assert len(args) == 2
    params = args[0]
    body = args[1]
    return ["func", params, body]
```

and the completed implementation of function call is:

```
def do_call(env, args):
    # Set up the call.
    assert len(args) >= 1
    name = args[0]
    values = [do(env, a) for a in args[1:]]

    # Find the function.
    func = env_get(env, name)
    assert isinstance(func, list) and (func[0] == "func")
    params, body = func[1], func[2]
    assert len(values) == len(params)

    # Run in new environment.
    env.append(dict(zip(params, values)))
    result = do(env, body)
    env.pop()

    # Report.
    return result
```

and our test program and its output are:

```
["seq",
  ["set", "double",
    ["func", ["num"],
      ["add", ["get", "num"], ["get", "num"]]
    ]
  ],
  ["set", "a", 1],
  ["repeat", 4, ["seq",
    ["set", "a", ["call", "double", ["get", "a"]]],
    ["print", ["get", "a"]]
  ]]
]
```

```
2
4
8
16
=> None
```

Unpacking One Line

`do_call` contains the line:

```
env.append(dict(zip(params, values)))
```

Working from the inside out, it uses the built-in function `zip` to create a list of pairs of corresponding items from `params` and `values`, then passes that list of pairs to `dict` to create a dictionary, which it then appends to the list `env`. The exercises will explore whether rewriting this would make it easier to read.

Once again, Python and other languages do more or less what we've done here. When we define a function, the interpreter saves the instructions in a lookup table. When we call a function at runtime, the interpreter finds the function in the table, creates a new stack frame, executes the instructions in the function, and pops the frame off the stack.

8.3   Closures

We normally define functions at the top level of our program, but Python and most other modern languages allow us to define functions within functions. Those inner functions have access to the variables defined in the enclosing function, just as the functions we've seen in earlier examples have access to things defined at the global level of the program:

```
def outer(value):
    def inner(current):
        print(f"inner sum is {current + value}")

    print(f"outer value is {value}")
    for i in range(3):
        inner(i)

outer(10)
```

```
outer value is 10
inner sum is 10
inner sum is 11
inner sum is 12
```

But since functions are just another kind of data, the outer function can return the inner function it defined as its result:

```
def make_hidden(thing):
    def _inner():
        return thing
    return _inner

has_secret = make_hidden(1 + 2)
print("hidden thing is", has_secret())
```

```
hidden thing is 3
```

The inner function still has access to the value of `thing`, but nothing else in the program does. A computer scientist would say that the inner function **captures** the variables in the enclosing function to create a **closure** (Figure 8.1). Doing this is a way to make data private: once `make_hidden` returns `_inner` and we assign it to `has_secret` in the example above, nothing else in our program has any way to access the value that was passed to `make_hidden` as `thing`.

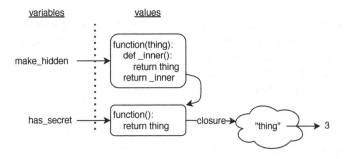

Figure 8.1: Closures.

One common use of closures is to turn a function that needs many arguments into one that needs fewer, i.e., to create a function *now* that remembers some values it's supposed to use *later*; we will explore this in Chapter 9. Closures are also another way to implement objects. Instead of building a dictionary ourselves as we did in Chapter 2, we use the one that Python creates behind the scenes to implement a closure. In the code below, for example, the function `make_object` creates a dictionary containing two functions:

```
def make_object(initial_value):
    private = {"value": initial_value}

    def getter():
        return private["value"]

    def setter(new_value):
        private["value"] = new_value

    return {"get": getter, "set": setter}

object = make_object(00)
print("initial value", object["get"]())
object["set"](99)
print("object now contains", object["get"]())
```

```
initial value 0
object now contains 99
```

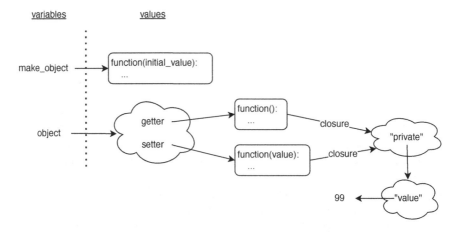

Figure 8.2: Implementing objects using closures.

When this code runs, Python creates a closure that is shared by the two functions (Figure 8.2). The closure has a key `"private"`; there is nothing special about this name, but nothing in the program can see the data in the closure except the two functions. We could add more keys to this dictionary to create more complex objects and build an entire system of objects and classes this way.

8.4   Summary

Figure 8.3 summarizes the ideas in this chapter, which is one of the most technically challenging in this book. In particular, don't be surprised if it takes several passes to understand closures: they are as subtle as they are useful.

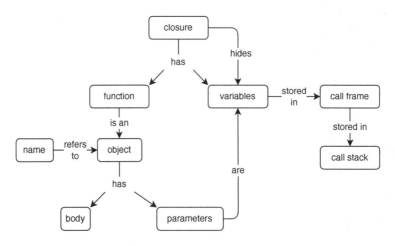

Figure 8.3: Concept map.

8.5   Exercises

Rewriting Environment Creation

Re-read the description of how this line in `do_call` works:

```
env.append(dict(zip(params, values)))
```

and then rewrite the line using a loop to insert parameter names and values into a dictionary. Do you find your rewritten code easier to read?

Chained Maps

Look at the documentation for the `ChainMap`[1] class and modify the interpreter to use that to manage environments.

Defining Named Functions

Modify `do_func` so that if it is given three arguments instead of two, it uses the first one as the function's name without requiring a separate `"set"` instruction.

Evaluating Parameters

`do_func` stores the new function's parameters and body without evaluating them. What would happen if it did evaluate them immediately?

Implicit Sequence

1. Modify `do_func` so that if it is given more than one argument, it uses all but the first as the body of the function (i.e., treats everything after the parameter list as an implicit `"seq"`).

2. Is there a way to make this work in combination with naming-at-creation from the previous exercise?

Preventing Redefinition

1. Modify the interpreter so that programs cannot redefine functions, i.e., so that once a function has been assigned to a variable, that variable's value cannot be changed.

2. Why might this be a good idea? What does it make more difficult?

Generalizing Closure-Based Objects

Modify the `getter`/`setter` example so that:

1. `make_object` accepts any number of named parameters and copies them into the `private` dictionary.

---

[1]https://docs.python.org/3/library/collections.html#collections.ChainMap

2. `getter` takes a name as an argument and returns the corresponding value from the dictionary.

3. `setter` takes a name and a new value as arguments and updates the dictionary.

What does your implementation of `getter` do if the name isn't already in the `private` dictionary? What does your `setter` do if the name isn't already there? What does it do if the update value has a different type than the current value?

What Can Change?

Explain why this program doesn't work:

```
def make_counter():
    value = 0
    def _inner():
        value += 1
        return value
    return _inner

c = make_counter()
for i in range(3):
    print(c())
```

Explain why this one does:

```
def make_counter():
    value = [0]
    def _inner():
        value[0] += 1
        return value[0]
    return _inner

c = make_counter()
for i in range(3):
    print(c())
```

How Private Are Closures?

If the data in a closure is private, explain why lines 1 and 2 are the same in the output of this program but lines 3 and 4 are different.

```
def wrap(extra):
    def _inner(f):
        return [f(x) for x in extra]
    return _inner

odds = [1, 3, 5]
first = wrap(odds)
print("1.", first(lambda x: 2 * x))

odds = [7, 9, 11]
print("2.", first(lambda x: 2 * x))

evens = [2, 4, 6]
second = wrap(evens)
print("3.", second(lambda x: 2 * x))
```

```
evens.append(8)
print("4.", second(lambda x: 2 * x))
```

```
1. [2, 6, 10]
2. [2, 6, 10]
3. [4, 8, 12]
4. [4, 8, 12, 16]
```

9

Protocols

- Temporarily replacing functions with mock objects can simplify testing.

- Mock objects can record their calls and/or return variable results.

- Python defines protocols so that code can be triggered by keywords in the language.

- Use the context manager protocol to ensure cleanup operations always execute.

- Use decorators to wrap functions after defining them.

- Use closures to create decorators that take extra parameters.

- Use the iterator protocol to make objects work with for loops.

Terms defined: **append mode**, **context manager**, **decorator**, **infinite recursion**, **iterator**, **Iterator pattern**, **mock object**, **protocol**

This book is supposed to teach software design by implementing small versions of real-world tools, but we have reached a point where we need to learn a little more about Python itself in order to proceed. Our discussion of closures in Chapter 8 was the first step; in this chapter, we will look at how Python allows users to tell it to do things at specific moments.

9.1 Mock Objects

We have already seen that functions are objects referred to by variable names just like other values. We can use this fact to change functions at runtime to make testing easier. For example, if the function we want to test uses the time of day, we can temporarily replace the real `time.time` function with one that returns a specific value so we know what result to expect in our test:

```
import time

def elapsed(since):
    return time.time() - since

def mock_time():
    return 200

def test_elapsed():
    time.time = mock_time
    assert elapsed(50) == 150
```

Temporary replacements like this are called **mock objects** because we usually use objects even if the thing we're replacing is a function. We can do this because Python lets us create objects that can be "called" just like functions. If an object `obj` has a `__call__` method, then `obj(...)` is automatically turned into `obj.__call__(...)` just as a `== b` is automatically turned into a.__eq__(b) (Chapter 5). For example, the code below defines a class Adder whose instances add a constant to their input:

```
class Adder:
    def __init__(self, value):
        self.value = value

    def __call__(self, arg):
        return arg + self.value

add_3 = Adder(3)
result = add_3(8)
print(f"add_3(8): {result}")
```

```
add_3(8): 11
```

Let's create a reusable mock object class that:

1. defines a __call__ method so that instances can be called like functions;

2. declares the parameters of that method to be *args and **kwargs so that it can be called with any number of regular or keyword arguments;

3. stores those arguments so we can see how the replaced function was called; and

4. returns either a fixed value or a value produced by a user-defined function.

The class itself is only 11 lines long:

```
class Fake:
    def __init__(self, func=None, value=None):
        self.calls = []
        self.func = func
        self.value = value

    def __call__(self, *args, **kwargs):
        self.calls.append([args, kwargs])
        if self.func is not None:
            return self.func(*args, **kwargs)
        return self.value
```

For convenience, let's also define a function that replaces some function we've already defined with an instance of our Fake class:

```
def fakeit(name, func=None, value=None):
    assert name in globals()
    fake = Fake(func, value)
    globals()[name] = fake
    return fake
```

To show how this works, we define a function that adds two numbers and write a test for it:

```
def adder(a, b):
    return a + b

def test_with_real_function():
    assert adder(2, 3) == 5
```

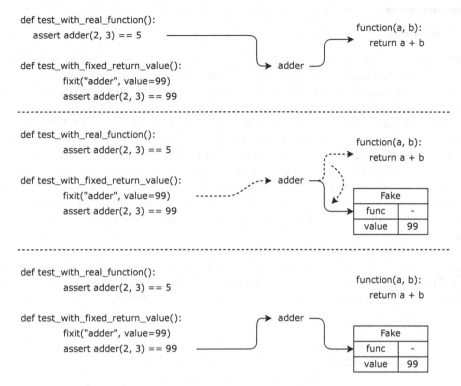

Figure 9.1: Timeline of mock operation.

We then use `fakeit` to replace the real `adder` function with a mock object that always returns 99 (Figure 9.1):

```
def test_with_fixed_return_value ():
    fakeit ("adder", value=99)
    assert adder (2, 3) == 99
```

Another test proves that our `Fake` class records all of the calls:

```
def test_fake_records_calls ():
    fake = fakeit ("adder", value=99)
    assert adder (2, 3) == 99
    assert adder (3, 4) == 99
    assert adder.calls == [[(2, 3), {}], [(3, 4), {}]]
```

And finally, the user can provide a function to calculate a return value:

```
def test_fake_calculates_result ():
    fakeit ("adder", func=lambda left, right: 10 * left + right)
    assert adder (2, 3) == 23
```

9.2 Protocols

Mock objects are very useful, but the way we're using them is going to cause strange errors. The problem is that each test replaces `adder` with a mock object that does something different. As a result, any test that *doesn't* replace `adder` will use whatever mock object was last put in place rather than the original `adder` function.

We could tell users it's their job to put everything back after each test, but people are forgetful. It would be better if Python did this automatically; luckily for us, it provides a **protocol** for exactly this purpose. A protocol is a rule that specifies how programs can tell Python to do specific things at specific moments. Giving a class a `__call__` method is an example of this: when Python sees `thing(...)`, it automatically checks if `thing` has that method. Defining an `__init__` method for a class is another example: if a class has a method with that name, Python calls it automatically when constructing a new instance of that class.

What we want for managing mock objects is a **context manager** that replaces the real function with our mock at the start of a block of code and then puts the original back at the end. The protocol for this relies on two methods called `__enter__` and `__exit__`. If the class is called `C`, then when Python executes a `with` block like this:

```
with C...(...args) as name:...
    do ...things
```

it does the following (Figure 9.2):

1. Call `C`'s constructor to create an object that it associates with the code block.

2. Call that object's `__enter__` method and assign the result to the variable `name`.

3. Run the code inside the `with` block.

4. Call `name.__exit__()` when the block finishes.

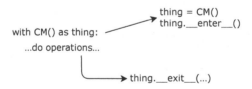

Figure 9.2: Operations performed by a context manager.

Here's a mock object that inherits all the capabilities of `Fake` and adds the two methods needed by `with`:

```
class ContextFake(Fake):
    def __init__(self, name, func=None, value=None):
        super().__init__(func, value)
        self.name = name
        self.original = None

    def __enter__(self):
        assert self.name in globals()
        self.original = globals()[self.name]
        globals()[self.name] = self
```

```
        return self

    def __exit__(self, exc_type, exc_value, exc_traceback):
        globals()[self.name] = self.original
```

Notice that `__enter__` doesn't take any extra parameters: anything it needs must be provided via the object's constructor. On the other hand, `__exit__` will always be called with three values that tell it whether an exception occurred, and if so, what the exception was. This test shows that our context manager is doing what it's supposed to:

```
def subber(a, b):
    return a - b

def check_no_lasting_effects():
    assert subber(2, 3) == -1
    with ContextFake("subber", value=1234) as fake:
        assert subber(2, 3) == 1234
        assert len(fake.calls) == 1
    assert subber(2, 3) == -1
```

Context managers can't prevent people from making mistakes, but they make it easier for people to do the right thing. They are also an example of how programming languages often evolve: eventually, if enough people are doing something the same way in enough places, support for that way of doing things is added to the language.

9.3 Decorators

Python programs rely on several other protocols, each of which gives user-level code a way to interact with some aspect of the Python interpreter. One of the most widely used is called a **decorator**, which allows us to wrap one function with another.

In order to understand how decorators work, we must take another look at closures (Chapter 8). Suppose we want to create a function called `logging` that prints a message before and after each call to some other arbitrary function. We could try to do it like this:

```
def original(value):
    print(f"original: {value}")

def logging(value):
    print("before call")
    original(value)
    print("after call")

original = logging
original("example")
```

but when we try to call `original` we wind up in an infinite loop. The wrapped version of our function refers to `original`, but Python looks up the function associated with that name *at the time of call*, which means it finds our wrapper function instead of the original function (Figure 9.3). We can prevent this **infinite recursion** by creating a closure to capture the original function for later use:

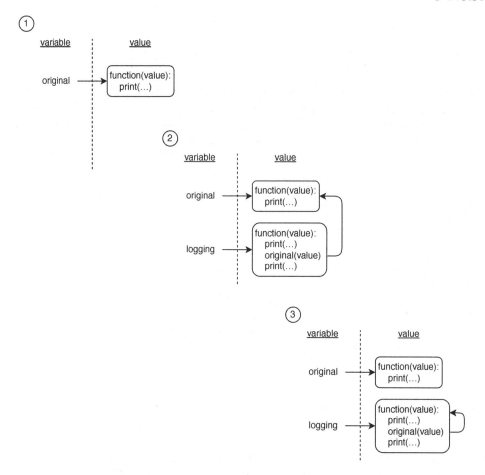

Figure 9.3: Infinite recursion caused by careless use of a wrapped function.

```
def original(value):
    print(f"original: {value}")

def logging(func):
    def _inner(value):
        print("before call")
        func(value)
        print("after call")
    return _inner

original = logging(original)
original("example")
```

```
before call
original: example
after call
```

Using a closure also gives us a way to pass extra arguments when we create the wrapped function:

```
def original(value):
    print(f"original: {value}")

def logging(func, label):
    def _inner(value):
        print(f"++ {label}")
        func(value)
        print(f"-- {label}")
    return _inner

original = logging(original, "call")
original("example")
```

```
++ call
original: example
-- call
```

Wrapping functions like this is so useful that Python has built-in support for doing it. We define the decorator function that does the wrapping as before, but then use @wrap to apply it rather than name = wrap(name):

```
def wrap(func):
    def _inner(*args):
        print("before call")
        func(*args)
        print("after call")
    return _inner

@wrap
def original(message):
    print(f"original: {message}")

original("example")
```

```
before call
original: example
after call
```

If we want to pass arguments at the time we apply the decorator, though, it seems like we're stuck: a Python decorator must take exactly one argument, which must be the function we want to decorate. The solution is to define a function inside a function *inside yet another function* to create a closure that captures the arguments:

```
def wrap(label):                    # function returning a decorator
    def _decorate(func):            # the decorator Python will apply
        def _inner(*args):          # the wrapped function
            print(f"++ {label}")    # 'label' is visible because
            func(*args)             # …it's captured in the closure
            print(f"-- {label}")    # …of '_decorate'
        return _inner
    return _decorate

@wrap("wrapping")                   # call 'wrap' to get a decorator
def original(message):              # decorator applied here
    print(f"original: {message}")

original("example")
```

```
++ wrapping
original: example
-- wrapping
```

Decorators didn't need to be this complicated. In order to define a method that takes N parameters in Python, we have to write a function of $N + 1$ parameters, the first of which represents the object for which the method is being called. Python could have done the same thing with decorators, i.e., allowed people to define a function of $N + 1$ parameters and have @ fill in the first automatically:

```
def decorator(func, label):
    def _inner(arg):
        print(f"entering {label}")
        func(arg)
    return _inner

@decorator("message")
def double(x):              # equivalent to
    return 2 * x            # double = decorator(double, "message")
```

But this isn't the path Python took, and as a result, decorators are harder to learn and use than they could have been.

9.4 Iterators

As a last example of how protocols work, consider the `for` loop. The statement `for thing in collection` assigns items from `collection` to the variable `thing` one at a time. Python implements this using a two-part **iterator** protocol, which is a version of the **Iterator** design pattern:

1. If an object has an `__iter__` method, that method is called to create an iterator object.

2. That iterator object must have a `__next__` method, which must return a value each time it is called. When there are no more values to return, it must raise a `StopIteration` exception.

   For example, suppose we have a class that stores a list of strings and we want to return the characters from the strings in order. (We will use a class like this to store lines of text in Chapter 23.) In our first attempt, each object is its own iterator, i.e., each object keeps track of what value to return next when looping:

```
class NaiveIterator:
    def __init__(self, text):
        self._text = text[:]

    def __iter__(self):
        self._row, self._col = 0, -1
        return self

    def __next__(self):
        self._advance()
        if self._row == len(self._text):
            raise StopIteration
        return self._text[self._row][self._col]
```

If we think of the text in terms of rows and columns, the `advance` method moves the column marker forward within the current row. When we reach the end of a row, we reset the column to 0 and advance the row index by one:

```python
def _advance(self):
    if self._row < len(self._text):
        self._col += 1
        if self._col == len(self._text[self._row]):
            self._row += 1
            self._col = 0
```

Our first test seems to work:

```python
def gather(buffer):
    result = ""
    for char in buffer:
        result += char
    return result


def test_naive_buffer():
    buffer = NaiveIterator(["ab", "c"])
    assert gather(buffer) == "abc"
```

However, our iterator doesn't work if the buffer contains an empty string:

```python
def test_naive_buffer_empty_string():
    buffer = NaiveIterator(["a", ""])
    with pytest.raises(IndexError):
        assert gather(buffer) == "a"
```

It also fails when we use a nested loop:

```python
def test_naive_buffer_nested_loop():
    buffer = NaiveIterator(["a", "b"])
    result = ""
    for outer in buffer:
        for inner in buffer:
            result += inner
    assert result == "abab"
```

We can fix the first problem with more careful bookkeeping—we leave that as an exercise—but fixing the second problem requires us to re-think our design. The problem is that we only have one pair of variables (the _row and _col attributes of the buffer) to store the current location, but two loops trying to use them. What we need to do instead is create a separate object for each loop to use:

```python
class BetterIterator:
    def __init__(self, text):
        self._text = text[:]

    def __iter__(self):
        return BetterCursor(self._text)
```

Each cursor keeps track of the current location for a single loop using code identical to what we've already seen (including the same bug with empty strings):

```python
class BetterCursor:
    def __init__(self, text):
        self._text = text
        self._row = 0
```

```
        self._col = -1

    def __next__(self):
        self._advance()
        if self._row == len(self._text):
            raise StopIteration
        return self._text[self._row][self._col]
```

With this change in place, our test of nested loops passes.

9.5   Summary

Figure 9.4 summarizes the ideas and tools introduced in this chapter.

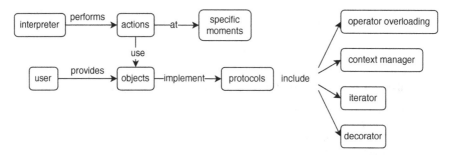

Figure 9.4: Concept map.

9.6   Exercises

Testing Exceptions

Create a context manager that works like `pytest.raises` from the `pytest`[1] module, i.e., that does nothing if an expected exception is raised within its scope but fails with an assertion error if that kind of exception is *not* raised.

Timing Blocks

Create a context manager called `Timer` that reports how long it has been since a block of code started running:

```
# your class goes here

with Timer() as start:
    # ...do some lengthy ...operation
    print(start.elapsed())  # time since the start of the block
```

---

[1] https://docs.pytest.org/

Handling Empty Strings

Modify the iterator example so that it handles empty strings correctly, i.e., so that iterating over the list ["a", ""] produces ["a"].

An Even Better Cursor

Rewrite the BetterCursor class so that it initializes self._row to 0 and self._col to −1 and always calls self._advance() as the first action in self.__next__. (You will need to make a few other changes as well.) Do you think this implementation is simpler than the one presented in this chapter?

Logging to a File

Create a decorator that takes the name of a file as an extra parameter and appends a log message to that file each time a function is called. (Hint: open the file in **append mode** each time it is needed.)

10

A File Archiver

> • Version control tools use hashing to uniquely identify each saved file.
>
> • Each snapshot of a set of files is recorded in a manifest.
>
> • Using a mock filesystem for testing is safer and faster than using the real thing.
>
> • Operations involving multiple files may suffer from race conditions.
>
> • Use a base class to specify what a component must be able to do and derive child classes to implement those operations.
>
> Terms defined: **atomic operation**, **base class**, **compression (of file)**, **Coordinated Universal Time**, **data migration**, **file locking**, **helper function**, **manifest**, **race condition**, **successive refinement**, **time of check - time of use**, **timestamp**, **top-down design**, **version control system**

We've written almost a thousand lines of Python so far. We could recreate it if we had to, but we'd rather not have to. We'd also like to be able to see what we've changed and to collaborate with other people.

A **version control system** like Git[1] solves all of these problems at once. It keeps track of changes to files so that we can see what we've changed, recover old versions, and merge our changes with those made by other people.

The core of a modern version control tool is a way to archive files that:

1. records which versions of which files existed at the same time, so that we can go back to a consistent previous state, and

2. stores any particular version of a file only once, so that we don't waste disk space.

This chapter builds a tool that does both tasks. It won't create and merge branches; if you would like to see how that works, please see Mary Rose Cook's[2] Gitlet[3] or Thibault Polge's Write yourself a Git[4].

10.1 Saving Files

Many files only change occasionally after they're created, or not at all. It would be wasteful for a version control system to make copies each time the user saved a snapshot of a project, so instead we will copy each unique file to something like `abcd1234.bck`, where `abcd1234` is the hash of the file's contents (Chapter 3). We will then record the filenames

---

[1] https://git-scm.com/
[2] https://maryrosecook.com/
[3] http://gitlet.maryrosecook.com/
[4] https://wyag.thb.lt/

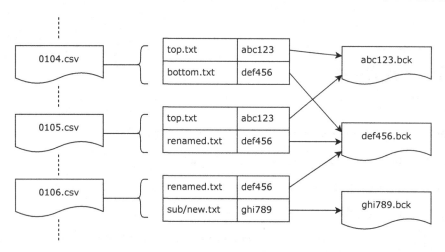

Figure 10.1: Organization of backup file storage.

and hash keys in each snapshot: The hash keys tell us which unique files existed at the time of the snapshot, while the filenames tell us what the file's contents were named when the snapshot was made. To restore a particular snapshot, we will copy the .bck files back to their original locations (Figure 10.1).

The first step is to find all the files in or below a given directory that we need to save. As described in Chapter 4, Python's glob[5] module can do this for us. Let's use this to create a table of files and hashes:

```
HASH_LEN = 16

def hash_all(root):
    result = []
    for name in glob("**/*.*", root_dir=root, recursive=True):
        full_name = Path(root, name)
        with open(full_name, "rb") as reader:
            data = reader.read()
            hash_code = sha256(data).hexdigest()[:HASH_LEN]
            result.append((name, hash_code))
    return result
```

Notice that we're truncating the hash code of each file to just 16 hexadecimal digits. This greatly increases the odds of collision, so real version control systems don't do this, but it makes our program's output easier to show on screen. For example, if our test directory looks like this:

```
sample_dir
|-- a.txt
|-- b.txt
`-- sub_dir
    `-- c.txt

1 directory, 3 files
```

then our program's output is:

```
python hash_all.py sample_dir
```

---
[5]https://docs.python.org/3/library/glob.html

```
filename,hash
b.txt,3cf9a1a81f6bdeaf
a.txt,17e682f060b5f8e4
sub_dir/c.txt,5695d82a086b6779
```

10.2 Testing

Before we go any further we need to figure out how we're going to test our code. The obvious approach is to create directories and sub-directories containing some files we can use as fixtures. However, we are going to change or delete those files as we back things up and restore them. To make sure early tests don't contaminate later ones, we would have to recreate those files and directories after each test.

As discussed in Chapter 9, a better approach is to use a mock object instead of the real filesystem. The `pyfakefs`[6] module replaces key functions like `open` with functions that behave the same way but act on "files" stored in memory (Figure 10.2). Using it prevents our tests from accidentally disturbing the filesystem; it also makes tests much faster since in-memory operations are thousands of times faster than ones that touch the disk.

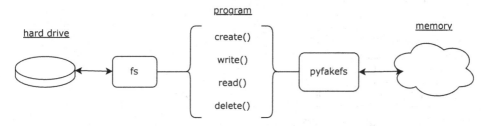

Figure 10.2: Using a mock filesystem to simplify testing.

If we `import pyfakefs`, we automatically get a fixture called `fs` that we can use to create files. We tell pytest[7] we want to use this fixture by passing it as an argument to our testing function:

```
from pathlib import Path

def test_simple_example(fs):
    sentence = "This file contains one sentence."
    with open("alpha.txt", "w") as writer:
        writer.write(sentence)
    assert Path("alpha.txt").exists()
    with open("alpha.txt", "r") as reader:
        assert reader.read() == sentence
```

We can use `fs` to create more complicated fixtures of our own with multiple directories and files:

```
from pathlib import Path
import pytest
```

---

[6]https://pytest-pyfakefs.readthedocs.io/
[7]https://docs.pytest.org/

```
@pytest.fixture
def our_fs(fs):
    fs.create_file("a.txt", contents="aaa")
    fs.create_file("b.txt", contents="bbb")
    fs.create_file("sub_dir/c.txt", contents="ccc")

def test_nested_example(our_fs):
    assert Path("a.txt").exists()
    assert Path("b.txt").exists()
    assert Path("sub_dir/c.txt").exists()

def test_deletion_example(our_fs):
    assert Path("a.txt").exists()
    Path("a.txt").unlink()
    assert not Path("a.txt").exists()
```

and then test that `hash_all` finds all the files:

```
import pytest

from hash_all import hash_all, HASH_LEN

@pytest.fixture
def our_fs(fs):
    fs.create_file("a.txt", contents="aaa")
    fs.create_file("b.txt", contents="bbb")
    fs.create_file("sub_dir/c.txt", contents="ccc")

def test_hashing(our_fs):
    result = hash_all(".")
    expected = {"a.txt", "b.txt", "sub_dir/c.txt"}
    assert {r[0] for r in result} == expected
    assert all(len(r[1]) == HASH_LEN for r in result)
```

and that hashes change when files change:

```
def test_change(our_fs):
    original = hash_all(".")
    original = [entry for entry in original if entry[0] == "a.txt"][0]
    with open("a.txt", "w") as writer:
        writer.write("this is new content for a.txt")
    changed = hash_all(".")
    changed = [entry for entry in changed if entry[0] == "a.txt"][0]
    assert original != changed
```

10.3 Tracking Backups

The second part of our backup tool keeps track of which files have and haven't been backed up already. It stores backups in a directory that contains files like `abcd1234.bck` (the hash followed by `.bck`) and creates a **manifest** that describes the content of each snapshot. A real system would support remote storage as well so that losing one hard drive wouldn't mean losing all our work, so we need to design our system with multiple back ends in mind.

For now, we will store manifests in CSV files named `ssssssssss.csv`, where `ssssssssss` is the **UTC timestamp** of the backup's creation.

> **Time of Check/Time of Use**
>
> Our naming convention for manifests will fail if we try to create two or more backups in the same second. This might seem unlikely, but many faults and security holes are the result of programmers assuming things weren't going to happen.
>
> We could try to avoid this problem by using a two-part naming scheme `sssssss-a.csv`, `sssssss-b.csv`, and so on, but this leads to a **race condition** called **time of check/time of use**. If two users run the backup tool at the same time, they will both see that there isn't a file (yet) with the current timestamp, so they will both try to create the first one. Ensuring that multi-file updates are **atomic operations** (i.e., that they always appear to be a single indivisible step) is a hard problem; **file locking** is a common approach, but complete solutions are out of the scope of this book.

This function creates a backup—or rather, it will once we fill in all the functions it depends on:

```
def backup(source_dir, backup_dir):
    manifest = hash_all(source_dir)
    timestamp = current_time()
    write_manifest(backup_dir, timestamp, manifest)
    copy_files(source_dir, backup_dir, manifest)
    return manifest
```

Writing a high-level function first and then filling in the things it needs is called **successive refinement** or **top-down design**. In practice, nobody designs code and then implements the design without changes unless they have solved closely-related problems before [Petre2016]. Instead, good programmers jump back and forth between higher and lower levels of design, adjusting their overall strategy as work on low-level details reveals problems or opportunities they hadn't foreseen.

When writing the manifest, we check that the backup directory exists, create it if it does not, and then save the manifest as CSV:

```
def write_manifest(backup_dir, timestamp, manifest):
    backup_dir = Path(backup_dir)
    if not backup_dir.exists():
        backup_dir.mkdir()
    manifest_file = Path(backup_dir, f"{timestamp}.csv")
    with open(manifest_file, "w") as raw:
        writer = csv.writer(raw)
        writer.writerow(["filename", "hash"])
        writer.writerows(manifest)
```

We then copy those files that *haven't* already been saved:

```
def copy_files(source_dir, backup_dir, manifest):
    for (filename, hash_code) in manifest:
        source_path = Path(source_dir, filename)
        backup_path = Path(backup_dir, f"{hash_code}.bck")
        if not backup_path.exists():
            shutil.copy(source_path, backup_path)
```

We have introduced several more race conditions here: for example, if two people are creating backups at the same time, they could both discover that the backup directory doesn't exist and then both try to create it. Whoever does so first will succeed, but whoever comes second will fail. We will look at ways to fix this in the exercises as well.

> **What Time Is It?**
>
> Our `backup` function relies on a **helper function** called `current_time` that does noth-
> ing but call `time.time` from Python's standard library:
>
> ```
> def current_time():
>     return f"{time.time()}".split(".")[0]
> ```
>
> We could call `time.time` directly, but wrapping it up like this makes it easier to replace
> with a mock for testing.

Let's do one test with real files:

```
BACKUPS=/tmp/backups
rm -rf $BACKUPS
python backup.py sample_dir $BACKUPS
tree --charset ascii $BACKUPS
```

```
/tmp/backups
|-- 1695482691.csv
|-- 17e682f060b5f8e4.bck
|-- 3cf9a1a81f6bdeaf.bck
`-- 5695d82a086b6779.bck

0 directories, 4 files
```

The rest of our tests use a fake filesystem and a mock replacement for the `current_time`
function (so that we know what the manifest file will be called). The setup is:

```
FILES = {"a.txt": "aaa", "b.txt": "bbb", "sub_dir/c.txt": "ccc"}

@pytest.fixture
def our_fs(fs):
    for name, contents in FILES.items():
        fs.create_file(name, contents=contents)
```

and an example of a single test is:

```
def test_nested_example(our_fs):
    with patch("backup.current_time", return_value=1234):
        manifest = backup(".", "/backup")
    for filename, hash_code in manifest:
        assert Path("/backup", f"{hash_code}.bck").exists()
        assert Path("/backup", "1234.csv").exists()
```

10.4   Refactoring

Now that we have a better idea of what we're doing, we can refactor to create a **base class**
that prescribes the general steps in creating a backup:

```
class Archive:
    def __init__(self, source_dir):
        self._source_dir = source_dir
```

```
def backup(self):
    manifest = hash_all(self._source_dir)
    self._write_manifest(manifest)
    self._copy_files(manifest)
    return manifest
```

We can then derive a child class to archive things locally and fill in its methods by re-using code from the functions we have just written. Once we've done this, we can create the specific archiver we want with a single line:

```
archiver = ArchiveLocal(source_dir, backup_dir)
```

Doing this makes life easier when we want to write archivers that behave the same way but work differently. For example, we could create an archiver that **compresses** the files it archives by deriving a new class from `ArchiveLocal` and writing a new `_copy_files` method. More importantly, other code can use an archiver *without knowing what it's doing*. For example, the function `analyze_and_save` reads some data, analyzes it, saves the results, and then creates an archive of those results. It doesn't know whether the archive is compressing files or whether they're being saved locally or remotely.

```
def analyze_and_save(options, archiver):
    data = read_data(options)
    results = analyze_data(data)
    save_everything(results)
    archiver.backup()
```

This example highlights one of the strengths of object-oriented programming: it allows old code to use new code without any changes.

10.5 Summary

Figure 10.3 summarizes the key ideas in this chapter, which are the foundation of most modern tools for doing backups and version control.

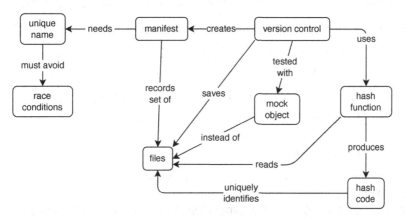

Figure 10.3: Concept map for hashing-based file backup.

10.6   Exercises

Sequencing Backups

Modify the backup program so that manifests are numbered sequentially as `00000001.csv`, `00000002.csv`, and so on rather than being timestamped. Why doesn't this solve the time of check/time of use race condition mentioned earlier?

JSON Manifests

1. Modify `backup.py` so that it can save JSON manifests as well as CSV manifests based on a command-line flag.

2. Write another program called `migrate.py` that converts a set of manifests from CSV to JSON. (The program's name comes from the term **data migration**.)

3. Modify `backup.py` programs so that each manifest stores the user name of the person who created it along with file hashes, and then modify `migrate.py` to transform old files into the new format.

Mock Hashes

1. Modify the file backup program so that it uses a function called `ourHash` to hash files.

2. Create a replacement that returns some predictable value, such as the first few characters of the data.

3. Rewrite the tests to use this function. How did you modify the main program so that the tests could control which hashing function is used?

Comparing Manifests

Write a program `compare-manifests.py` that reads two manifest files and reports:

• Which files have the same names but different hashes (i.e., their contents have changed).

• Which files have the same hashes but different names (i.e., they have been renamed).

• Which files are in the first hash but neither their names nor their hashes are in the second (i.e., they have been deleted).

• Which files are in the second hash but neither their names nor their hashes are in the first (i.e., they have been added).

From One State to Another

1. Write a program called `from_to.py` that takes a directory and a manifest file as command-line arguments, then adds, removes, and/or renames files in the directory to restore the state described in the manifest. The program should only perform file operations when it needs to, e.g., it should not delete a file and re-add it if the contents have not changed.

2. Write some tests for `from_to.py` using pytest and a mock filesystem.

File History

1. Write a program called `file_history.py` that takes the name of a file as a command-line argument and displays the history of that file by tracing it back in time through the available manifests.

2. Write tests for your program using pytest and a mock filesystem.

Pre-commit Hooks

Modify `backup.py` to load and run a function called `pre_commit` from a file called `pre_commit.py` stored in the root directory of the files being backed up. If `pre_commit` returns `True`, the backup proceeds; if it returns `False` or raises an exception, no backup is created.

11

An HTML Validator

- HTML consists of text and of elements represented by tags with attributes.

- HTML is represented in memory as a Document Object Model (DOM) tree.

- Trees are usually processed using recursion.

- The Visitor design pattern is often used to perform an action for each member of a data structure.

- We can summarize and check the structure of an HTML page by visiting each node and recording what we find there.

Terms defined: **attribute**, **child (in a tree)**, **closing tag**, **DOM**, **DOM tree**, **element (in HTML)**, **HTML**, **node**, **opening tag**, **self-closing tag**, **tag (in HTML)**, **tree**, **Visitor pattern**

Suppose we want to generate web pages to show the results of data analyses. We want to check that these pages all have the same structure so that people can find things in them, and that they meet accessibility standards so that *everyone* can find things in them. This chapter builds a small tool to do this checking, which introduces ideas we will use in building a page generator (Chapter 12) and another to check the structure and style of our code (Chapter 13).

11.1 HTML and the DOM

An **HTML** document is made up of **elements** and text. (It can actually contain other things, but we'll ignore those for now.) Elements are represented using **tags** enclosed in < and >. An **opening tag** like <p> starts an element, while a **closing tag** like </p> ends it. If the element is empty, we can use a **self-closing tag** like <br/> to save some typing. Tags must be properly nested, i.e., they must be closed in the reverse of the order in which they were opened. This rule means that things like <a><b></a></b> are not allowed; it also means that a document's elements form a **tree** of **nodes** and text like the one shown in Figure 11.1.

This figure also shows that opening and self-closing tags can have **attributes**, which are written as key="value". For example, if we want to put an image in an HTML page, we specify the image file's name using the src attribute of the img tag:

```
<img src="banner.png" />
```

The objects that represent the nodes and text in an HTML tree are called the Document Object Model or **DOM**. Hundreds of tools have been written to convert HTML text to DOM; our favorite is a Python module called Beautiful Soup[1], which can handle messy real-world documents as well as those that conform to every rule of the standard.

---

[1] https://beautiful-soup-4.readthedocs.io/

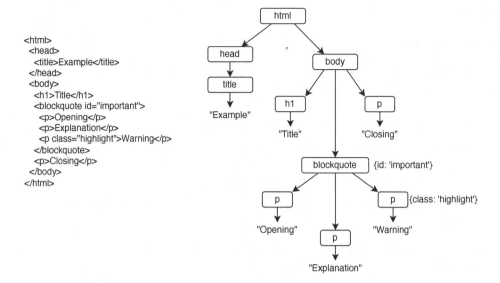

```
<html>
  <head>
    <title>Example</title>
  </head>
  <body>
    <h1>Title</h1>
    <blockquote id="important">
      <p>Opening</p>
      <p>Explanation</p>
      <p class="highlight">Warning</p>
    </blockquote>
    <p>Closing</p>
  </body>
</html>
```

Figure 11.1: Representing HTML elements as a DOM tree.

Beautiful Soup's DOM has two main classes: `NavigableString` for text and `Tag` for elements. To parse a document, we import what we need and call `BeautifulSoup` with the text to be parsed and a string specifying exactly what kind of parsing we want to do. (In practice, this is almost always `"html.parser"`.)

```
from bs4 import BeautifulSoup, NavigableString, Tag

doc = BeautifulSoup(text, "html.parser")
display(doc)
```

Tag nodes have two properties `name` and `children` to tell us what element the tag represents and to give us access to the node's **children**, i.e., the nodes below it in the tree. We can therefore write a short recursive function to show us everything in the DOM:

```
def display(node):
    if isinstance(node, NavigableString):
        print(f"string: {repr(node.string)}")
        return
    else:
        print(f"node: {node.name}")
        for child in node:
            display(child)
```

We can test this function with a short example:

```
text = """<html>
<body>
<h1>Title</h1>
<p>paragraph</p>
</body>
</html>"""
```

```
node: [document]
node: html
string: '\n'
```

```
node: body
string: '\n'
node: h1
string: 'Title'
string: '\n'
node: p
string: 'paragraph'
string: '\n'
string: '\n'
```

In order to keep everything in one file, we have written the HTML "page" as a multiline Python string; we will do this frequently when writing unit tests so that the HTML fixture is right beside the test code. Notice in the output that the line breaks in the HTML have been turned into text nodes containing only a newline character. It's easy to forget about these when writing code that processes pages.

The last bit of the DOM that we need is its representation of attributes. Each Tag node has a dictionary called attrs that stores the node's attributes. The values in this dictionary are either strings or lists of strings depending on whether the attribute has a single value or multiple values:

```
def display(node):
    if isinstance(node, Tag):
        print(f"node: {node.name} {node.attrs}")
        for child in node:
            display(child)
```

```
text = """<html lang="en">
<body class="outline narrow">
<p align="left" align="right">paragraph</p>
</body>
</html>"""
```

```
node: [document] {}
node: html {'lang': 'en'}
node: body {'class': ['outline', 'narrow']}
node: p {'align': 'right'}
```

11.2 The Visitor Pattern

Before building an HTML validator, let's build something to tell us which elements appear inside which others in a document. Our recursive function takes two arguments: the current node and a dictionary whose keys are node names and whose values are sets containing the names of those nodes' children. Each time it encounters a node, the function adds the names of the child nodes to the appropriate set and then calls itself once for each child to collect their children:

```
def recurse(node, catalog):
    assert isinstance(node, Tag)

    if node.name not in catalog:
        catalog[node.name] = set()
```

```
    for child in node:
        if isinstance(child, Tag):
            catalog[node.name].add(child.name)
            recurse(child, catalog)

    return catalog
```

When we run our function on this page:

```
<html>
  <head>
    <title>Software Design by Example</title>
  </head>
  <body>
    <h1>Main Title</h1>
    <p>introductory paragraph</p>
    <ul>
      <li>first item</li>
      <li>second item is <em>emphasized</em></li>
    </ul>
  </body>
</html>
```

it produces this output (which we print in sorted order to make things easier to find):

```
body: h1, p, ul
em:
h1:
head: title
html: body, head
li: em
p:
title:
ul: li
```

At this point we have written several recursive functions that have almost exactly the same control flow. A good rule of software design is that if we have built something three times, we should make what we've learned reusable so that we never have to write it again. In this case, we will rewrite our code to use the **Visitor** design pattern.

A visitor is a class that knows how to get to each element of a data structure and call a user-defined method when it gets there. Our visitor will have three methods: one that it calls when it first encounters a node, one that it calls when it is finished with that node, and one that it calls for text (Figure 11.2):

```
class Visitor:
    def visit(self, node):
        if isinstance(node, NavigableString):
            self._text(node)
        elif isinstance(node, Tag):
            self._tag_enter(node)
            for child in node:
                self.visit(child)
            self._tag_exit(node)

    def _tag_enter(self, node): pass

    def _tag_exit(self, node): pass

    def _text(self, node): pass
```

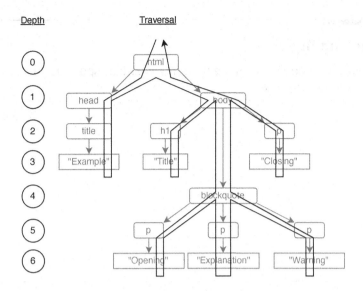

Figure 11.2: Visitor checking each node in depth-first order.

We provide do-nothing implementations of the three action methods rather than having them raise a `NotImplementedError` because a particular use of our `Visitor` class may not need some of these methods. For example, our catalog builder didn't need to do anything when leaving a node or for text nodes, and we shouldn't require people to implement things they don't need.

Here's what our catalog builder looks like when re-implemented on top of our `Visitor` class:

```python
class Catalog(Visitor):
    def __init__(self):
        super().__init__()
        self.catalog = {}

    def _tag_enter(self, node):
        if node.name not in self.catalog:
            self.catalog[node.name] = set()
        for child in node:
            if isinstance(child, Tag):
                self.catalog[node.name].add(child.name)
```

```python
with open(sys.argv[1], "r") as reader:
    text = reader.read()
doc = BeautifulSoup(text, "html.parser")

cataloger = Catalog()
cataloger.visit(doc.html)
result = cataloger.catalog

for tag, contents in sorted(result.items()):
    print(f"{tag}: {', '.join(sorted(contents))}")
```

It is only a few lines shorter than the original, but the more complicated the data structure is, the more helpful the Visitor pattern becomes.

11.3   Checking Style

To wrap up our style checker, let's create a manifest that specifies which types of nodes can be children of which others:

```
body:
- section
head:
- title
html:
- body
- head
section:
- h1
- p
- ul
ul:
- li
```

We've chosen to use YAML for the manifest because it's a relatively simple way to write nested rules. JSON would have worked just as well, but as we said in Chapter 5, we shouldn't invent a syntax of our own: there are already too many in the world.

Our `Check` class needs a constructor to set everything up and a `_tag_enter` method to handle nodes:

```python
class Check(Visitor):
    def __init__(self, manifest):
        self.manifest = manifest
        self.problems = {}

    def _tag_enter(self, node):
        actual = {child.name for child in node
                  if isinstance(child, Tag)}
        errors = actual - self.manifest.get(node.name, set())
        if errors:
            errors |= self.problems.get(node.name, set())
            self.problems[node.name] = errors
```

To run this, we load a manifest and an HTML document, create a checker, ask the checker to visit each node, then print out every problematic parent-child combination it found:

```python
def read_manifest(filename):
    with open(filename, "r") as reader:
        result = yaml.load(reader, Loader=yaml.FullLoader)
        for key in result:
            result[key] = set(result[key])
        return result

manifest = read_manifest(sys.argv[1])
with open(sys.argv[2], "r") as reader:
    text = reader.read()
doc = BeautifulSoup(text, "html.parser")

checker = Check(manifest)
checker.visit(doc.html)
for key, value in checker.problems.items():
    print(f"{key}: {', '.join(sorted(value))}")
```

```
body: h1, p, ul
li: em
```

The output tells us that content is supposed to be inside a `section` element, not directly inside the `body`, and that we're not supposed to *emphasize* words in lists. Other users' rules may be different, but we now have the tool we need to check that any HTML we generate conforms to our intended rules. More importantly, we have a general pattern for building recursive code that we can use in upcoming chapters.

11.4 Summary

HTML is probably the most widely used data format in the world today; Figure 11.3 summarizes how it is represented and processed.

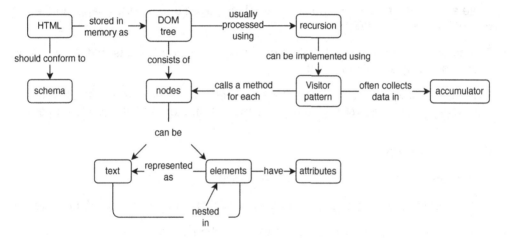

Figure 11.3: Concept map for checking HTML using the Visitor pattern.

11.5 Exercises

Simplify the Logic

1. Trace the operation of `Check._tag_enter` and convince yourself that it does the right thing.

2. Rewrite it to make it easier to understand.

Detecting Empty Elements

Write a visitor that builds a list of nodes that could be written as self-closing tags but aren't, i.e., node that are written as `<a></a>`. The `Tag.sourceline` attribute may help you make your report more readable.

Eliminating Newlines

Write a visitor that deletes any text nodes from a document that only contains newline characters. Do you need to make any changes to `Visitor`, or can you implement this using the class as it is?

Linearize the Tree

Write a visitor that returns a flat list containing all the nodes in a **DOM tree** in the order in which they would be traversed. When you are done, you should be able to write code like this:

```
for node in Flatten(doc.html).result():
    print(node)
```

Reporting Accessibility Violations

1. Write a program that reads one or more HTML pages and reports images in them that do *not* have an `alt` attribute.

2. Extend your program so that it also reports any `figure` elements that do *not* contain exactly one `figcaption` element.

3. Extend your program again so that it warns about images with redundant text (i.e., images in figures whose `alt` attribute contains the same text as the figure's caption).

Ordering Headings

Write a program that checks the ordering of headings in a page:

1. There should be exactly one `h1` element, and it should be the first heading in the page.

2. Heading levels should never increase by more than 1, i.e., an `h1` should only ever be followed by an `h2`, an `h2` should never be followed directly by an `h4`, and so on.

Report Full Path

Modify the checking tool so that it reports the full path for style violations when it finds a problem, e.g., reports 'div.div.p (meaning "a paragraph in a div in another div") instead of just p‘.

12

A Template Expander

> • Static site generators create HTML pages from templates, directives, and data.
>
> • A static site generator has the same core features as a programming language.
>
> • Special-purpose mini-languages quickly become as complex as other languages.
>
> • Static methods are a convenient way to group functions together.
>
> Terms defined: **abstract class**, **abstract method**, **Application Programming Interface**, **Boolean expression**, **static site generator**, **truthy**

Every program needs documentation, and the best place to put documentation is on the web. Writing and updating HTML pages by hand is time-consuming and error-prone, particularly when many parts are the same. Most modern websites therefore use some kind of **static site generator** (SSG) to create pages from templates.

Hundreds of SSGs[1] have been written in every popular programming language, and languages like PHP[2] have been invented primarily for this purpose. Most of these systems use one of three designs (Figure 12.1):

1. Mix commands in an existing language such as JavaScript with the HTML or Markdown using some kind of marker to indicate which parts are commands and which parts are to be taken as-is. This approach is taken by EJS[3].

2. Create a mini-language with its own commands like Jekyll[4]. Mini-languages are appealing because they are smaller and safer than general-purpose languages, but eventually they acquire most of the features of a general-purpose language. Again, some kind of marker must be used to show which parts of the page are code and which are ordinary text.

3. Put directives in specially-named attributes in the HTML. This approach is the least popular, but it eliminates the need for a special parser.

This chapter builds a simple page templating system using the third strategy. We will process each page independently by parsing the HTML and walking the DOM to find nodes with special attributes. Our program will execute the instructions in those nodes to implement loops and if/else statements; other nodes will be copied as-is to create text.

---

[1] https://jamstack.org/generators/
[2] https://www.php.net/
[3] https://ejs.co/
[4] https://jekyllrb.com/

EJS	Jekyll	Argon
<ul>	<ul>	<ul *z-loop="item:items"*>
<% items.forEach(item => { %>	{% for item in items %}	<li><span *z-var="item"*/></li>
<li><%- item.title %></li>	<li>{{ item.title }}</li>	</ul>
<% } %>	{% endfor %}	
</ul>	</ul>	

Figure 12.1: Three different ways to implement page templating.

12.1 Syntax

Let's start by deciding what "done" looks like. Suppose we want to turn an array of strings into an HTML list. Our template will look like this:

```
<html>
  <body>
    <ul z-loop="item:names">
      <li><span z-var="item"/></li>
    </ul>
  </body>
</html>
```

The attribute `z-loop` tells the tool to repeat the contents of that node; the loop variable and the collection being looped over are separated by a colon. The `span` with the attribute `z-var` tells the tool to fill in the node with the value of the variable. When our tool processes this page, the output will be standard HTML without any traces of how it was created:

```
<html>
<body>
<ul>
<li><span>Johnson</span></li>

<li><span>Vaughan</span></li>

<li><span>Jackson</span></li>
</ul>
</body>
</html>
```

Human-Readable vs. Machine-Readable

Putting the loop variable and target in a single attribute makes loops easy to type but hides information from standard HTML tools, which can't know that this attribute contains multiple values separated by a colon. We should use two attributes like this:

```
<ul z-loop="names" z-loop-var="item">
```

but we decided to save ourselves a little typing. We should also call our attributes `data-something` instead of `z-something` to conform with the HTML5 specification[5], but again, decided to save ourselves a bit of typing.

---

[5]https://developer.mozilla.org/en-US/docs/Learn/HTML/Howto/Use_data_attributes

The next step is to define the **Application Programming Interface** (API) for filling in templates. Our tool needs the template itself, somewhere to write its output, and the set of variables to use in the expansion. Those variables might come from a configuration file from a header in the file itself, or from somewhere else entirely, so we will assume the calling program has gotten them somehow and have it pass them into the expansion function as a dictionary (Figure 12.2):

```
data = {"names": ["Johnson", "Vaughan", "Jackson"]}

dom = read_html("template.html")
expander = Expander(dom, data)
expander.walk()
print(expander.result)
```

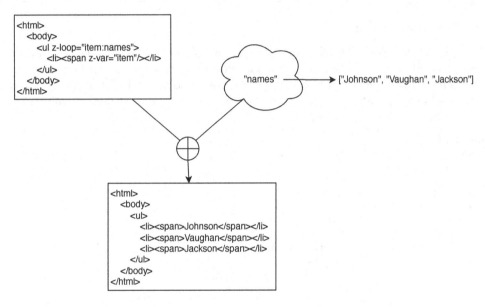

Figure 12.2: Combining text and data in templating.

12.2 Managing Variables

As soon as we have variables, we need a way to track their values. We also need to maintain multiple sets of variables so that (for example) variables used inside a loop don't conflict with ones used outside of it. As in Chapter 7, we will use a stack of environments, each of which is a dictionary.

Our stack-handling class Env has methods to push and pop new stack frames and find a variable given its name. If the variable can't be found, Env.find returns None instead of raising an exception:

```
class Env:
    def __init__(self, initial):
        self.stack = [initial.copy()]

    def push(self, frame):
```

```
        self.stack.append(frame)

    def pop(self):
        self.stack.pop()

    def find(self, name):
        for frame in reversed(self.stack):
            if name in frame:
                return frame[name]
        return None
```

12.3   Visiting Nodes

As Chapter 11 explained, HTML pages are usually stored in memory as trees and processed using the Visitor pattern. We therefore create a `Visitor` class whose constructor
takes the root node of the DOM tree as an argument and saves it. Calling `Visitor.walk`
without a value starts recursion from that saved root; when `.walk` is given a value (as it is
during recursive calls), it uses that instead.

```
class Visitor:
    def __init__(self, root):
        self.root = root

    def walk(self, node=None):
        if node is None:
            node = self.root
        if self.open(node):
            for child in node.children:
                self.walk(child)
        self.close(node)

    def open(self, node):
        raise NotImplementedError("open")

    def close(self, node):
        raise NotImplementedError("close")
```

`Visitor` defines two **abstract methods** `open` and `close` that are called when we first
arrive at a node and when we are finished with it. These methods are called "abstract"
because we can't actually use them: any attempt to do so will raise an exception, which
means child classes *must* override them. (In object-oriented terminology, this means that
`Visitor` is an **abstract class**.) This approach is different from that of the visitor in Chapter 11, where we defined do-nothing methods so that derived classes could override only
the ones they needed.

The `Expander` class is specialization of `Visitor` that uses an `Env` to keep track of
variables. It imports handlers for each type of special node—we will explore those in a
moment—and saves them along with a newly-created environment and a list of strings
making up the output:

```
class Expander(Visitor):
    def __init__(self, root, variables):
        super().__init__(root)
        self.env = Env(variables)
        self.handlers = HANDLERS
        self.result = []
```

When recursion encounters a new node, it calls open to do one of three things:

1. If the node is plain text, copy it to the output.

2. If there is a handler for the node, call the handler's open or close method.

3. Otherwise, open a regular tag.

```
def open(self, node):
    if isinstance(node, NavigableString):
        self.output(node.string)
        return False
    elif self.hasHandler(node):
        return self.getHandler(node).open(self, node)
    else:
        self.showTag(node, False)
        return True
```

Expander.close works much the same way. Both methods find handlers by comparing the DOM node's attributes to the keys in the dictionary of handlers built during construction:

```
def hasHandler(self, node):
    return any(
        name in self.handlers
        for name in node.attrs
    )

def getHandler(self, node):
    possible = [
        name for name in node.attrs
        if name in self.handlers
    ]
    assert len(possible) == 1, "Should be exactly one handler"
    return self.handlers[possible[0]]
```

Finally, we need a few helper methods to show tags and generate output:

```
def showTag(self, node, closing):
    if closing:
        self.output(f"</{node.name}>")
        return
    self.output(f"<{node.name}")
    for name in node.attrs:
        if not name.startswith("z-"):
            self.output(f' {name}="{node.attrs[name]}"')
    self.output(">")

def output(self, text):
    self.result.append("UNDEF" if text is None else text)

def getResult(self):
    return "".join(self.result)
```

Notice that `Expander` adds strings to an array and joins them all right at the end rather than concatenating strings repeatedly. Doing this is more efficient; it also helps with debugging, since each string in the array corresponds to a single method call.

12.4 Implementing Handlers

Our last task is to implement the handlers for filling in variables' values, looping, and so on. We could define an abstract class with `open` and `close` methods, derive one class for each of the template expander's capabilities, and then construct one instance of each class for `Expander` to use, but there's a simpler way. When Python executes the statement `import something` it executes the file `something.py`, saves the result in a specialized dictionary-like object, and assigns that object to the variable `something`. That object can also be saved in data structures like lists and dictionaries or passed as an argument to a function just like numbers, functions, and classes—remember, programs are just data.

Let's write a pair of functions that each take an expander and a node as inputs and expand a DOM node with a `z-num` attribute to insert a number into the output:

```
def open(expander, node):
    expander.showTag(node, False)
    expander.output(node.attrs["z-num"])

def close(expander, node):
    expander.showTag(node, True)
```

When we enter a node like `<span z-num="123"/>` this handler asks the expander to show an opening tag followed by the value of the `z-num` attribute. When we exit the node, the handler asks the expander to close the tag. The handler doesn't know whether things are printed immediately, added to an output list, or something else; it just knows that whoever called it implements the low-level operations it needs.

Here's how we connect this handler (and others we're going to write in a second) to the expander:

```
import z_if
import z_loop
import z_num
import z_var

HANDLERS = {
    "z-if": z_if,
    "z-loop": z_loop,
    "z-num": z_num,
    "z-var": z_var
}
```

The `HANDLERS` dictionary maps the names of special attributes in the HTML to modules, each of which defines `open` and `close` functions for the expander to call. In other words, we are using modules to prevent name collision just as we would use classes or functions.

The handlers for variables are:

```
def open(expander, node):
    expander.showTag(node, False)
    expander.output(expander.env.find(node.attrs["z-var"]))

def close(expander, node):
    expander.showTag(node, True)
```

This code is almost the same as the previous example. The only difference is that instead of copying the attribute's value directly to the output, we use it as a key to look up a value.

These two pairs of handlers look plausible, but do they work? To find out, we can build a program that loads variable definitions from a JSON file, reads an HTML template using the Beautiful Soup[6] module, and does the expansion:

```
import json
import sys
from bs4 import BeautifulSoup
from expander import Expander

def main():
    with open(sys.argv[1], "r") as reader:
        variables = json.load(reader)

    with open(sys.argv[2], "r") as reader:
        doc = BeautifulSoup(reader.read(), "html.parser")
        template = doc.find("html")

    expander = Expander(template, variables)
    expander.walk()
    print(expander.getResult())

if __name__ == "__main__":
    main()
```

We added new variables for our test cases one by one as we were writing this chapter. To avoid repeating text repeatedly, here's the entire set:

```
{
  "firstVar": "firstValue",
  "secondVar": "secondValue",
  "varName": "varValue",
  "yes": true,
  "no": false,
  "names": ["Johnson", "Vaughan", "Jackson"]
}
```

Our first test checks whether static text is copied over as-is:

```
<html>
  <body>
    <h1>Static Text</h1>
    <p>test</p>
  </body>
</html>
```

```
<html>
<body>
<h1>Static Text</h1>
<p>test</p>
</body>
</html>
```

---

[6]https://beautiful-soup-4.readthedocs.io/

Good. Now, does the expander handle constants?

```
<html>
  <body>
    <p><span z-num="123"/></p>
  </body>
</html>
```

```
<html>
<body>
<p><span>123</span></p>
</body>
</html>
```

What about a single variable?

```
<html>
  <body>
    <p><span z-var="varName"/></p>
  </body>
</html>
```

```
<html>
<body>
<p><span>varValue</span></p>
</body>
</html>
```

What about a page containing multiple variables? There's no reason it should fail if the single-variable case works, but we should still check—again, software isn't done until it has been tested.

```
<html>
  <body>
    <p><span z-var="firstVar" /></p>
    <p><span z-var="secondVar" /></p>
  </body>
</html>
```

```
<html>
<body>
<p><span>firstValue</span></p>
<p><span>secondValue</span></p>
</body>
</html>
```

Generating Element IDs

It's often handy to have a unique identifier for every element in a page, so some templating engines automatically generate `id` attributes for elements that don't specify IDs explicitly. If you do this, please do not generate random numbers, because then Git and other version control systems will think a regenerated page has changed when it actually hasn't. Generating sequential IDs is equally problematic: if you add an item to a list at the top of the page, for example, that might change the IDs for all of the items in subsequent (unrelated) lists.

12.5   Control Flow

Our tool supports conditional expressions and loops. Since we're not implementing **Boolean expressions** like and and or, all we have to do for a condition is look up a variable and then expand the node if Python thinks the variable's value is **truthy**:

```
def open(expander, node):
    check = expander.env.find(node.attrs["z-if"])
    if check:
        expander.showTag(node, False)
    return check

def close(expander, node):
    if expander.env.find(node.attrs["z-if"]):
        expander.showTag(node, True)
```

Let's test it:

```
<html>
  <body>
    <p z-if="yes">Should be shown.</p>
    <p z-if="no">Should <em>not</em> be shown.</p>
  </body>
</html>
```

```
<html>
<body>
<p>Should be shown.</p>
</body>
</html>
```

> **Spot the Bug**
>
> This implementation of if contains a subtle bug. open and close both check the value of the control variable. If something inside the body of the if changes that value, the result could be an opening tag without a matching closing tag or vice versa. We haven't implemented an assignment operator, so right now there's no way for that to happen, but it's a plausible thing for us to add later, and tracking down a bug in old code that is revealed by new code is always a headache.

Finally we have loops. For these, we need to get the array we're looping over from the environment and do the following for each item it contains:

1. Create a new stack frame holding the current value of the loop variable.

2. Expand all of the node's children with that stack frame in place.

3. Pop the stack frame to get rid of the temporary variable.

```
def open(expander, node):
    index_name, target_name = node.attrs["z-loop"].split(":")
    expander.showTag(node, False)
    target = expander.env.find(target_name)
    for value in target:
        expander.env.push({index_name: value})
        for child in node.children:
```

```
            expander.walk(child)
        expander.env.pop()
    return False

def close(expander, node):
    expander.showTag(node, True)
```

Once again, it's not done until we test it:

```
<html>
  <body>
    <ul z-loop="item:names">
      <li><span z-var="item"/></li>
    </ul>
  </body>
</html>
```

```
<html>
<body>
<ul>
<li><span>Johnson</span></li>

<li><span>Vaughan</span></li>

<li><span>Jackson</span></li>
</ul>
</body>
</html>
```

We have just implemented another simple programming language like the one in Chapter 7. It's unlikely that anyone would want to use it as-is, but adding a new feature is now as simple as writing a matching pair of `open` and `close` functions.

12.6   Summary

Figure 12.3 summarizes the key ideas in this chapter, some of which we first encountered in Chapter 7. Please see Appendix B for extra material related to these ideas.

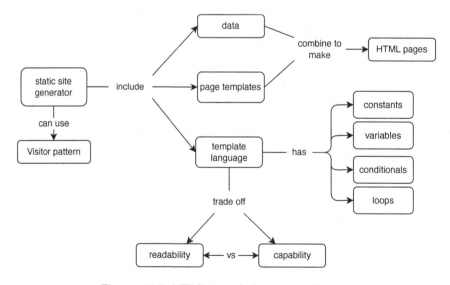

Figure 12.3: HTML templating concept map.

12.7 Exercises

Tracing Execution

Add a directive `<span z-trace="variable"/>` that prints the current value of a variable for debugging.

Unit Tests

Write unit tests for template expansion using pytest[7].

Sub-keys

Modify the template expander so that a variable name like `person.name` looks up the `"name"` value in a dictionary called `"person"` in the current environment.

Literal Text

Add a directive `<div z-literal="true">...</div>` that copies the enclosed text as-is without interpreting or expanding any contained directives. (A directive like this would be needed when writing documentation for the template expander.)

Including Other Files

1. Add a directive `<div z-include="filename.html"/>` that includes another file in the file being processed.

2. Should included files be processed and the result copied into the including file, or should the text be copied in and then processed? What difference does it make to the way variables are evaluated?

HTML Snippets

Add a directive `<div z-snippet="variable">...</div>` that saves some text in a variable so that it can be displayed later. For example:

```
<html>
  <body>
    <div z-snippet="prefix"><strong>Important:</strong></div>
    <p>Expect three items</p>
    <ul>
      <li z-loop="item:names">
        <span z-var="prefix"><span z-var="item"/>
      </li>
    </ul>
  </body>
</html>
```

would print the word "Important:" in bold before each item in the list.

---

[7]https://docs.pytest.org/

YAML Headers

Modify the template expander to handle variables defined in a YAML header in the page being processed. For example, if the page is:

```
---
name: "Dorothy Johnson Vaughan"
---
<html>
  <body>
    <p><span z-var="name"/></p>
  </body>
</html>
```

will create a paragraph containing the given name.

Expanding All Files

Write a program `expand_all.py` that takes two directory names as command-line arguments and builds a website in the second directory by expanding all of the HTML files found in the first or in sub-directories of the first.

Counting Loops

Add a directive `<div z-index="indexName" z-limit="limitName">...</div>` that loops from zero to the value in the variable `limitName`, putting the current iteration index in `indexName`.

Boolean Expression

Design and implement a way to express the Boolean operators `and` and `or`.

Element IDs

The callout earlier said that templating systems should not generate random or sequential IDs for elements. A colleague of yours has proposed generating the IDs by hashing the element's content, since this will stay the same as long as the content does. What are the pros and cons of doing this?

13

A Code Linter

- A linter checks that a program conforms to a set of style and usage rules.

- Linters typically use the Visitor design pattern to find nodes of interest in an abstract syntax tree.

- Programs can modify a program's AST and then unparse it to create modified versions of the original program.

- Dynamic code modification is very powerful, but the technique can produce insecure and unmaintainable code.

Terms defined: **false negative**, **linter**

This book relies on about 1800 lines of Python to turn Markdown into HTML, fill in cross-references, and so on. To keep that code readable, we use `black`[1], `flake8`[2], and `isort`[3] to check that lines aren't too long, that classes and functions have consistent names, that modules are imported in a consistent order, and dozens of other things.

Checking tools are often called **linters** because an early tool like this that found fluff in C programs was called `lint`. Many projects insist that code pass linting checks before being committed to version control. To show how linters work, this chapter builds a trio of tools that find duplicate keys in dictionaries, look for unused variables, and create a table showing which classes in a hierarchy define which methods.

13.1 Machinery

Chapter 11 represented HTML as a DOM tree. We can also represent the structure of a program as an abstract syntax tree (AST) whose nodes represent functions, statements, variables, array indexing operations, and so on.

Python's `ast`[4] module will parse Python source code and produce an AST for us. For example, Figure 13.1 shows key parts of the AST for the short program shown below:

```
def double(x):
    return 2 * x

result = double(3)
print(result)
```

We said "key parts of the AST" because the complete structure contains many details that we haven't bothered to draw. To see them, let's use `ast.parse` to turn our example code into an AST and `ast.dump` to display it:

---

[1] https://black.readthedocs.io/
[2] https://flake8.pycqa.org/
[3] https://pycqa.github.io/isort/
[4] https://docs.python.org/3/library/ast.html

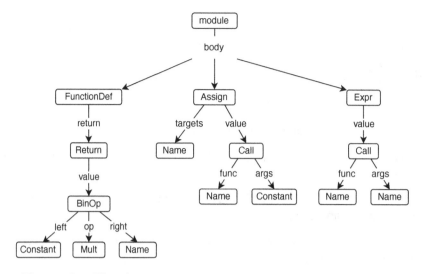

Figure 13.1: The abstract syntax tree for a simple Python program.

```
import ast
import sys

with open(sys.argv[1], "r") as reader:
    source = reader.read()

tree = ast.parse(source)
print(ast.dump(tree, indent=4))
```

```
python dump_ast.py simple.py
```

```
Module(
    body=[
        FunctionDef(
            name='double',
            args=arguments(
                posonlyargs=[],
                args=[
                    arg(arg='x')],
                kwonlyargs=[],
                kw_defaults=[],...
```

The node representing the definition of the function double is a FunctionDef node with a name and an arguments sub-node that stores information about the function's arguments; other nodes that we have left out represent its return value, the call to double, the assignment to result, and so on.

If we want a list of all the functions defined in this module, we can walk through this tree to find all the FunctionDef nodes and record their name properties. Since each node's structure is a little different, we would have to write one function for each type of node that knew which fields of that node were worth exploring.

Luckily for us the ast module has tools to do this for us. The class ast.NodeVisitor uses the now-familiar Visitor design pattern to recurse through a structure like the one in Figure 13.1. Each time the visitor reaches a node of type Thing, it looks for a method called visit_Thing; for example, when it reaches a FunctionDef node it looks for visit_FunctionDef. If that method has been defined, NodeVisitor calls it with the node as an argument. The class CollectNames uses this machinery to create a list of the function and variable names defined in a program:

```python
class CollectNames(ast.NodeVisitor):
    def __init__(self):
        super().__init__()
        self.names = {}

    def visit_Assign(self, node):
        for var in node.targets:
            self.add(var, var.id)
        self.generic_visit(node)

    def visit_FunctionDef(self, node):
        self.add(node, node.name)
        self.generic_visit(node)

    def add(self, node, name):
        loc = (node.lineno, node.col_offset)
        self.names[name] = self.names.get(name, set())
        self.names[name].add(loc)

    def position(self, node):
        return ({node.lineno}, {node.col_offset})
```

A few things worth noting about this class are:

1. The constructor of CollectNames invokes the constructor of NodeVisitor using super().__init__() before doing anything else.

2. The methods visit_Assign and visit_FunctionDef must call self.generic_visit (node) explicitly to recurse down through their children. By requiring this to be explicit, NodeVisitor gives programmers control on whether and when recursion takes place.

3. The method position relies on the fact that every node in the AST keeps track of where in the source code it came from.

To use this class, we read the source of the program that we want to analyze, parse it, and then call the visit method of our class to trigger recursion:

```python
with open(sys.argv[1], "r") as reader:
    source = reader.read()
tree = ast.parse(source)
collector = CollectNames()
collector.visit(tree)
print(collector.names)
```

```
python walk_ast.py simple.py
```

```
{'double': {(1, 0)}, 'result': {(4, 0)}}
```

With a little more work we could record class names as well, and then check that (for example) class names use CamelCase, while function and variable names use pothole_case. We'll tackle this in the exercises.

13.2 Finding Duplicate Keys

Many programs store their configuration in dictionaries. As those dictionaries grow larger, it's easy for programmers to redefine values by accident. For example, the dictionary in this short piece of code has two entries for the key "third":

```
has_duplicates = {
    "third": 3,
    "fourth": 4,
    "fourth": 5,
    "third": 6
}
print(has_duplicates)
```

Python could treat this as an error, keep the first entry, keep the last entry, or concatenate the entries somehow. As the output below shows, it chooses the third option:

```
{'third': 6, 'fourth': 5}
```

We can build a linter that finds dictionaries like `has_duplicates` with just a few lines of code and the `Counter` class from Python's `collections`[5] module (which implements a specialized dictionary that counts how many times a key has been seen). We define a `visit_Dict` method for `NodeVisitor` that adds each constant key to the counter, then look for keys that have been seen more than once:

```
class FindDuplicateKeys(ast.NodeVisitor):
    def visit_Dict(self, node):
        seen = Counter()
        for key in node.keys:
            if isinstance(key, ast.Constant):
                seen[key.value] += 1
        problems = {k for (k, v) in seen.items() if v > 1}
        self.report(node, problems)
        self.generic_visit(node)

    def report(self, node, problems):
        if problems:
            msg = ", ".join(p for p in problems)
            print(f"duplicate key(s) {{{msg}}} at {node.lineno}")
```

When we parse `has_duplicate_keys.py` and pass the AST to `FindDuplicateKeys`, we get:

```
duplicate key(s) {fourth, third} at 1
```

As Far as We Can Go

`FindDuplicateKeys` only considers constant keys, which means it won't find duplicate keys that are created on the fly like this:

```
def label():
    return "label"

actually_has_duplicate_keys = {
```

---
[5]https://docs.python.org/3/library/collections.html

```
        "label": 1,
        "la" + "bel": 2,
        label(): 3,
        "".join(["l", "a", "b", "e", "l"]): 4,
}
```

We could try adding more code to handle this, but there are so many different ways to generate keys on the fly that our linter couldn't possibly catch them all. The possibility of **false negatives** doesn't mean that linting is useless, though: every problem that linting catches gives programmers more time to check for things that linters can't find.

13.3 Finding Unused Variables

Finding unused variables—ones that are assigned values but never used—is more challenging than our previous examples. The problem is scope: a variable defined in a function or method might have the same name as one defined elsewhere, but they are different variables.

Let's start by defining a class that handles variables in modules and functions. Since functions can be defined inside modules and other functions, the constructor for our class creates a list that we will use as a stack to keep track of what scopes we're currently in:

```python
class FindUnusedVariables(ast.NodeVisitor):
    def __init__(self):
        super().__init__()
        self.stack = []

    def visit_Module(self, node):
        self.search("global", node)

    def visit_FunctionDef(self, node):
        self.search(node.name, node)
```

We could just use a list of three values to record information for each scope, but using namedtuple (which also comes from Python's collections module) tells readers explicitly what each scope consists of:

```python
Scope = namedtuple("Scope", ["name", "load", "store"])
```

Each time we encounter a new scope we push a new Scope triple onto the stack with a name, a set to hold the variables that are used in the scope, and another set to hold the variables that are defined in the scope. We then call NodeVisitor.generic_visitor to trigger recursion, pop the record we just pushed off the stack, and report any problems:

```python
def search(self, name, node):
    self.stack.append(Scope(name, set(), set()))
    self.generic_visit(node)
    scope = self.stack.pop()
    self.check(scope)

def check(self, scope):
    unused = scope.store - scope.load
    if unused:
        names = ", ".join(sorted(unused))
        print(f"unused in {scope.name}: {names}")
```

The last part of the puzzle is `visit_Name`. If the variable's value is being read, the node will have a property `.ctx` (short for "context") of type `ast.Load`. If the variable is being written to, the node's `.ctx` property will be an instance of `ast.Store`. Checking this property allows us to put the name in the right set in the scope that's at the top of the stack:

```
def visit_Name(self, node):
    if isinstance(node.ctx, ast.Load):
        self.stack[-1].load.add(node.id)
    elif isinstance(node.ctx, ast.Store):
        self.stack[-1].store.add(node.id)
    else:
        assert False, f"Unknown context"
    self.generic_visit(node)
```

Once again, we can run this by reading the source of a program, converting it to an AST, constructing an instance of `FindUnusedVariables`, and running its `visit` method:

```
with open(sys.argv[1], "r") as reader:
    source = reader.read()
tree = ast.parse(source)
finder = FindUnusedVariables()
finder.visit(tree)
```

To test our code, let's create a program that has some unused variables:

```
used = 3
distractor = 2
not_used = used + distractor


def no_unused(param):
    result = 2 * param
    return result


def has_unused(param):
    used = 3 * param
    not_used = 2 * param
    distractor = "distraction"
    return used
```

When we run our linter we get:

```
unused in has_unused: distractor, not_used
unused in global: not_used
```

13.4   Summary

Figure 13.2 summarizes the ideas introduced in this chapter; please see Appendix B for some more related material.

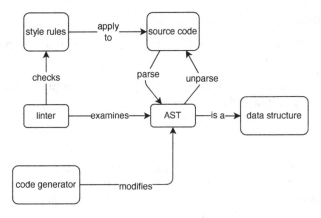

Figure 13.2: Concepts for code manipulation.

13.5 Exercises

Finding Unused Parameters

Modify the code that finds unused variables to report unused function parameters as well.

Finding Redundant Assignments

Write a linter that looks for redundant assignments to variables, i.e., assignments that are immediately overwritten:

```
x = 1   # redundant
x = 2
```

(Redundant assignments are a common result of copying and pasting.)

Checking Names

Write a linter that checks that class names are written in CamelCase but function and variable names are in pothole_case.

Missing Documentation

Write a linter that complains about modules, classes, methods, and functions that don't have docstrings.

Missing Tests

Write a linter that takes two files as input: one that defines one or more functions and another that defines one or more tests of those functions. The linter looks through the tests to see what functions are being called, then reports any functions from the first file that it hasn't seen.

Chaining Methods

1. Modify the code that injects methods into `NodeVisitor` so that any previously injected methods are also called.

2. Modify the methods again so that each one signals whether or not it has handled recursion (either directly or indirectly).

Sorting Imports

`isort`[6] checks that the imports in a file are sorted correctly: modules from Python's standard library come first (in alphabetical order), then installed modules (also in alphabetical order) and finally local imports (ditto). Write a linter that reports violations of these rules. How did you distinguish between the three cases?

---

[6]https://pycqa.github.io/isort/

14

Page Layout

- A layout engine places page elements based on their size and organization.

- Page elements are organized as a tree of basic blocks, rows, and columns.

- The layout engine calculates the position of each block based on its size and the position of its parent.

- Drawing blocks on top of each other is an easy way to render them.

- Use multiple inheritance and mixin classes to inject methods into classes.

Terms defined: **accidental complexity**, **block (on page)**, **confirmation bias**, **easy mode**, **intrinsic complexity**, **layout engine**, **Liskov Substitution Principle**, **mixin class**, **z-buffering**

You might be reading this as HTML in your browser, as an e-book, or on the printed page. In all three cases a **layout engine** took some text and some layout instructions and decided where to put each character and image. To explore how they work, we will build a small layout engine based on Matt Brubeck's[1] tutorial[2] and on Pavel Panchekha[3] and Chris Harrelson's[4] book *Web Browser Engineering*[5]. Since our focus is layout, we will create objects ourselves to represent DOM nodes rather than parsing HTML.

14.1 Sizing

Let's start on **easy mode** without margins, padding, line-wrapping, or other complications. Everything we can put on the screen is represented as a rectangular cell, and every cell is either a row, a column, or a **block**. A block has a fixed width and height:

```python
class Block:
    def __init__(self, width, height):
        self.width = width
        self.height = height

    def get_width(self):
        return self.width

    def get_height(self):
        return self.height
```

---

[1] https://limpet.net/mbrubeck/
[2] https://limpet.net/mbrubeck/2014/08/08/toy-layout-engine-1.html
[3] https://pavpanchekha.com/
[4] https://twitter.com/chrishtr
[5] https://browser.engineering/

```
     0  1  2  3  4  5
                         ➤ X
   0 F  i  r  s  t

   1 S  e  c  o  n  d

   2 T  h  i  r  d

     Y
```

Figure 14.1: Coordinate system with (0, 0) in the upper-left corner.

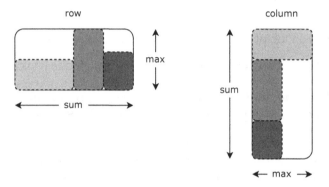

Figure 14.2: Calculating sizes of blocks with fixed width and height.

Upside Down

The coordinate systems for screens puts (0, 0) in the upper-left corner instead of the lower-left, so Y increases as we go down, rather than up (Figure 14.1). This convention dates back to teletype terminals that printed on rolls of paper; as Mike Hoye[6] has observed[7], the past is all around us.

A row arranges one or more cells horizontally; its width is the sum of the widths of its children, while its height is the height of its tallest child (Figure 14.2):

```
class Row:
    def __init__(self, *children):
        self.children = list(children)

    def get_width(self):
        return sum([c.get_width() for c in self.children])

    def get_height(self):
        return max(
            [c.get_height() for c in self.children],
            default=0
        )
```

---

[6]http://exple.tive.org/blarg/
[7]http://exple.tive.org/blarg/2020/11/26/punching-holes/

Finally, a column arranges one or more cells vertically: its width is the width of its widest child and its height is the sum of the heights of its children. (Here and elsewhere, we use the abbreviation `col` when referring to columns.)

```
class Col:
    def __init__(self, *children):
        self.children = list(children)

    def get_width(self):
        return max(
            [c.get_width() for c in self.children],
            default=0
        )

    def get_height(self):
        return sum([c.get_height() for c in self.children])
```

Rows and columns nest inside one another: a row cannot span two or more columns, and a column cannot cross the boundary between two rows. We can therefore represent our document as a tree and calculate the width and height of each cell every time we need it. This is simple but inefficient: we could calculate both width and height at the same time and cache those values to avoid recalculation, but we called this "easy mode" for a reason.

As simple as it is, this code could still contain errors (and did during development), so we write some tests to check that it works properly before trying to build anything more complicated. One such test is:

```
def test_lays_out_a_grid_of_rows_of_columns():
    fixture = Col(
        Row(Block(1, 2), Block(3, 4)),
        Row(Block(5, 6), Col(Block(7, 8), Block(9, 10)))
    )
    assert fixture.get_width() == 14
    assert fixture.get_height() == 22
```

14.2 Positioning

Once we know how big cells are, we can figure out where to put them. Suppose we start with the upper-left corner of the browser: upper because we lay out the page top-to-bottom and left because we are doing left-to-right layout. If the cell is a block, we place it there. If the cell is a row, on the other hand, we get its height and then calculate its lower edge as y1 = y0 + height. We then place the first child's upper-left corner at (x0, y1-height0), the second child's at (x0 + width0, y1-height0), and so on (Figure 14.3). Similarly, if the cell is a column, we place the first child at (x0, y0), the next at (x0, y0 + height0), and so on.

To save ourselves some work, we will derive the classes that know how to do layout from the classes we wrote before. Basic blocks are:

```
class PlacedBlock(Block):
    def __init__(self, width, height):
        super().__init__(width, height)
        self.x0 = None
        self.y0 = None

    def place(self, x0, y0):
```

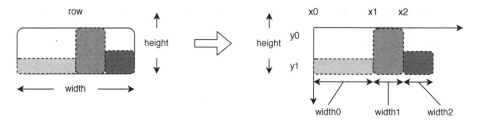

Figure 14.3: Laying out rows and columns of fixed-size blocks.

```
    self.x0 = x0
    self.y0 = y0

def report(self):
    return [
        "block",
        self.x0, self.y0,
        self.x0 + self.width, self.y0 + self.height
    ]
```

The constructor and reporting method for the `PlacedCol` class looks much the same. Its placement method is:

```
def place(self, x0, y0):
    self.x0 = x0
    self.y0 = y0
    y_current = self.y0
    for child in self.children:
        child.place(x0, y_current)
        y_current += child.get_height()
```

while the placement method for rows is:

```
def place(self, x0, y0):
    self.x0 = x0
    self.y0 = y0
    y1 = self.y0 + self.get_height()
    x_current = x0
    for child in self.children:
        child_y = y1 - child.get_height()
        child.place(x_current, child_y)
        x_current += child.get_width()
```

Once again, we write and run some tests to check that everything is doing what it's supposed to. One such test is:

```
def test_places_a_column_of_two_blocks():
    fixture = Col(Block(1, 1), Block(2, 4))
    fixture.place(0, 0)
    assert fixture.report() == [
        "col",
        0, 0, 2, 5,
        ["block", 0, 0, 1, 1],
        ["block", 0, 1, 2, 5],
    ]
```

14.3 Rendering

We drew blocks on graph paper to figure out the expected answers for the tests shown above. We can do something similar in software by creating a "screen" of space characters and having each block draw itself in the right place. If we start at the root of the tree, children will overwrite the marks made by their parents, which will automatically produce the right appearance (Figure 14.4). (A more sophisticated version of this called **z-buffering** used in 3D graphics keeps track of the visual depth of each pixel to draw objects correctly regardless of their order.)

Our "screen" is a list of lists of characters, with one inner list for each a row on the screen. (We use lists rather than strings so that we can overwrite characters in place.)

```
def make_screen(width, height):
    screen = []
    for i in range(height):
        screen.append([" "] * width)
    return screen
```

We will use successive lower-case characters to show each block, i.e., the root block will draw itself using 'a', while its children will be 'b', 'c', and so on.

```
def draw(screen, node, fill=None):
    fill = next_fill(fill)
    node.render(screen, fill)
    if hasattr(node, "children"):
        for child in node.children:
            fill = draw(screen, child, fill)
    return fill

def next_fill(fill):
    return "a" if fill is None else chr(ord(fill) + 1)
```

To teach each kind of cell to render itself, we derive new classes from the ones we have and give each of those new classes a `render` method with the same signature. Since Python supports multiple inheritance, we can do this with a **mixin class** (Figure 14.5). The `Renderable` mixin is:

```
class Renderable:
    def render(self, screen, fill):
        for ix in range(self.get_width()):
            for iy in range(self.get_height()):
                screen[self.y0 + iy][self.x0 + ix] = fill
```

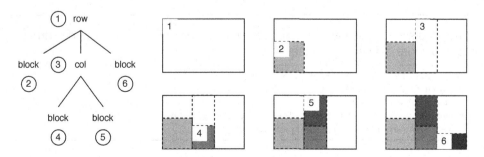

Figure 14.4: Render blocks by drawing child nodes on top of parent nodes.

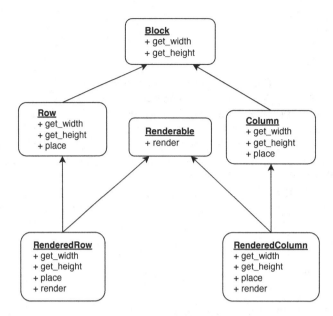

Figure 14.5: Using multiple inheritance and a mixin class to add methods.

Using it, the new cell classes are simply:

```
class RenderedBlock(PlacedBlock, Renderable):
    pass

class RenderedCol(PlacedCol, Renderable):
    pass

class RenderedRow(PlacedRow, Renderable):
    pass
```

(Not) The Right Way to Do It

If we were building a real layout engine, we would go back and create a class called
`Cell` with this `render` method, then derive our `Block`, `Row`, and `Col` classes from that.
In general, if two or more classes need to be able to do something, we should add the
required method to their lowest common ancestor. We've chosen not to do that in this
case both to show when and why mixin classes are sometimes useful, and so that we
can build and test code incrementally.

Simple tests are a little easier to read using rendering, though we still had to draw things
on paper to figure out what to expect:

```
def test_renders_a_column_of_two_blocks():
    fixture = Col(Block(1, 1), Block(2, 4))
    fixture.place(0, 0)
    expected = "\n".join(["ba", "cc", "cc", "cc", "cc"])
    assert render(fixture) == expected
```

The fact that our tests are difficult to understand is a sign that we should do more testing. It would be very easy for us to get a wrong result and convince ourselves that it was correct; this kind of **confirmation bias** is very common in software development.

14.4   Wrapping

One of the biggest differences between a browser and a printed page is that the text in the browser wraps automatically as the window is resized. (The other, these days, is that the printed page doesn't spy on us, though someone is undoubtedly working on that.)

The first step in adding wrapping to our layout engine is to fix the width of a row. If the total width of the children is greater than the row's width, the layout engine needs to wrap the children around. This assumes that columns can be made as tall as they need to be, i.e., that we can grow vertically to make up for limited space horizontally. It also assumes that none of a row's children is wider than the width of the row so that each can fit in a row of its own if necessary. We will look at what happens when this isn't true in the exercises.

Our layout engine manages wrapping by transforming the tree. The height and width of blocks are fixed, so they become themselves. Columns become themselves as well, but since they have children that might need to wrap, the class representing columns needs a new method:

```
class WrappedBlock(PlacedBlock):
    def wrap(self):
        return self

class WrappedCol(PlacedCol):
    def wrap(self):
        return PlacedCol(*[c.wrap() for c in self.children])
```

(The * in front of the list being passed to PlacedCol in the last line of the code above is another use of the spreading introduced in Chapter 2.)

Rows do all the hard work. Each original row is replaced with a new row that contains a single column with one or more rows, each of which is one "line" of wrapped cells (Figure 14.6). This replacement is unnecessary when everything will fit on a single row, but it's easiest to write the code that does it every time; we will look at making this more efficient in the exercises.

Our new wrappable row's constructor takes a fixed width followed by the children and returns that fixed width when asked for its size:

```
class WrappedRow(PlacedRow):
    def __init__(self, width, *children):
        super().__init__(*children)
        assert width >= 0, "Need non-negative width"
        self.width = width

    def get_width(self):
        return self.width
```

Wrapping puts the row's children into buckets, and then converts the buckets to a row of a column of rows:

```
def wrap(self):
    children = [c.wrap() for c in self.children]
    rows = self._bucket(children)
```

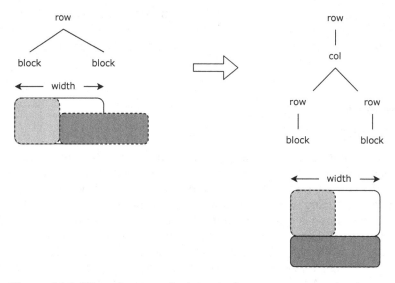

Figure 14.6: Wrapping rows by introducing a new row and column.

```
new_rows = [PlacedRow(*r) for r in rows]
new_col = PlacedCol(*new_rows)
return PlacedRow(new_col)
```

To bucket the children, we add them one at a time to a temporary list. If adding another node would make the total width of the nodes in that list too large, we use that node to start a new temporary list:

```
def _bucket(self, children):
    result = []
    current_row = []
    current_x = 0

    for child in children:
        child_width = child.get_width()
        if (current_x + child_width) <= self.width:
            current_row.append(child)
            current_x += child_width
        else:
            result.append(current_row)
            current_row = [child]
            current_x = child_width
    result.append(current_row)

    return result
```

Once again, we bring forward all the previous tests and write some new ones to test the functionality we've added:

```
def test_wrap_a_row_of_two_blocks_that_do_not_fit_on_one_row():
    fixture = WrappedRow(3, WrappedBlock(2, 1), WrappedBlock(2, 1))
    wrapped = fixture.wrap()
    wrapped.place(0, 0)
    assert wrapped.report() == [
        "row",
        0, 0, 2, 2,
        [
```

```
        "col",
        0, 0, 2, 2,
        ["row", 0, 0, 2, 1, ["block", 0, 0, 2, 1]],
        ["row", 0, 1, 2, 2, ["block", 0, 1, 2, 2]],
    ],
]
```

We could have had columns handle resizing rather than rows, but we (probably) don't need to make both resizeable. This is an example of **intrinsic complexity**: the problem really is this hard, so something has to deal with it somewhere. Programs often contain **accidental complexity** as well, which can be removed if people are willing to accept change. In practice, that often means that it sticks around longer than it should.

The Liskov Substitution Principle

We are able to re-use tests as our code evolved because of the **Liskov Substitution Principle**, which states that it should be possible to replace objects in a program with objects of derived classes without breaking anything. In order to satisfy this principle, new code must handle the same set of inputs as the old code, though it may be able to process more inputs as well. Conversely, its output must be a subset of what the old code produced so that whatever is downstream from it won't be surprised. Thinking in these terms leads to the methodology called design by contract discussed in Chapter 2.

14.5 Summary

Figure 14.7 summarizes the ideas introduced in this chapter. Real page layout systems do far more than what we have described, but all of them implement some kind of negotiation between containers and content.

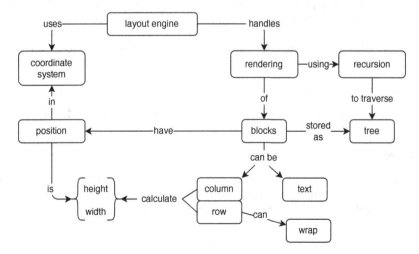

Figure 14.7: Page layout concept map.

14.6   Exercises

Refactoring

Refactor the classes used to represent blocks, rows, and columns so that:

1. They all derive from a common parent class.

2. All common behavior is defined in that parent (if only with placeholder methods).

Removing Spreads

The code shown in this chapter makes heavy use of varargs and spreading, i.e., uses `*` to spread the values of lists to match parameters and `*children` to capture multiple arguments. Rewrite the code to use lists instead. Do you find your rewritten code easier to understand?

Recycling

Modify the wrapping code so that new rows and columns are only created if needed. For example, if a row of width 10 contains a text node that is only 4 characters wide, a new row and column are *not* inserted.

Rendering a Clear Background

Modify the rendering code so that only the text in block nodes is shown, i.e., so that the empty space in rows and columns is rendered as spaces.

Clipping Text

1. Modify the wrapping and rendering so that if a block of text is too wide for the available space, the extra characters are clipped. For example, if a column of width 5 contains a line "unfittable", only "unfit" appears.

2. Extend your solution to break lines on spaces as needed in order to avoid clipping.

Bidirectional Rendering

Modify the existing software to do either left-to-right or right-to-left rendering upon request.

Equal Sizing

Modify the existing code to support elastic columns, i.e., so that all of the columns in a row are automatically sized to have the same width. If the number of columns does not divide evenly into the width of the row, allocate the extra space as equally as possible from left to right.

Properties

Look at the documentation for Python's `@property`[8] decorator and modify the block classes to replace the `get_width` and `get_height` methods with properties called `width` and `height`.

Drawing Borders

1. Modify the existing code so that elements are drawn with borders like this:

```
+----+
|text|
+----+
```

Padding Elements

Modify the existing code so that:

1. Authors can define a `padding` attribute for row and column elements.

2. When the node is rendered, that many blank spaces are added on all four sides of the contents.

For example, string `"text"` with a padding of 1 would render as:

```
+------+
|      |
| text |
|      |
+------+
```

where the lines show the outer border of the rendering.

Tables

Add another node type `Table` such that:

1. All the children of a table must be rows.

2. Every row must contain exactly the same number of columns.

3. When the table is rendered, every column has the same width in every row.

---

[8]https://docs.python.org/3/library/functions.html#property

15

Performance Profiling

- Create abstract classes to specify interfaces.

- Store two-dimensional data as rows or as columns.

- Use reflection to match data to function parameters.

- Measure performance to evaluate engineering tradeoffs.

Terms defined: **batch processing**, **benchmark**, **column-wise storage**, **data engineer**, **dataframe**, **docstring**, **immutable**, **index (a database)**, **join (tables)**, **online analytical processing**, **online transaction processing**, **parameter sweeping**, **profiling**, **row-wise storage**

One peril of publishing a book online is obsessing over analytics. How many people visited the site today? Which pages did they look at, and for how long? Whether we use Excel, SQL, or Python, we will almost certainly be analyzing tables with named columns and multiple rows. Such tables are called **dataframes**, and their performance is important when we are working with large data sets. This chapter therefore implements dataframes in two ways and shows how to compare their performance.

15.1 Options

To start, let's create an abstract class that defines the methods our dataframe classes will support. This class requires concrete classes to implement the methods shown below:

```
class DataFrame:
    def ncol(self):
        """Report the number of columns."""

    def nrow(self):
        """Report the number of rows."""

    def cols(self):
        """Return the set of column names."""

    def eq(self, other):
        """Check equality with another dataframe."""

    def get(self, col, row):
        """Get a scalar value."""

    def select(self, *names):
        """Select a named subset of columns."""

    def filter(self, func):
        """Select a subset of rows by testing values."""
```

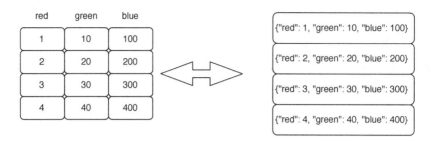

Figure 15.1: Storing a dataframe's data in rows.

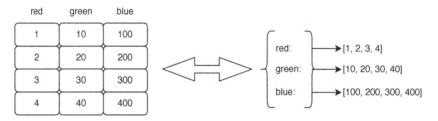

Figure 15.2: Storing a dataframe's data in columns.

Docstrings Are Enough

Every method in Python needs a body, so many programmers will write `pass` (Python's "do nothing" statement). However, a **docstring** also counts as a body, so if we write those (which we should) there's no need to write `pass`.

For our first usable implementation, we will derive a class `DfRow` that uses **row-wise** storage (Figure 15.1). The dataframe is stored as a list of dictionaries, each of which represents a row. All of the dictionaries must have the same keys so that the concept of "column" is meaningful, and the values associated with a particular key must all have the same type.

Our second implementation, `DfCol`, will use **column-wise** storage (Figure 15.2). Each column is stored as a list of values, all of which are of the same type. The dataframe itself is a dictionary of such lists, all of which have the same length so that there are no holes in any of the rows. How we store the data determines which methods are easy to implement and which are hard, and which are fast or slow.

15.2 Row-Wise Storage

We start by deriving `DfRow` from `DataFrame` and writing its constructor, which takes a list of dictionaries as an argument, checks that they're consistent with each other, and saves them:

```
from df_base import DataFrame
from util import dict_match

class DfRow(DataFrame):
```

```
    def __init__(self, rows):
        assert len(rows) > 0
        assert all(dict_match(r, rows[0]) for r in rows)
        self._data = rows
```

The helper function to check that a bunch of dictionaries all have the same keys and the same types of values associated with those keys is:

```
def dict_match(d, prototype):
    if set(d.keys()) != set(prototype.keys()):
        return False
    return all(type(d[k]) == type(prototype[k]) for k in d)
```

Notice that DfRow's constructor compares all of the rows against the first row. Doing this means that we can't create an empty dataframe, i.e., one that has no rows. This restriction wasn't part of our original design: it's an accident of implementation that might surprise our users. It's OK not to fix this while we're prototyping, but we will look at ways to address it in the exercises.

Four of the methods required by DataFrame are easy to implement on top of row-wise storage, though once again our implementation assumes there is at least one row:

```
def ncol(self):
    return len(self._data[0])

def nrow(self):
    return len(self._data)

def cols(self):
    return set(self._data[0].keys())

def get(self, col, row):
    assert col in self._data[0]
    assert 0 <= row < len(self._data)
    return self._data[row][col]
```

Checking equality is also relatively simple. Two dataframes are the same if they have exactly the same columns and the same values in every column:

```
def eq(self, other):
    assert isinstance(other, DataFrame)
    for (i, row) in enumerate(self._data):
        for key in row:
            if key not in other.cols():
                return False
            if row[key] != other.get(key, i):
                return False
    return True
```

Notice that we use other.cols() and other.get() rather than reaching into the other dataframe. We are planning to implement dataframes in several different ways, and we might want to compare instances of those different implementations. Since they might have different internal data structures, the only safe way to do this is to rely on the interface defined in the base class.

Our final operations are selection, which returns a subset of the original dataframe's columns, and filtering, which returns a subset of its rows. Since we don't know how many columns the user might want, we give the select method a single parameter *names that will capture zero or more positional arguments. We then build a new list of dictionaries that only contain the fields with those names (Figure 15.3):

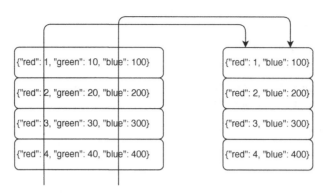

Figure 15.3: Selecting columns from data stored as rows.

```
def select(self, *names):
    assert all(n in self._data[0] for n in names)
    rows = [{key: r[key] for key in names} for r in self._data]
    return DfRow(rows)
```

We now need to decide how to filter rows. Typical filtering conditions include, "Keep rows where red is non-zero," "Keep rows where red is greater than green," and, "Keep rows where red+green is within 10% of blue." Rather than trying to anticipate every possible rule, we require users to define functions whose parameters match the names of the table's columns. For example, if we have this test fixture:

```
def odd_even():
    return DfRow([{"a": 1, "b": 3}, {"a": 2, "b": 4}])
```

then we should be able to write this test:

```
def test_filter():
    def odd(a, b):
        return (a % 2) == 1

    df = odd_even()
    assert df.filter(odd).eq(DfRow([{"a": 1, "b": 3}]))
```

We can implement this by using ** to spread the row across the function's parameters (Chapter 2). If there are keys in the row that don't match parameters in the function or vice versa, Python will throw an exception, but that's probably what we want. Using this, the implementation of DfRow.filter is:

```
def filter(self, func):
    result = [r for r in self._data if func(**r)]
    return DfRow(result)
```

Notice that the dataframe created by filter re-uses the rows of the original dataframe (Figure 15.4). This is safe and efficient as long as dataframes are **immutable**, i.e., as long as their contents are never changed in place. Most dataframe libraries work this way: while recycling memory can save a little time, it usually also makes bugs much harder to track down.

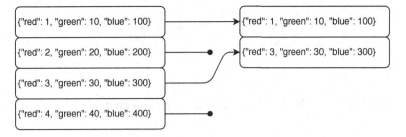

Figure 15.4: Filtering data stored as rows.

15.3   Column-Wise Storage

Having done all of this thinking, our column-wise dataframe class is somewhat easier to write. We start as before with its constructor:

```
from df_base import DataFrame
from util import all_eq

class DfCol(DataFrame):
    def __init__(self, **kwargs):
        assert len(kwargs) > 0
        assert all_eq(len(kwargs[k]) for k in kwargs)
        for k in kwargs:
            assert all_eq(type(v) for v in kwargs[k])
        self._data = kwargs
```

and use a helper function `all_eq` to check that all of the values in any column have the same types:

```
def all_eq(*values):
    return (not values) or all(v == values[0] for v in values)
```

> **One Allowable Difference**
>
> Notice that `DfCol`'s constructor does *not* have the same signature as `DfRow`'s. At some point in our code we have to decide which of the two classes to construct. If we design our code well, that decision will be made in exactly one place and everything else will rely solely on the common interface defined by `DataFrame`. But since we have to type a different class name at the point of construction, it's OK for the constructors to be different.

The four methods that were simple to write for `DfRow` are equally simple to write for `DfCol`, though once again our prototype implementation accidentally disallows empty dataframes:

```
def ncol(self):
    return len(self._data)

def nrow(self):
    n = list(self._data.keys())[0]
    return len(self._data[n])
```

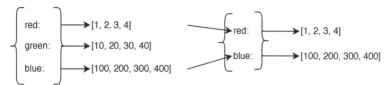

Figure 15.5: Column-wise selection.

```
def cols(self):
    return set(self._data.keys())

def get(self, col, row):
    assert col in self._data
    assert 0 <= row < len(self._data[col])
    return self._data[col][row]
```

As with `DfRow`, the method that checks equality relies on the internal details of its own class but uses the interface defined by `DataFrame` to access the other object:

```
def eq(self, other):
    assert isinstance(other, DataFrame)
    for n in self._data:
        if n not in other.cols():
            return False
        for i in range(len(self._data[n])):
            if self.get(n, i) != other.get(n, i):
                return False
    return True
```

To select columns, we pick the ones named by the caller and use them to create a new dataframe. Again, this recycles the existing storage:

```
def select(self, *names):
    assert all(n in self._data for n in names)
    return DfCol(**{n: self._data[n] for n in names})
```

Finally, we need to filter the rows of a column-wise dataframe. Doing this is complex: since values are stored in columns, we have to extract the ones belonging to each row to pass them into the user-defined filter function (Figure 15.6). And if that wasn't enough, we want to do this solely for the columns that the user's function needs.

For now, we will solve this problem by requiring the user-defined filter function to define parameters to match all of the dataframe's columns regardless of whether they are used for filtering or not. We will then build a temporary dictionary with all the values in a "row"

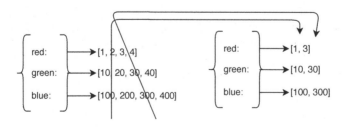

Figure 15.6: Extracting values from columns to create temporary rows.

(i.e., the corresponding values across all columns) and use ** to spread it across the filter function. Appendix B looks at a safer, but more complex, way to do this.

```
def filter(self, func):
    result = {n: [] for n in self._data}
    for i in range(self.nrow()):
        args = {n: self._data[n][i] for n in self._data}
        if func(**args):
            for n in self._data:
                result[n].append(self._data[n][i])
    return DfCol(**result)
```

Time to write some tests. This one checks that we can construct a dataframe with some values:

```
def test_construct_with_two_pairs():
    df = DfCol(a=[1, 2], b=[3, 4])
    assert df.get("a", 0) == 1
    assert df.get("a", 1) == 2
    assert df.get("b", 0) == 3
    assert df.get("b", 1) == 4
```

while this one checks that `filter` works correctly:

```
def test_filter():
    def odd(a, b):
        return (a % 2) == 1

    df = DfCol(a=[1, 2], b=[3, 4])
    assert df.filter(odd).eq(DfCol(a=[1], b=[3]))
```

15.4   Performance

Our two implementations of dataframes have identical interfaces, so how can we choose which to use?

Transactions vs. Analysis

Regardless of data volumes, different storage schemes are better (or worse) for different kinds of work. **Online transaction processing** (OLTP) refers to adding or querying individual records, such as online sales. **Online analytical processing** (OLAP), on the other hand, processes selected columns of a table in bulk to do things like find averages over time. Row-wise storage is usually best for OLTP, but column-wise storage is better suited for OLAP. If data volumes are large, **data engineers** will sometimes run two databases in parallel, using **batch processing** jobs to copy new or updated records from the OLTP databases over to the OLAP database.

To compare the speed of these classes, let's write a short program to create dataframes of each kind and time how long it takes to select their columns and filter their rows. To keep things simple, we will create dataframes whose columns are called `label_1`, `label_2`, and so on, and whose values are all integers in the range 0–9. A thorough set of **benchmarks** would create columns with other datatypes as well, but this example is enough to illustrate the technique.

```
RANGE = 10

def make_col(nrow, ncol):
    def _col(n, start):
        return [((start + i) % RANGE) for i in range(n)]
    fill = {f"label_{c}": _col(nrow, c) for c in range(ncol)}
    return DfCol(**fill)

def make_row(nrow, ncol):
    labels = [f"label_{c}" for c in range(ncol)]
    def _row(r):
        return {
            c: ((r + i) % RANGE) for (i, c) in enumerate(labels)
        }
    fill = [_row(r) for r in range(nrow)]
    return DfRow(fill)
```

To time `filter`, we arbitrarily decide to keep rows with an even value in the first column:

```
FILTER = 2

def time_filter(df):
    def f(label_0, **args):
        return label_0 % FILTER == 1
    start = time.time()
    df.filter(f)
    return time.time() - start
```

Since `DfCol` and `DfRow` derive from the same base class, `time_filter` doesn't care which we give it. Again, if we were doing this for real, we would look at actual programs to see what fraction of rows filtering usually kept and simulate that.

To time `select`, we arbitrarily decide to keep one-third of the columns:

```
SELECT = 3

def time_select(df):
    indices = [i for i in range(df.ncol()) if ((i % SELECT) == 0)]
    labels = [f"label_{i}" for i in indices]
    start = time.time()
    df.select(*labels)
    return time.time() - start
```

Finally, we write a function that takes a list of strings like 3x3 or 100x20, creates dataframes of each size, times operations, and reports the results. We call this function `sweep` because executing code multiple times with different parameters to measure performance is called **parameter sweeping**:

```
def sweep(sizes):
    result = []
    for (nrow, ncol) in sizes:
        df_col = make_col(nrow, ncol)
        df_row = make_row(nrow, ncol)
        times = [
            time_filter(df_col),
            time_select(df_col),
            time_filter(df_row),
            time_select(df_row),
        ]
        result.append([nrow, ncol, *times])
    return result
```

The results are shown in Table 15.1 and Figure 15.7. For a 1000×1000 dataframe, selection is over 250 times faster with column-wise storage than with row-wise, while filtering is 1.8 times slower.

nrow	ncol	filter col	select col	filter row	select row
10	10	8.87e-05	7.70e-05	4.41e-05	2.50e-05
100	100	0.00275	4.10e-05	0.00140	8.76e
1000	1000	0.146	0.000189	0.0787	0.0508
10000	10000	19.0	0.00234	9.97	5.57

Table 15.1: Dataframe timings.

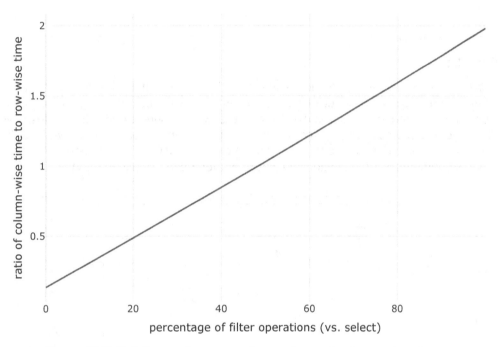

Figure 15.7: Relative performance of row-wise and column-wise storage.

We can get much more insight by **profiling** our code using Python cProfile[1] module, which collects detailed information on how long each function runs and reports the result:

```
python -m cProfile --sort=tottime \
    timing.py --silent 10x10 50x50 100x100 500x500 1000x1000
```

```
        3007281 function calls (3003108 primitive calls) in 2.120 seconds

   Ordered by: internal time

   ncalls  tottime  percall  cumtime  percall filename:lineno(function)
  2319840    0.671    0.000    0.671    0.000 util.py:10(<genexpr>)
        5    0.271    0.054    0.521    0.104 df_col.py:50(filter)
     1660    0.261    0.000    0.261    0.000 timing.py:20(<dictcomp>)
8066/3916    0.213    0.000    1.056    0.000 {built-in method builtins.all}
     1660    0.191    0.000    0.191    0.000 df_col.py:53(<dictcomp>)…
```

[1] https://docs.python.org/3/library/profile.html

The profiler's output tells us the number of times each function or method was called, the total time spent in those calls (which is what we care about most), the time spent per call, and the cumulative time spent in that call and all the things it calls. We can see right away that the `dict_match` function that checks the consistency of the rows in a row-oriented dataframe is eating up a lot of time. It's only called in the constructor, but since we're constructing a new dataframe for each `filter` and `select`, removing that safety check would speed things up.

Looking down a little further, the dictionary comprehension in `DfCol.filter` takes a lot of time as well. That isn't surprising: we're copying the values out of the columns into a temporary dictionary for every row when we filter, and building all those temporary dictionaries adds up to a lot of time.

15.5 Summary

Figure 15.8 summarizes the key ideas introduced in this chapter. The most important is that experiments can help us decide how to implement key features of our software, but the results of those experiments depend on exactly what we measure. Good software designers collect and analyze data all the time to find out whether one website design works better than another [Kohavi2020] or to improve the performance of CPUs [Patterson2017]. A few simple experiments like these can save weeks or months of misguided effort.

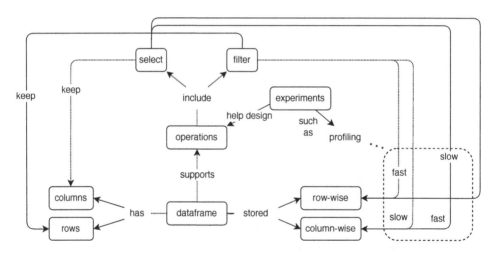

Figure 15.8: Concepts for dataframes.

15.6 Exercises

More Efficient Filtering

Derive a class from `DfCol` and override its `filter` method so that the user-defined filtering functions take zero or more columns and a row index called `i_row` as parameters and return `True` or `False` to signal whether the row passes the test.

1. How much faster does this make filtering?

2. When would it be useful for filtering functions to take no column at all as parameters?

Empty Dataframes

An empty dataframe is as reasonable and as useful as an empty string or an empty list. DfCol can represent this, but DfRow cannot: if the list of dictionaries is empty, we cannot ask for column names. Derive another dataframe class from DF that uses row-wise storage but can represent a dataframe with no rows.

Unified Constructors

Modify the constructors of DfRow and DfCol to have the same signatures. Where and why might this be useful?

Fixture Functions

Read the documentation for the @fixture decorator in pytest[2] and modify the tests in this chapter to use it.

Using Arrays

Derive another dataframe class from DF that uses Python's array[3] module for column-wise storage. How does it perform compared to other implementations?

Crossover

1. At what ratio of filter operations to select operations are DfRow and DfCol equally fast? (Your answer may depend on the size of the dataframe.)

2. How does the relative performance of the two classes change if tables have a fixed number of columns (such as 10 or 20) but an increasing numbers of rows? Is this scenario more realistic?

Conversion

Write a function to convert a DfRow into a DfCol and another to do the opposite. Which one is faster? How does the difference in performance depend on the size and shape of the dataframes being converted?

Filtering by Strings

Modify the comparison of filter and select to work with tables that contain columns of strings instead of columns of numbers and see how that changes performance. For testing, create random 4-letter strings using the characters A-Z and then filter by:

---

[2]https://docs.pytest.org/
[3]https://docs.python.org/3/library/array.html

- an exact match,

- strings starting with a specific character, and

- strings that contain a specific character.

Inspection

Rewrite `DfCol.filter` using Python's `inspect`[4] module so that users' filtering functions only need to define parameters for the columns of interest.

Join Performance

A join combines data from two tables based on matching keys. For example, if the two tables are:

Key	Left
A	a1
B	b1
C	c1

and:

Key	Right
A	a2
A	a3
B	b2

then the join is:

Key	Left	Right
A	a1	a2
A	a1	a3
B	b1	b2

Write a test to compare the performance of row-wise vs. column-wise storage when joining two tables based on matching numeric keys. Does the answer depend on the fraction of keys that match?

Join Optimization

The simplest way to **join** two tables is to look for matching keys using a double loop. An alternative is to build an **index** for each table and then use it to construct matches. For example, suppose the tables are:

Key	Left
A	a1
B	b1
C	c1

---

[4]https://docs.python.org/3/library/inspect.html

and:

Key	Right
A	a2
A	a3
B	b2

The first step is to create a `Map` showing where each key is found in the first table:

```
{A: [0], B: [1], C: [2]}
```

The second step is to create a similar `Map` for the second table:

```
{A: [0, 1], B: [2]}
```

We can then loop over the keys in one of the maps, look up values in the second map, and construct all of the matches.

Write a function that joins two tables this way. Is it faster or slower than using a double loop? How does the answer depend on the number of keys and the fraction that match?

16

Object Persistence

> - A persistence framework saves and restores objects.
>
> - Persistence must handle aliasing and circularity.
>
> - Users should be able to extend persistence to handle objects of their own types.
>
> - Software designs should be open for extension but closed for modification.
>
> Terms defined: **atomic value**, **list comprehension**, **Open-Closed Principle**, **persistence**

Version control can keep track of our files, but what should we put in them? Plain text works well for things like this chapter, but the data structures used to represent HTML (Chapter 11) or the state of a game aren't easy to represent in prose.

Another option is to store objects, i.e., to save a list of dictionaries as-is rather than flattering it into rows and columns. Python's `pickle`[1] module does this in a Python-specific way, while the `json`[2] module saves some kinds of data as text formatted like JavaScript objects. As odd as it may seem, this has become a cross-language standard.

The phrase "some kinds of data" is the most important part of the preceding paragraph. Since programs can define new classes, a **persistence framework** has to choose one of the following:

1. Only handle built-in types, or even more strictly, only handle types that are common across many languages, so that data saved by Python can be read by JavaScript and vice versa.

2. Provide a way for programs to convert from user-defined types to built-in types and then save those. This option is less restrictive than the first but can lead to some information being lost. For example, if instances of a program's `User` class are saved as dictionaries, the program that reads data may wind up with dictionaries instead of users.

3. Save class definitions as well as objects' values so that when a program reads saved data it can reconstruct the classes and then create fully functional instances of them. This choice is the most powerful, but it is also the hardest to implement, particularly across languages. It is also the riskiest: if a program is running third-party code in order to restore objects, it has to trust that code not to do anything malicious.

This chapter starts by implementing the first option (built-in types only), then extends it to handle objects that the data structure refers to in several places (which JSON does not). To keep parsing and testing simple, our framework will store everything as text with one value per line; we will look at non-text options in Chapter 17, and at how to handle user-defined types in Appendix B.

---

[1]https://docs.python.org/3/library/pickle.html
[2]https://docs.python.org/3/library/json.html

16.1   Built-in Types

The first thing we need to do is specify our data format. We will store each **atomic value** on a line of its own with a type name and a value separated by a colon:

```
bool:True
int:123
```

Since we are storing things as text, we have to handle strings carefully: for example, we might need to save the string `"str:something"` and later be able to tell that it *isn't* the string `"something"`. We do this by splitting strings on newline characters and saving the number of lines, followed by the actual data:

```
# input
this is
two lines
```

```
# output
str:2
this is
two lines
```

The function `save` handles three of Python's built-in types to start with:

```
def save(writer, thing):
    if isinstance(thing, bool):
        print(f"bool:{thing}", file=writer)

    elif isinstance(thing, float):
        print(f"float:{thing}", file=writer)

    elif isinstance(thing, int):
        print(f"int:{thing}", file=writer)

    else:
        raise ValueError(f"unknown type of thing {type(thing)}")
```

The function that loads data starts by reading a single line, stripping off the newline at the end (which is added automatically by the `print` statement in `save`), and then splitting the line on colons. After checking that there are two fields, it uses the type name in the first field to decide how to handle the second:

```
def load(reader):
    line = reader.readline()[:-1]
    assert line, "Nothing to read"
    fields = line.split(":", maxsplit=1)
    assert len(fields) == 2, f"Badly-formed line {line}"
    key, value = fields

    if key == "bool":
        names = {"True": True, "False": False}
        assert value in names, f"Unknown Boolean {value}"
        return names[value]

    elif key == "float":
        return float(value)

    elif key == "int":
```

```
        return int(value)

    else:
        raise ValueError(f"unknown type of thing {line}")
```

Saving a list is almost as easy: we save the number of items in the list, with a recursive _call_. For example, the list [55, True, 2.71] is saved as shown in Figure 16.1. The code to do this is:

```
elif isinstance(thing, list):
    print(f"list:{len(thing)}", file=writer)
    for item in thing:
        save(writer, item)
```

while to load a list, we just read the specified number of items:

```
elif key == "list":
    return [load(reader) for _ in range(int(value))]
```

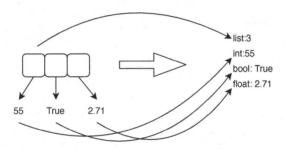

Figure 16.1: Saving nested data structures.

Notice that `save` and `load` don't need to know what kinds of values are in the list. Each recursive call advances the input or output stream by precisely as many lines as it needs to. As a result, this approach should handle empty lists and nested lists without any extra work.

Our functions handle sets in exactly the same way as lists; the only difference is using the keyword `set` instead of the keyword `list` in the opening line. To save a dictionary, we save the number of entries and then save each key and value in turn:

```
elif isinstance(thing, dict):
    print(f"dict:{len(thing)}", file=writer)
    for (key, value) in thing.items():
        save(writer, key)
        save(writer, value)
```

The code to load a dictionary is analogous. With this machinery in place, we can save our first data structure:

```
save(sys.stdout, [False, 3.14, "hello", {"left": 1, "right": [2, 3]}])
```

```
list:4
bool:False
float:3.14
str:1
hello
dict:2
str:1
```

```
left
int:1
str:1
right
list:2
int:2
int:3
```

We now need to write some unit tests. We will use two tricks when doing this:

1. The `StringIO` class from Python's io[3] module allows us to read from strings and write to them using the functions we normally use to read and write files. Using this lets us run our tests without creating lots of little files as a side effect.

2. The `dedent` function from Python's `textwrap`[4] module removes leading indentation from the body of a string. As the example below shows, `dedent` allows us to indent a fixture the same way we indent our Python code, which makes the test easier to read.

```
def test_save_list_flat():
    fixture = [0, False]
    expected = dedent("""\
    list:2
    int:0
    bool:False
    """)
    output = StringIO()
    save(output, fixture)
    assert output.getvalue() == expected
```

16.2   Converting to Classes

The `save` and `load` functions we built in the previous section work, but as we were extending them we had to modify their internals every time we wanted to do something new.

The **Open-Closed Principle** states that software should be open for extension but closed for modification, i.e., that it should be possible to extend functionality without having to rewrite existing code. This allows old code to use new code, but only if our design permits the kinds of extensions people are going to want to make. (Even then, it often leads to deep class hierarchies that can be hard for the next programmer to understand.) Since we can't anticipate everything, it is normal to have to revise a design the first two or three times we try to extend it. As [Brand1995] said of buildings, the things we make learn how to do things better as we use them.

In this case, we can follow the Open-Closed Principle by rewriting our functions as classes and by using yet another form of dynamic dispatch to handle each item so that we don't have to modify a multi-way `if` statement each time we add a new capability. If we have an object `obj`, then `hasattr(obj, "name")` tells us whether that object has an attribute called `"name"`. If it does, `getattr(obj, "name")` returns that attribute's value; if that attribute happens to be a method, we can then call it like a function:

---

[3] https://docs.python.org/3/library/io.html
[4] https://docs.python.org/3/library/textwrap.html

```
class Example:
    def __init__(self, label):
        self.label = label

    def get_size(self):
        return len(self.label)

ex = Example("thing")
print("ex has missing", hasattr(ex, "missing"))
print("ex has label", hasattr(ex, "label"), "with value", getattr(ex, "label"))
print("ex has get_size", hasattr(ex, "get_size"))
method = getattr(ex, "get_size")
print("result of calling method", method())
```

```
ex has missing False
ex has label True with value thing
ex has get_size True
result of calling method 5
```

Using this, the core of our saving class is:

```
class SaveObjects:
    def __init__(self, writer):
        self.writer = writer

    def save(self, thing):
        typename = type(thing).__name__
        method = f"save_{typename}"
        assert hasattr(self, method), \
            f"Unknown object type {typename}"
        getattr(self, method)(thing)
```

We have called this class SaveObjects instead of just Save because we are going to create other variations on it. SaveObjects.save figures out which method to call to save a particular thing by constructing a name based on the thing's type, checking whether that method exists, and then calling it. As in _our_ previous example, the methods that handle specific items must all have the same signature so that they can be called interchangeably. For example, the methods that write integers and strings are:

```
def save_int(self, thing):
    self._write("int", thing)

def save_str(self, thing):
    lines = thing.split("\n")
    self._write("str", len(lines))
    for line in lines:
        print(line, file=self.writer)
```

LoadObjects.load combines dynamic dispatch with the string handling of our original load function:

```
class LoadObjects:
    def __init__(self, reader):
        self.reader = reader

    def load(self):
        line = self.reader.readline()[:-1]
        assert line, "Nothing to read"
        fields = line.split(":", maxsplit=1)
```

```
        assert len(fields) == 2, f"Badly-formed line {line}"
        key, value = fields
        method = f"load_{key}"
        assert hasattr(self, method), f"Unknown object type {key}"
        return getattr(self, method)(value)
```

The methods that load individual items are even simpler. For example, we load a floating-point number like this:

```
def load_float(self, value):
    return float(value)
```

16.3 Aliasing

Consider the two lines of code below, which created the data structure shown in Figure 16.2. If we save this structure and then reload it using what we have built so far, we will wind up with two copies of the list containing the string `"content"` instead of one. This won't be a problem if we only ever read the reloaded data, but if we modify the new copy of `fixture[0]`, we won't see that change reflected in `fixture[1]`, where we *would* have seen the change in the original data structure:

```
shared = ["content"]
fixture = [shared, shared]
```

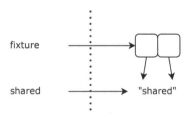

Figure 16.2: Saving aliased data without respecting aliases.

The problem is that the list `shared` is aliased, i.e., there are two or more references to it. To reconstruct the original data correctly, we need to:

1. keep track of everything we have saved;

2. save a marker instead of the object itself when we try to save it a second time; and

3. reverse this process when loading data.

We can keep track of the things we have saved using Python's built-in `id` function, which returns a unique ID for every object in the program. For example, even if two lists contain exactly the same values, `id` will report different IDs for those lists because they're stored in different locations in memory. We can use this to:

1. store the IDs of all the objects we've already saved in a set, and then

2. write a special entry with the keyword `alias` and its unique ID when we see an object for the second time.

Here's the start of `SaveAlias`:

```python
class SaveAlias(SaveObjects):
    def __init__(self, writer):
        super().__init__(writer)
        self.seen = set()

    def save(self, thing):
        thing_id = id(thing)
        if thing_id in self.seen:
            self._write("alias", thing_id, "")
            return

        self.seen.add(id(thing))
        typename = type(thing).__name__
        method = f"save_{typename}"
        assert hasattr(self, method), f"Unknown object type {typename}"
        getattr(self, method)(thing)
```

Its constructor creates an empty set of IDs seen so far. If `SaveAlias.save` notices that the object it's about to save has been saved before, it writes a line like this:

```
alias:12345678:
```

where `12345678` is the object's ID. (The exercises will ask why the trailing colon needs to be there.) If the object hasn't been seen before, `SaveAlias` saves the object's type, its ID, and either its value or its length:

```python
def save_list(self, thing):
    self._write("list", id(thing), len(thing))
    for item in thing:
        self.save(item)
```

`SaveAlias._list` is a little different from `SaveObjects._list` because it has to save each object's identifier along with its type and its value or length. Our `LoadAlias` class needs a similar change compared to `LoadObjects`. The first version is shown below; as we will see, it contains a subtle bug:

```python
class LoadAlias(LoadObjects):
    def __init__(self, reader):
        super().__init__(reader)
        self.seen = {}

    def load(self):
        line = self.reader.readline()[:-1]
        assert line, "Nothing to read"
        fields = line.split(":", maxsplit=2)
        assert len(fields) == 3, f"Badly-formed line {line}"
        key, ident, value = fields

        # the lines below contain a bug
        if key == "alias":
            assert ident in self.seen
            return self.seen[ident]

        method = f"load_{key}"
        assert hasattr(self, method), f"Unknown object type {key}"
        result = getattr(self, method)(value)
        self.seen[ident] = result
        return result
```

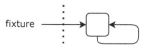

Figure 16.3: A data structure that contains a reference to itself.

The first test of our new code is:

```
def test_aliasing_no_aliasing():
    fixture = ["a", {"b": True, 7: {"c": "d"}}]
    assert roundtrip(fixture) == fixture
```

which uses this helper function:

```
def roundtrip(fixture):
    writer = StringIO()
    SaveAlias(writer).save(fixture)
    reader = StringIO(writer.getvalue())
    return LoadAlias(reader).load()
```

There isn't any aliasing in the test case, but that's deliberate: we want to make sure we haven't broken code that was working before we move on. Here's a test that actually includes some aliasing:

```
def test_aliasing_shared_child():
    shared = ["content"]
    fixture = [shared, shared]
    result = roundtrip(fixture)
    assert result == fixture
    assert id(result[0]) == id(result[1])
    result[0][0] = "changed"
    assert result[1][0] == "changed"
```

It checks that the aliased sub-list is actually aliased after the data is restored, then checks that changes to the sub-list through one alias show up through the other. The second check ought to be redundant, but it's still comforting.

There's one more case to check, and unfortunately it reveals a bug. The two lines:

```
fixture = []
fixture.append(fixture)
```

create the data structure shown in Figure 16.3, in which an object contains a reference to itself. Our code ought to handle this case but doesn't: when we try to read in the saved data, LoadAlias.load sees the alias line but then says it can't find the object being referred to. The problem is these lines in LoadAlias.load marked as containing a bug, in combination with these lines inherited from LoadObjects:

```
def load_list(self, value):
    return [self.load() for _ in range(int(value))]
```

Let's trace execution for the saved data:

```
list:4484025600:1
alias:4484025600:
```

1. The first line tells us that there's a list whose ID is 4484025600 so we LoadObjects._list to load a list of one element.

2. `LoadObjects._list` called `LoadAlias.load` recursively to load that one element.

3. `LoadAlias.load` reads the second line of saved data, which tells it to re-use the data whose ID is 4484025600. But `LoadObjects._list` hasn't created that list yet—it is still reading the elements—so `LoadAlias.load` hasn't added the list to `seen`.

   The solution is to reorder the operations, which unfortunately means writing new versions of all the methods defined in `LoadObjects`. The new implementation of `_list` is:

```python
def load_list(self, ident, length):
    result = []
    self.seen[ident] = result
    for _ in range(int(length)):
        result.append(self.load())
    return result
```

This method creates the list it's going to return, adds that list to the `seen` dictionary immediately, and *then* loads list items recursively. We have to pass it the ID of the list to use as the key in `seen`, and we have to use a loop rather than a **list comprehension**, but the changes to `save_set` and `save_dict` follow exactly the same pattern.

```python
word = "word"
child = [word, word]
parent = []
parent.append(parent)
parent.append(child)

saver = SaveAlias(sys.stdout)
saver.save(parent)
```

```
list:4539747200:2
alias:4539747200:
list:4539552960:2
str:4539552048:1
word
alias:4539552048:
```

16.4 Summary

Figure 16.4 summarizes the ideas introduced in this chapter, while Appendix B shows how to extend our framework to handle user-defined classes.

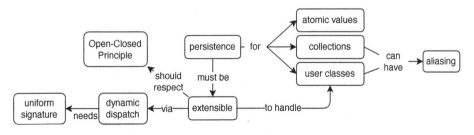

Figure 16.4: Concepts for persistence.

16.5   Exercises

Dangling Colon

Why is there a colon at the end of the line `alias:12345678:` when we create an alias marker?

Versioning

We now have several versions of our data storage format. Early versions of our code can't read the archives created by later ones, and later ones can't read the archives created early on (which used two fields per line rather than three). This problem comes up all the time in long-lived libraries and applications, and the usual solution is to include some sort of version marker at the start of each archive to indicate what version of the software created it (and therefore how it should be read). Modify the code we have written so far to do this.

Strings

Modify the framework so that strings are stored using escape characters like \n instead of being split across several lines.

Who Calculates?

Why doesn't `LoadAlias.load` calculate object IDs? Why does it use the IDs saved in the archive instead?

Using Globals

The lesson on unit testing introduced the function `globals`, which can be used to look up everything defined at the top level of a program.

1. Modify the persistence framework so that it looks for `save_` and `load_` functions using `globals`.

2. Why is this a bad idea?

17

Binary Data

- Programs usually store integers using two's complement rather than sign and magnitude.

- Characters are usually encoded as bytes using either ASCII, UTF-8, or UTF-32.

- Programs can use bitwise operators to manipulate the bits representing data directly.

- Low-level compiled languages usually store raw values, while high-level interpreted languages use boxed values.

- Sets of values can be packed into contiguous byte arrays for efficient transmission and storage.

Terms defined: **ANSI character encoding, ASCII character encoding, bit mask, bit shifting, bitwise operation, boxed value, buffer (in memory), character encoding, code point, continuation byte, control code, escape sequence, exclusive or, format string, sign and magnitude, two's complement, Unicode, UTF-32, UTF-8, variable-length encoding**

Python and other high-level languages shield programmers from the low-level details of how computers actually store and manipulate data, but sooner or later someone has to worry about bits and bytes. This chapter explores how computers represent numbers and text and shows how to work with data at this level.

17.1 Integers

Let's start by looking at how integers are stored. The natural way to do this with ones and zeroes uses base 2, so 1001 in binary is $(1{\times}8) + (0{\times}4) + (0{\times}2) + (1{\times}1)$ or 9 base 10. We can handle negative numbers by reserving the top bit for the sign, so that 01001 is $+9$ and 11001 is -9.

This representation has two drawbacks. The less important one is that it gives us two zeroes, one positive and one negative. The larger one is that the hardware needed to do arithmetic on this **sign and magnitude** representation is more complicated than the hardware needed for another scheme called **two's complement**. Instead of mirroring positive values, two's complement rolls over when going below zero like an odometer. For example, three-bit integers give us the values in Table 17.1.

We can still tell whether a number is positive or negative by looking at the first bit: negative numbers have 1, positive numbers have 0. However, two's complement is asymmetric: since 0 counts as a positive number, numbers go from -4 to 3, or -16 to 15, and so on. As a result, even if x is a valid number, -x may not be.

Base 10	Base 2
3	011
2	010
1	001
0	000
-1	111
-2	110
-3	101
-4	100

Table 17.1: 3-bit integer values using two's complement.

Decimal	Hexadecimal	Bits	Decimal	Hexadecimal	Bits
0	0	0000	8	8	1000
1	1	0001	9	9	1001
2	2	0010	10	A	1010
3	3	0011	11	B	1011
4	4	0100	12	C	1100
5	5	0101	13	D	1101
6	6	0110	14	E	1110
7	7	0111	15	F	1111

Table 17.2: Hexadecimal digits.

We can write binary numbers directly in Python using the `0b` prefix:

```
print(0b101101)   # (1 * 32) + (1 * 8) + (1 * 4) + 1
```

```
45
```

As noted in Chapter 3, programmers usually use hexadecimal instead: the digits 0–9 have the usual meaning, and the letters A–F (or a–f) are used to represent the digits 11–15. We signal that we're using hexadecimal with a `0x` prefix, so `0xF7` is $(15 \times 16) + 7$ or 247 base 10. Each hexadecimal digit corresponds to four bits (Table 17.2), so two hexadecimal digits are exactly one byte, which makes it easy to translate bits to digits and vice versa: for example, `0xF7` is `0b11110111`.

17.2   Bitwise Operations

Like most languages based on C, Python has **bitwise operations** for working directly with 1's and 0's: & (and), | (or), ^ (xor), ~ (not). & yields a 1 only if both its inputs are 1's, while | yields 1 if either or both are 1. ^, called **exclusive or** or "xor" (pronounced "ex-or"), produces 1 if the bits are different, i.e., it produces 1 if either input bit is 1 but not both. Finally, ~ flips its argument: 1 becomes 0, and 0 becomes 1. When these operators are applied on multi-bit values they work on corresponding bits independently as shown in Table 17.3.

We can set individual bits to 0 or 1 with these operators. To set a particular bit to 1, create a value in which that bit is 1 and the rest are 0. When this is or'd with a value, the bit we set is guaranteed to come out 1; the other bits will be left as they are. Similarly, to set a

Expression	Bitwise	Result (bits)	Result (decimal)
12 & 6	1100 & 0110	0100	4
12 | 6	1100 | 0110	1110	14
12 ^ 6	1100 ^ 0110	1010	10
~ 6	~ 0110	1001	9
12 << 2	1100 << 2	110000	48
12 >> 2	1100 >> 2	0011	3

Table 17.3: Bitwise operations.

bit to zero, create a **mask** in which that bit is 0 and the others are 1, then use & to combine the two. To make things easier to read, programmers often set a single bit, negate it with ~, and then use &:

```
mask = ~0x0100    # binary 1111 1110 1111 1111
val = val & mask  #    clears this ^ bit
```

Finally, Python has **bit shifting** operators that move bits left or right. Shifting the bits 0110 left by one place produces 1100, while shifting it right by one place produces 0011. In Python, this is written x << 1 or x >> 1. Just as shifting a decimal number left corresponds to multiplying by 10, shifting a binary number left is the same as multiplying it by 2. Similarly, shifting a number right corresponds to dividing by 2 and throwing away the remainder, so 17 >> 3 is 2.

But what if the top bit of an integer changes from 1 to 0 or vice versa as a result of shifting? If we're using two's complement, then the bits 1111 represent the value −1; if we shift right we get 0111 which is 7. Similarly, if we shift 0111 to the left we get 1110 (assuming we fill in the bottom with 0), which is −6.

Different languages deal with this problem in different ways. Python always fills with zeroes, while Java provides two versions of right shift: >> fills in the high end with zeroes, while >>> copies in the topmost (sign) bit of the original value. C (and by extension C++) lets the underlying hardware decide, which means that if you want to be sure of getting a particular answer, you have to handle the top bit yourself.

17.3   Text

The rules for storing text make integers look simple. By the early 1970s most programs used **ASCII**, which represented unaccented Latin characters using the numbers from 32 to 127. (The numbers 0 to 31 were used for **control codes** such as newline, carriage return, and bell.) Since computers use 8-bit bytes and the numbers 0–127 only need 7 bits, programmers were free to use the numbers 128–255 for other characters. Unfortunately, different programmers used them to represent different symbols: non-Latin characters, graphic characters like boxes, and so on. The chaos was eventually tamed by the **ANSI standard** which (for example) defined the value 231 to mean the character "ç".

A standard that specifies how characters are represented in memory is called a **character encoding**, and the ANSI standard encoding only solved a small part of a large problem. It didn't include characters from Turkish, Devanagari, and many other alphabets, much less the thousands of characters used in some East Asian writing systems. One solution would have been to use 16 or even 32 bits per character, but:

1. existing text files using ANSI would have to be transcribed, and

2. documents would be two or four times larger.

The solution was a new two-part standard called **Unicode**. The first part defined a **code point** for every character: U+0065 for an upper-case Latin "A", U+2605 for a black star, and so on. (The Unicode Consortium site[1] offers a complete list.) The second part defined ways to store these values in memory. The simplest of these is **UTF-32**, which stores every character as a 32-bit number. This scheme wastes a lot of memory if the text is written in a Western European language, since it uses four times as much storage as is absolutely necessary, but it's easy to process.

The most popular encoding is **UTF-8**, which is **variable length**. Every code point from 0 to 127 is stored in a single byte whose high bit is 0, just as it was in the original ASCII standard. If the top bit in the byte is 1, on the other hand, the number of 1's after the high bit but before the first 0 tells UTF-8 how many more bytes are used by that character's representation. For example, if the first byte of the character is 11101101 then:

- the first 1 signals that this is a multi-byte character;

- the next two 1's signal the character includes bits from the following two bytes as well;

- the 0 separates the byte count from the first few bits used in the character; and

- the final 1101 is the first four bits of the character.

But that's not all: every byte that's a continuation of a character starts with the bits 10. (Such bytes are, unsurprisingly, called **continuation bytes**.) This rule means that if we look at any byte in a string we can immediately tell if it starts a character or continues a character. Thus, to represent the character whose code point is 1789:

- We convert decimal 1789 to binary 11011111101.

- We count and realize that we'll need two bytes: the first storing the high 5 bits of the character, the second storing the low 6 bits.

- We encode the high 5 bits as 11011011: "start of a character with one continuation byte and 5 payload bits 11011".

- We encode the low 6 bits as 10111101: "a continuation byte with 6 payload bits 111101".

Internal vs. External

Since UTF-8 uses a varying number of bytes per character, the only way to get to a particular character in a string is to scan the string from the beginning, which means that indexing a string is $O(N)$. However, when Python loads text into memory, it converts the variable-length encoding to a fixed-length encoding, with the same number of bytes per character. This allows it to jump directly to any character in the string in constant time, which a computer scientist would say is $O(1)$.

---

[1] https://www.unicode.org/

17.4   And Now, Persistence

Chapter 16 showed how to store data as human-readable text. There are generally three reasons to store it in formats that people can't easily read:

1. Size. The string "10239472" is 8 bytes long, but the 32-bit integer it represents only needs 4 bytes in memory. This doesn't matter for small data sets, but it does for large ones, and it definitely does when data has to move between disk and memory or between different computers.

2. Speed. Adding the integers 34 and 56 is a single machine operation. Adding the values represented by the strings "34" and "56" is dozens; we'll explore this in the exercises. Most programs that read and write text files convert the values in those files into binary data using something like the `int` or `float` functions, but if we're going to process the data many times, it makes sense to avoid paying the conversion cost over and over.

3. Lack of anything better. It's possible to represent images as ASCII art, but sound? Or video? It would be possible, but it would hardly be sensible.

Finally, no matter how values are eventually stored, someone, somewhere, has to convert the signals from a digital thermometer to numbers. Those signals almost certainly arrive as a stream of 1's and 0's, and the bitwise operations shown above are almost certainly used to do the conversion.

The first step toward saving and loading binary data is to write it and read it correctly. If we open a file for reading using `open("filename", "r")` then Python assumes we want to read character strings from the file. It therefore:

- asks the operating system for the default character encoding (which is almost always UTF-8);

- uses this to convert bytes to characters; and

- converts Windows end-of-line markers to the Unix standard if necessary. For historical reasons, Windows uses both a carriage return "\r" and a newline "\n" to mark the end of a line, while Unix uses only the latter. Python converts from Windows to Unix on the way in and vice versa on the way out so that programs (usually) don't have to worry about the difference.

These translations are handy when we're working with text, but they mess up binary data: we probably don't want the pixels in our PNG image translated in these ways. As mentioned in Chapter 3, if we open a file in binary mode using `open(filename, "rb")` with a lower-case 'b' after the 'r', Python gives us back the file's contents as a `bytes` object instead of as character strings. In this case we will almost always get data using `reader.read(N)` to read N bytes at a time rather than `for line in reader` because there aren't actually lines of text in the file.

But what values should we actually store? C and Fortran manipulate "naked" values: programs use what the hardware provides directly. Python and other dynamic languages, on the other hand, put each value in a data structure that keeps track of its type along with a bit of extra administrative information (Figure 17.1). Something stored this way is called a **boxed value**, and this extra information is what allows the interpreter to do introspection at runtime.

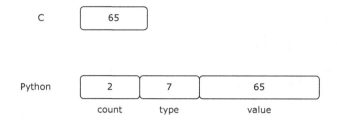

Figure 17.1: Using boxed values to store metadata.

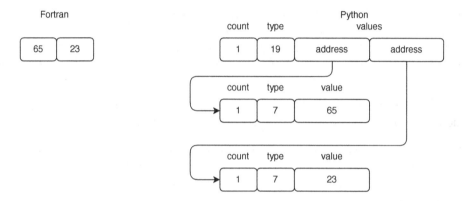

Figure 17.2: Low-level and high-level array storage.

The same is true of collections. For example, Fortran stores all the values in an array side by side in memory (Figure 17.2). Writing this to disk is easy: if the array starts at location L in memory and has N values, each of which is B bytes long, we just copy the bytes from L to $L + NB - 1$ to the file.

A Python list, on the other hand, stores references to values rather than the values themselves. To put the values in a file, we can either write them one at a time or pack them into a contiguous block and write that. Similarly, when reading from a file, we can either grab the values one by one or read a larger block and then unpack it in memory.

Packing data is a lot like formatting strings using Python's str.format method. The **format string** specifies what types of data are being packed, how big they are (e.g., is this a 32-bit or 64-bit floating point number?), and how many values there are, which in turn exactly determines how much memory is required by the packed representation.

Unpacking reverses this process. After reading data into memory, we can unpack it according to a format. The most important thing is that *we can unpack data any way we want*. We might pack an integer and then unpack it as four characters, since both are 32 bits long (Figure 17.3). Or we might save two characters, an integer, and two more characters, then unpack it as a 64-bit floating point number. The bits are just bits: it's our responsibility to make sure we keep track of their meaning when they're down there on disk.

Python's struct[2] module packs and unpacks data for us. The function pack(format, val_1, val_2, ...) takes a format string and a bunch of values as arguments and packs them into a bytes object. The inverse function, unpack(format, string), takes some bytes and a format and returns a tuple containing the unpacked values. Here's an example:

---

[2]https://docs.python.org/3/library/struct.html

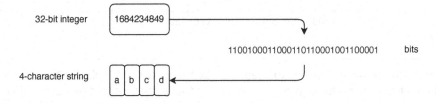

Figure 17.3: Packing and unpacking binary values.

Format	Meaning
"c"	Single character (i.e., string of length 1)
"B"	Unsigned 8-bit integer with all 8 bits used for value
"h"	16-bit integer
"i"	32-bit integer
"d"	64-bit float

Table 17.4: struct package formats.

```
import struct

fmt = "ii"  # two 32-bit integers
x = 31
y = 65

binary = struct.pack(fmt, x, y)
print("binary representation:", repr(binary))

normal = struct.unpack(fmt, binary)
print("back to normal:", normal)
```

```
binary representation: b'\x1f\x00\x00\x00A\x00\x00\x00'
back to normal: (31, 65)
```

What is \x1f and why is it in our data? If Python finds a byte in a string that doesn't correspond to a printable character, it prints a 2-digit **escape sequence** in hexadecimal. Python is therefore telling us that our string contains the eight bytes ['\x1f', '\x00', '\x00', '\x00', 'A', '\x00', '\x00', '\x00']. 1F in hex is $(1\times16^1) + (15\times16^0)$, or 31; 'A' is our 65, because the ASCII code for an upper-case letter A is the decimal value 65. All the other bytes are zeroes ("\x00") because each of our integers is 32 bits long and the significant digits only fill one byte's worth of each.

The struct module offers a lot of different formats, some of which are shown in Table 17.4. Some of the formats, like "c" for a single character, are self-explanatory. The "B" format packs or unpacks the least significant 8 bits of an integer; the "h" format takes the least significant 16 bits and does likewise. They are needed because binary data formats often store only as much data as they need to, so we need a way to get 8- and 16-bit values out of files. (Many audio formats, for example, only store 16 bits per sample.)

Any format can be preceded by a count, so the format "3i" means "three integers":

```
from struct import pack

print(pack("3i", 1, 2, 3))
print(pack("5s", bytes("hello", "utf-8")))
print(pack("5s", bytes("a longer string", "utf-8")))
```

```
b'\x01\x00\x00\x00\x02\x00\x00\x00\x03\x00\x00\x00'
b'hello'
b'a lon'
```

We get the wrong answer in the last call because we only told Python to pack five characters. How can we tell it to pack all the data that's there regardless of length?

The short answer is that we can't: we must specify how much we want packed. But that doesn't mean we can't handle variable-length strings; it just means that we have to construct the format on the fly using an expression like this:

```
format = f"{len(str)}s"
```

If str contains the string "example", the expression above will assign "7s" to format, which just happens to be exactly the right format to use to pack it *provided all the characters can be represented in a single byte each*. We will explore packing and unpacking strings with other characters in the exercises.

Saving the format when we are writing solves half of the problem, but how do we know how much data to get when we're reading? For example, suppose we have the two strings "hello" and "Python". We can pack them like this:

```
pack('5s6s', 'hello', 'Python')
```

but how do we know how to unpack 5 characters then 6? The trick is to save the size along with the data. If we always use exactly the same number of bytes to store the size, we can read it back safely, then use it to figure out how big our string is:

```
def pack_string(as_string):
    as_bytes = bytes(as_string, "utf-8")
    header = pack("i", len(as_bytes))
    format = f"{len(as_bytes)}s"
    body = pack(format, as_bytes)
    return header + body
```

```
if __name__ == "__main__":
    result = pack_string("hello!")
    print(repr(result))
```

```
b'\x06\x00\x00\x00hello!'
```

The unpacking function is analogous. We break the **memory buffer** into a header that's exactly four bytes long (i.e., the right size for an integer) and a body made up of whatever's left. We then unpack the header, whose format we know, to determine how many characters are in the string. Once we've got that, we use the trick shown earlier to construct the right format on the fly and then unpack the string and return it.

```
def unpack_string(buffer):
    header, body = buffer[:4], buffer[4:]
    length = unpack("i", header)[0]
    format = f"{length}s"
    result = unpack(format, body)[0]
    return str(result, "utf-8")

buffer = pack_string("hello!")
result = unpack_string(buffer)
print(result)
```

```
hello!
```

In practice, programmers use the `struct` module's `calcsize` function to figure out how large (in bytes) the data represented by a format is:

```
from struct import calcsize

for format in ["4s", "3i4s5d"]:
    print(f"format '{format}' needs {calcsize(format)} bytes")
```

```
format '4s' needs 4 bytes
format '3i4s5d' needs 56 bytes
```

Binary data is to programming what chemistry is to biology: you don't want to spend any more time thinking at its level than you have to, but there's no substitute when you *do* have to. Please remember that libraries already exist to handle almost every binary format ever created and to read data from almost every instrument on the market. You shouldn't worry about 1's and 0's unless you really have to.

17.5 Summary

Figure 17.4 summarizes the ideas introduced in this chapter. Please see Appendix B for extra material related to floating-point numbers.

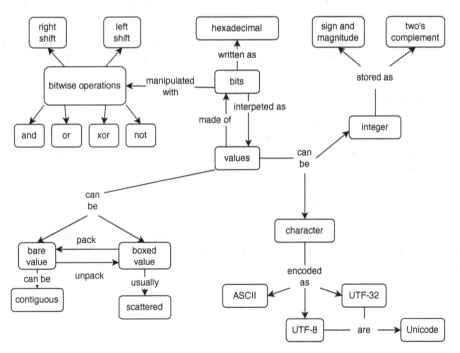

Figure 17.4: Concepts for binary data.

17.6   Exercises

Adding Strings

Write a function that takes two strings of digits and adds them as if they were numbers *without* actually converting them to numbers. For example, `add_str("12", "5")` should produce the string `"17"`.

File Types

The first eight bytes of a PNG image file always contain the following (base-10) values:

```
137 80 78 71 13 10 26 10
```

Write a program that determines whether a file is a PNG image or not.

Converting Integers to Bits

Using Python's bitwise operators, write a function that returns the binary representation of a non-negative integer. Write another function that converts a string of 1's and 0's into an integer (treating it as unsigned).

Encoding and Decoding

1. Write a function that takes a list of integers representing Unicode code points as input and returns a list of single-byte integers with their UTF-8 encoding.

2. Write the complementary function that turns a list of single-byte integers into the corresponding code points and reports an error if anything is incorrectly formatted.

Storing Arrays

Python's `array`[3] module manages a block of basic values (characters, integers, or floating-point numbers). Write a function that takes a list as input, checks that all values in the list are of the same basic type, and if so, packs them into an array and then uses the `struct` module to pack that.

Performance

Getting a single value out of an array created with the `array` module takes time, since the value must be boxed before it can be used. Write some tests to see how much slower working with values in arrays is compared to working with values in lists.

---

[3]https://docs.python.org/3/library/array.html

18

A Database

> - Database stores records so that they can be accessed by key.
>
> - Log-structured database appends new records to database and invalidates older versions of records.
>
> - Classes are data structures that can be saved like any other data.
>
> - The filesystem saves data in fixed-size pages.
>
> - We can improve the efficiency of a database by saving records in blocks.
>
> Terms defined: **block (of memory)**, **compact (data or files)**, **garbage collection**, **key-value store**, **log-structured database**, **null byte**, **page**

Persisting objects (Chapter 16) lets us save and restore program state, but we often want to be able to look things up quickly without reloading all of our data. We would also like applications written in different languages to be able to get at our data, which might be easier if we choose a different storage format.

This chapter therefore builds a very simple **log-structured database**. The phrase "log-structured" means that records a log of operations, i.e., every new record is appended to the end of the database. Programmers have invented many other ways to store large amounts of data, but this is one of the easiest to understand.

18.1   Starting Point

Our starting point is a simple **key-value store** that lets us save records and look them up later. To use it, we have to provide a function that takes a record and returns its key. We store that function in the Database object for later use:

```
class Database:
    def __init__(self, key_func):
        """Initialize with function to get key."""
        self._key_func = key_func

    def add(self, record):
        """Store the given record."""
        raise NotImplementedError("add")

    def get(self, key):
        """Return record associated with key or None."""
        raise NotImplementedError("get")
```

If we want a dictionary that only stores things in memory, we can derive a class from Database that uses a dictionary with the values returned by the user's key function for lookup (Figure 18.1):

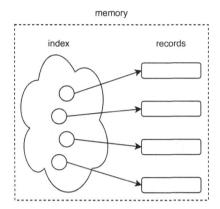

Figure 18.1: Storing a database as a single dictionary in memory.

```python
from interface_original import Database

class JustDict(Database):
    def __init__(self, key_func):
        super().__init__(key_func)
        self._data = {}

    def add(self, record):
        key = self._key_func(record)
        self._data[key] = record

    def get(self, key):
        return self._data.get(key, None)
```

This simple class is enough to let us start writing some tests. Let's create a class to store experimental records:

```python
class BasicRec:
    MAX_NAME_LEN = 6      # length of name in chars
    TIMESTAMP_LEN = 8     # length of timestamp in chars
    MAX_READING = 10      # maximum reading value
    MAX_READING_LEN = 2   # length of reading in chars
    MAX_READINGS_NUM = 2  # maximum number of readings

    @staticmethod
    def key(record):
        assert isinstance(record, BasicRec)
        return record._name

    def __init__(self, name, timestamp, readings):
        assert 0 < len(name) <= self.MAX_NAME_LEN
        assert 0 <= len(readings) <= self.MAX_READINGS_NUM
        assert all((0 <= r <= self.MAX_READING) for r in readings)
        self._name = name
        self._timestamp = timestamp
        self._readings = readings
```

and use the `pytest.fixture` decorator (Chapter 9) to create a database and two records:

```
@pytest.fixture
def db():
    return JustDict(BasicExperiment.key)

@pytest.fixture
def ex01():
    return BasicExperiment("ex01", 12345, [1, 2])

@pytest.fixture
def ex02():
    return BasicExperiment("ex02", 67890, [3, 4])
```

Our first few tests are then:

```
def test_construct(db):
    assert db

def test_get_nothing_from_empty_db(db):
    assert db.get("something") is None

def test_add_then_get(db, ex01):
    db.add(ex01)
    assert db.get("ex01") == ex01

def test_add_two_then_get_both(db, ex01, ex02):
    db.add(ex01)
    db.add(ex02)
    assert db.get("ex01") == ex01
    assert db.get("ex02") == ex02

def test_add_then_overwrite(db, ex01):
    db.add(ex01)
    ex01._timestamp = 67890
    db.add(ex01)
    assert db.get("ex01") == ex01
```

Our next step is to save the user's records in the database without tying the database to a particular type of record. The cleanest way to solve this problem is to require records to know how to convert themselves into something storable. Rather than passing a second function to the database's constructor, we will refactor the database so that we pass in the object that represents the record class:

```
class Database:
    def __init__(self, record_cls):
        """Initialize with data manipulation functions."""
        self._record_cls = record_cls

    def add(self, record):
        """Store the given record."""
        raise NotImplementedError("add")

    def get(self, key):
        """Return record associated with key or None."""
        raise NotImplementedError("get")
```

We can now refactor our database to use a static method of the record class provided to its constructor when it needs a key:

```
from interface import Database

class JustDictRefactored(Database):
    def __init__(self, record_cls):
        super().__init__(record_cls)
        self._data = {}

    def add(self, record):
        key = self._record_cls.key(record)
        self._data[key] = record

    def get(self, key):
        return self._data.get(key, None)
```

18.2   Saving Records

The next step in building a usable database is to have it store records rather than just refer to the user's objects. Since we don't want the database tied to any particular kind of record, records must know how to pack and unpack themselves. We could have used the techniques of Chapter 17, but to make our test and sample output a little more readable, we will pack numbers as strings with a **null byte** \0 between each string:

```
@staticmethod
def pack(record):
    assert isinstance(record, Experiment)
    readings = "\0".join(str(r) for r in record._readings)
    result = f"{record._name}\0{record._timestamp}\0{readings}"
    if len(result) < Experiment.RECORD_LEN:
        result += "\0" * (Experiment.RECORD_LEN - len(result))
    return result
```

The corresponding method to unpack a stored record is:

```
@staticmethod
def unpack(raw):
    assert isinstance(raw, str)
    parts = raw.split("\0")
    name = parts[0]
    timestamp = int(parts[1])
    readings = [int(r) for r in parts[2:] if len(r)]
    return Experiment(name, timestamp, readings)
```

These records look like the example below (which uses . to show null bytes):

```
from record import Experiment

ex = Experiment("abcdef", 12345, [6, 7])
print(Experiment.pack(ex).replace('\0', '.'))
```

```
abcdef.12345.6.7.....
```

Notice that our packing and unpacking methods are static, i.e., they're part of the class but don't require an object to work. More importantly, they don't handle strings that contain null bytes. This limitation wasn't part of our original design, but is instead an accident of implementation. We will look at ways around it in the exercises.

To finish off, we write methods to pack and unpack multiple records at once by joining and splitting single-record data:

```
@staticmethod
def pack_multi(records):
    return ''.join([Experiment.pack(r) for r in records])

@staticmethod
def unpack_multi(raw):
    size = Experiment.size()
    split = [raw[i:i + size] for i in range(0, len(raw), size)]
    return [Experiment.unpack(s) for s in split]
```

and give our record class a static method that calculates the size of a single record:

```
class Experiment(BasicRec):
    RECORD_LEN = BasicRec.MAX_NAME_LEN + 1 \
        + BasicRec.TIMESTAMP_LEN + 1 \
        + (BasicRec.MAX_READING_LEN * BasicRec.MAX_READINGS_NUM) \
        + (BasicRec.MAX_READINGS_NUM - 1)

    @staticmethod
    def size():
        return Experiment.RECORD_LEN
```

Tradeoffs

We're assuming that every record is the same size. If we want to save records with variable-length fields such as strings, we can either set a maximum size and always save that much data or make our implementation more complicated (and probably slower) by saving each record's size and then scanning records in the same way that we scanned the bytes making up Unicode characters in Chapter 17. The first choice spends space (i.e., memory and disk) to save time; the second spends time to save space. As [Bentley1982] pointed out over 40 years ago, a lot of performance optimizations in programming come down to trading space for time or vice versa.

18.3   A File-Backed Database

We now have what we need to extend our dictionary-based implementation to write records to a file and load them as needed:

```
class FileBacked(Database):
    def __init__(self, record_cls, filename):
        super().__init__(record_cls)
        self._filename = Path(filename)
        if not self._filename.exists():
            self._filename.touch()
        self._load()

    def add(self, record):
```

```
        key = self._record_cls.key(record)
        self._data[key] = record
        self._save()

    def get(self, key):
        return self._data.get(key, None)
```

This implementation stores everything in a single file, whose name must be provided to the database's constructor (Figure 18.2). If that file doesn't exist when the database object is created, we use Path.touch to create an empty file; either way, we then load the entire database into memory. When we add a record, we save it in the dictionary and call a helper method _save to write the entire database back to the file. When we get a record, we simply get it from the in-memory dictionary.

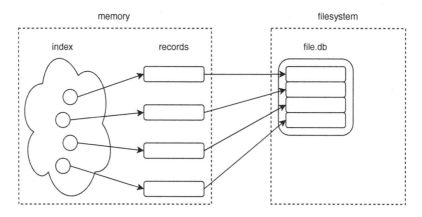

Figure 18.2: Saving the entire database in a single file.

The two helper methods we need to make this work are:

```
def _save(self):
    packed = self._record_cls.pack_multi(self._data.values())
    with open(self._filename, "w") as writer:
        writer.write(packed)

def _load(self):
    assert self._filename.exists()
    with open(self._filename, "r") as reader:
        raw = reader.read()
    records = self._record_cls.unpack_multi(raw)
    self._data = {self._record_cls.key(r): r for r in records}
```

It isn't very efficient—we are loading the entire database the first time we want a single record, and saving the entire database every time we add a record—but we are getting closer to something we might actually use.

18.4 Playing with Blocks

How can we make our file-backed implementation more efficient? One option would be to save each record in a file of its own, in the same way that we saved each version of a file in

Chapter 10. However, this strategy won't give us as much of a performance boost as we'd like. The reason is that computers do file I/O in **pages** that are typically 2 or 4 kilobytes in size. Even when we want to read a single byte, the operating system always reads a full page and then gives us just the byte we asked for.

A more efficient strategy is to group records together in **blocks of memory**, each of which is the same size as a page, and to create an index in memory to tell us which records are in which blocks. When we add a record, we only write its block to disk; similarly, when we need a record whose block isn't already in memory, we only read that block.

At this point we need to address an issue we should have tackled earlier. How do we handle updates to records? For example, suppose we already have a record with the ID 12345; what do we do when we get another record with the same ID? If we are storing the entire database in a single dictionary, the dictionary takes care of that for us, but if we are storing things in blocks, we will have multiple dictionaries.

This is where the "log-structured" part of our design comes in. Whenever we add a record to the database, we append it to the current block or start another block if the current one is full (Figure 18.3). We give each record a sequence number as we add it, and our overall index keeps track of the mapping from record IDs to sequence IDs. Since we know how many records there are in a block, we can quickly calculate which block contains the record with a particular sequence ID.

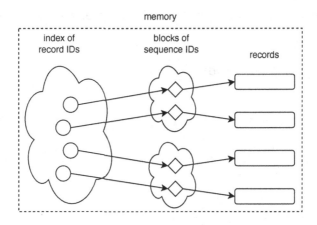

Figure 18.3: Mapping records to blocks.

Let's create a new in-memory database using one dictionary for each block. The constructor creates `self._next` to store the sequence ID of the next record, `self._index` to map record IDs to sequence IDs, and a list `self._blocks` to store blocks:

```python
class Blocked(Database):
    RECORDS_PER_BLOCK = 2

    @staticmethod
    def size():
        return Blocked.RECORDS_PER_BLOCK

    def __init__(self, record_cls):
        super().__init__(record_cls)
        self._next = 0
        self._index = {}
        self._blocks = []

    def num_blocks(self):
```

```
        return len(self._blocks)

    def num_records(self):
        return len(self._index)
```

To add a record, we:

1. get the sequence ID for the record;

2. store the key-to-sequence mapping in the index;

3. find or create the right block; and

4. add the record.

```
def add(self, record):
    key = self._record_cls.key(record)
    seq_id = self._next_seq_id()
    self._index[key] = seq_id
    block_id = self._get_block_id(seq_id)
    block = self._get_block(block_id)
    block[seq_id] = record
```

To get a record given a record ID, we first ask if we even have that record. If we do, we:

1. find its current sequence ID;

2. find the corresponding block; and

3. get the record.

```
def get(self, key):
    if key not in self._index:
        return None
    seq_id = self._index[key]
    block_id = self._get_block_id(seq_id)
    block = self._get_block(block_id)
    return block[seq_id]
```

The three helper methods that add and get rely on are:

```
def _next_seq_id(self):
    seq_id = self._next
    self._next += 1
    return seq_id

def _get_block_id(self, seq_id):
    return seq_id // Blocked.RECORDS_PER_BLOCK

def _get_block(self, block_id):
    while block_id >= len(self._blocks):
        self._blocks.append({})
    return self._blocks[block_id]
```

18.5 Persisting Blocks

We now have working prototypes of the two parts of our design: saving data to file and dividing records into blocks. In order to combine them, we will inherit from our block-based implementation and extend the `add` and `get` methods to save and load data:

```
class BlockedFile(Blocked):
    def __init__(self, record_cls, db_dir):
        super().__init__(record_cls)
        self._db_dir = Path(db_dir)
        self._build_index()

    def add(self, record):
        super().add(record)
        self._save(record)

    def get(self, key):
        if key not in self._index:
            return None
        self._load(key)
        return super().get(key)
```

We will explain the call to `self._build_index()` in a few paragraphs.

One at a Time

Exploring ideas one at a time and then combining them is a common tactic among experienced designers [Petre2016]. Creating classes like the all-in-one-file database that we don't put into production may feel like a waste of time, but it usually saves us effort in the long run by reducing cognitive load.

Saving a block is mostly a matter of bookkeeping at this point. Given the record, we figure out which block it belongs in, save it, pack the block, and write the result to a file:

```
def _save(self, record):
    key = self._record_cls.key(record)
    seq_id = self._index[key]
    block_id = self._get_block_id(seq_id)

    block = self._get_block(block_id)
    packed = self._record_cls.pack_multi(block.values())

    filename = self._get_filename(block_id)
    with open(filename, "w") as writer:
        writer.write(''.join(packed))
```

Loading involves almost the same steps, but our implementation splits it into two pieces:

```
def _load(self, key):
    seq_id = self._index[key]
    block_id = self._get_block_id(seq_id)
    filename = self._get_filename(block_id)
    self._load_block(block_id, filename)

def _load_block(self, block_id, filename):
    with open(filename, "r") as reader:
```

```
        raw = reader.read()

    records = self._record_cls.unpack_multi(raw)
    base = self.size() * block_id
    block = self._get_block(block_id)
    for i, r in enumerate(records):
        block[base + i] = r
```

We put the code to load a single block in a method of its own because we need to initialize the in-memory index when restarting the database:

```
def _build_index(self):
    seq_id = 0
    for (block_id, filename) in enumerate(
            sorted(self._db_dir.iterdir())
    ):
        self._load_block(block_id, filename)
        for record in self._get_block(block_id).values():
            key = self._record_cls.key(record)
            self._index[key] = seq_id
            seq_id += 1
```

An obvious extension to our design is to save the index in a separate file each time we add or modify a record. However, we should profile this change before putting it into production to see if it actually improves performance (Chapter 15), since many small writes might cost more than one large multi-file read. We would also have to do something to avoid creating a race condition; as in Chapter 10, operating on two files (one for the index and one for the block) could lead to harmful inconsistencies.

18.6   Cleaning Up

The final step in our implementation is to clean up blocks that are no longer needed because we have a more recent version of every record they contain. Reclaiming unused space this way is another form of **garbage collection**. Python and most other modern languages do it automatically to recycle unused memory, but it's our responsibility to do it for the files our database creates.

The steps in cleanup are:

1. Calculate a new sequence ID for each record.

2. Figure out which blocks contain records that we need to retain.

3. Generate new block IDs for those blocks while also creating a set of IDs of blocks we can delete because all of their records are out of date.

4. Delete and rename blocks.

5. Generate a new in-memory index.

The implementation of these steps is mostly a matter of bookkeeping:

```
def _cleanup(self):
    new_seq = {
        o: i for i, o in enumerate(self._index.values())
```

```
    }
    keep = {self._get_block_id(o) for o in new_seq}

    renaming = {o: i for i, o in enumerate(list(sorted(keep)))}
    garbage_ids = {
        i for i in range(len(self._blocks))
        if i not in renaming
    }

    self._delete_blocks(garbage_ids)
    self._rename_blocks(renaming)

    new_index = {
        k: new_seq[self._index[k]] for k in self._index
    }
    self._index = new_index
    self._next = len(self._index)
```

This method doesn't **compact** storage, i.e., it doesn't move records around to get rid of stale blocks within records. Production-quality databases do this periodically in order to use the disk more efficiently; we will explore this idea in the exercises.

18.7   Summary

Figure 18.4 summarizes the key ideas introduced in this chapter. Most real databases use different data structures than ours, but must deal with the same challenges: making data access fast without ever losing data or allowing it to become inconsistent.

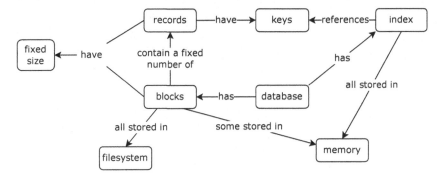

Figure 18.4: Concept map for a log-structured database.

18.8   Exercises

Packing Null Bytes

Modify the experimental record class so that records are packed as strings but can safely contain null bytes.

Packing in Binary

1. Modify the experimental record class so that it packs itself in a fixed-size binary record.

2. How does this change the file I/O operations in the database class?

3. Should those operations be moved into the record class or not?

Implement Compaction

Add a static method to the database that compacts blocks, i.e., rewrites all of the blocks so that only live records are stored.

Save the Index Separately

1. Modify the database so that it saves the entire index in a single file.

2. Design and run an experiment to determine if this change improves performance or not.

19

A Build Manager

- Build managers track dependencies between files and update files that are stale.

- Every build rule has a target, some dependencies, and a recipe for updating the target.

- Build rules form a directed graph which must not contain cycles.

- Pattern rules describe the dependencies and recipes for sets of similar files.

- Pattern rules can use automatic variables to specify targets and dependencies in recipes.

Terms defined: **affordance, build manager, build recipe, build rule, circular dependency, compiled language, cycle, dependency (in build), directed acyclic graph, dry run, link (a program), phony target, stable sort, stale (in build), target (in build), Template Method pattern, topological order**

Suppose that `plot.py` produces `result.svg` from `collated.csv`, that `collated.csv` is produced from `samples.csv` and `controls.csv` by `analyze.py`, and that `samples.csv` depends on `normalize.py` and `raw.csv`. If `raw.csv` changes we want to re-run all three programs; if `controls.csv` changes, on the other hand, we only need to re-run the analysis and plotting programs. If we try to manage this ourselves we will inevitably make mistakes. Instead, we should use a **build manager** to keep track of which files depend on which and what actions to take to create or update files. This chapter shows how a simple build manager works; along the way, it introduces some algorithms for working with graphs.

19.1 Concepts

The first build manager, Make[1], was written by a student intern at Bell Labs in the 1970s. Many others now exist (such as SCons[2] and Snakemake[3]), but they all perform the same basic operations. If a **target** is **stale** with respect to any of its **dependencies**, the build manager runs a **recipe** to refresh it.

The build manager runs recipes in an order that respects dependencies, and it only runs each recipe once (if at all). In order for this to be possible, targets and dependencies must form a **directed acyclic graph**, i.e., there cannot be a **cycle** of links leading from a node back to itself. The build manager constructs a **topological ordering** of that graph, i.e., arranges nodes so that each one comes after everything it depends on and then builds what it needs to in that order (Figure 19.1).

---

[1]https://www.gnu.org/software/make/
[2]https://www.scons.org/
[3]https://snakemake.readthedocs.io/

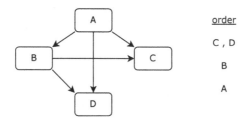

Figure 19.1: Dependencies and topological order.

A Bit of History

Make was created to manage programs in **compiled languages** like C and Java, which have to be translated into lower-level forms before they can run. There are usually two stages to the translation: compiling each source file into some intermediate form, and then **linking** the compiled modules to each other and to libraries to create a runnable program. If a source file hasn't changed, we don't need to recompile it before linking. Skipping unnecessary work in this way can save a lot of time when we are working with programs that contain thousands or tens of thousands of files.

19.2   Initial Design

Our first step is to decide how we are going to represent **build rules**. We could invent a special-purpose syntax to fit the problem, but as we said in Chapter 5, the world has enough data formats. Instead, we will represent our recipes as JSON. For example, this file describes two targets A and B and states that the former depends on the latter:

```
{
  "A": {"depends": ["B"], "rule": "build A"},
  "B": {"depends": [], "rule": "build B"}
}
```

As in Chapter 10, we will use successive refinement to create our first build manager. Our BuildBase class takes a configuration file as a constructor argument, loads it, creates a topological ordering, and then refreshes each target in order. For now, "refreshing" means "prints the update rule"; we will come back and make this more sophisticated later.

```
class BuildBase:
    def build(self, config_file):
        config = self._configure(config_file)
        ordered = self._topo_sort(config)
        for node in ordered:
            self._refresh(config, node)

    def _refresh(self, config, node):
        assert node in config, f"Unknown node {node}"
        print(config[node]["rule"])
```

To load a configuration file, we read in the JSON, build a set of known targets, and then verify each rule using a helper method called _check:

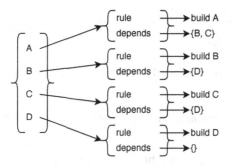

Figure 19.2: Representing dependency graph.

```python
def _configure(self, config_file):
    with open(config_file, "r") as reader:
        config = json.load(reader)
        known = set(config.keys())
        return {
            n: self._check(n, d, known)
            for n, d in config.items()
        }
```

To check a rule, we make sure the dictionary that represents it has the required keys and that we have a rule for every dependency it mentions. We also transform the rule's structure a bit to simplify later processing:

```python
def _check(self, name, details, known):
    assert "rule" in details, f"Missing rule for {name}"
    assert "depends" in details, f"Missing depends for {name}"
    depends = set(details["depends"])
    assert depends.issubset(known), \
        f"Unknown depends for {name}"
    return {"rule": details["rule"], "depends": depends}
```

It's Not Extra Work

We have to implement the consistency checks for our build rules because JSON is a generic format that knows nothing about dependencies, rules, and required keys. There is a format called JSON Schema[4] for specifying these things and a Python module[5] that implements its checks, but using it here would trade seven lines of code for 10 minutes of explanation. We will explore its use in the exercises, but the most important point is that whether we write code by hand or use a library with a bit of configuration, *someone* has to write these checks.

---

[4]https://json-schema.org/
[5]https://python-jsonschema.readthedocs.io/

19.3   Topological Sorting

The next step is to figure out a safe order in which to build things. Figure 19.3 shows how
our algorithm works:

1. We find all the nodes in the dependency graph that don't have any outstanding dependencies.

2. We append those to the result and then remove them from the dependencies of all the
   other nodes in the graph.

3. If anything is still in the graph, we go back to the first step.

4. If at any point the graph isn't empty but nothing is available, we have found a **circular
   dependency**, so we report the problem and fail.

   The code that implements this algorithm is:

```
def _topo_sort(self, config):
    graph = {n: config[n]["depends"] for n in config}
    result = []
    while graph:
        available = {n for n in graph if not graph[n]}
        assert available, f"Circular graph {graph.keys()}"
        result.extend(available)
        graph = {
            n: graph[n] - available
            for n in graph
            if n not in available
        }
    return result
```

   With all of this in place, we can run our first test:

```
{
    "A": {"depends": ["B"], "rule": "build A"},
    "B": {"depends": [], "rule": "build B"}
}
```

```
build B
build A
```

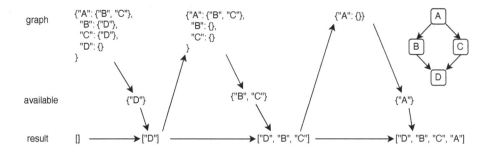

Figure 19.3: Topological Sort.

19.4 A Better Design

Our implementation works, but we can do better:

1. The configuration might not come directly from a JSON file—for example, it might be embedded in a larger file or generated by another program—so we should modify the constructor to take a configuration as input.

2. Printing actions to the screen isn't very useful, so we should collect them and return an ordered list of the commands for the build manager.

3. `assert` isn't a friendly way to handle user errors; we should raise `ValueError` (or a custom exception of our own) to indicate a problem.

4. Our topological sort isn't **stable**, i.e., there's no way to predict the order in which two "equal" nodes will be added to the ordering. We will explore the reason for this in the exercises, but for now, we should sort node names when appending to the `result` list so that our tests can know what to check for.

5. We might want to add other keys to rules, so we should put that check in a separate method that we can override.

The top level of our better build manager looks like this:

```
class BuildBetter:
    def build(self, config):
        config = self._configure(config)
        ordered = self._topo_sort(config)
        actions = []
        for node in ordered:
            self._refresh(config, node, actions)
        return actions

    def _refresh(self, config, node, actions):
        assert node in config, f"Unknown node {node}"
        actions.append(config[node]["rule"])

    def _must(self, condition, message):
        if not condition:
            raise ValueError(message)
```

The revised configuration code is:

```
def _configure(self, config):
    known = set(config.keys())
    return {n: self._check(n, d, known)
            for n, d in config.items()}

def _check(self, name, details, known):
    self._check_keys(name, details)
    depends = set(details["depends"])
    self._must(
        depends.issubset(known), f"Unknown depends for {name}"
    )
    result = details.copy()
    result["depends"] = depends
    return result
```

```
def _check_keys(self, name, details):
    self._must("rule" in details, f"Missing rule for {name}")
    self._must(
        "depends" in details, f"Missing depends for {name}"
    )
```

and the updated topological sorting method is

```
def _topo_sort(self, config):
    graph = {n: config[n]["depends"] for n in config}
    result = []
    while graph:
        available = {n for n in graph if not graph[n]}
        self._must(
            available,
            f"Circular graph {list(graph.keys())}",
        )
        result.extend(sorted(available))
        graph = {
            n: graph[n] - available
            for n in graph
            if n not in available
        }
    return result
```

We can now test that the code detects circularities in the dependency graph:

```
def test_circular():
    action_A = "build A"
    action_B = "build B"
    config = {
        "A": {"depends": ["B"], "rule": action_A},
        "B": {"depends": ["A"], "rule": action_B},
    }
    try:
        Builder().build(config)
        assert False, "should have had exception"
    except ValueError:
        pass
```

and that it builds what it's supposed to:

```
def test_no_dep():
    action_A = "build A"
    action_B = "build B"
    config = {
        "A": {"depends": [], "rule": action_A},
        "B": {"depends": [], "rule": action_B},
    }
    assert Builder().build(config) == [action_A, action_B]
```

We can also extend it. For example, suppose we only want to update targets that are older than their dependencies (which is, after all, the whole point of a build manager). If the targets are actual files we can check their timestamps, but for testing purposes we would like to specify pretended times in the configuration:

```
def test_diamond_dep():
    action_A = "build A"
    action_B = "build B"
    action_C = "build C"
```

```
        action_D = "build D"
        config = {
            "A": {"depends": ["B", "C"], "rule": action_A, "time": 0},
            "B": {"depends": ["D"], "rule": action_B, "time": 0},
            "C": {"depends": ["D"], "rule": action_C, "time": 1},
            "D": {"depends": [], "rule": action_D, "time": 1},
        }
        assert Builder().build(config) == [action_B, action_A]
```

Starting from the class we have written so far, we need to override three methods:

```
class BuildTime(BuildBetter):
    def _check_keys(self, name, details):
        super()._check_keys(name, details)
        self._must("time" in details, f"No time for {name}")

    def _refresh(self, config, node, actions):
        assert node in config, f"Unknown node {node}"
        if self._needs_update(config, node):
            actions.append(config[node]["rule"])

    def _needs_update(self, config, node):
        return any(
            config[node]["time"] < config[d]["time"]
            for d in config[node]["depends"]
        )
```

How We Actually Did It

Our final design uses the **Template Method** pattern: a method in a parent class defines the control flow, while child classes implement those operations. We didn't know in advance exactly how to divide our code into methods; instead, as we were creating a class that loaded and used timestamps, we reorganized the parent class to create the **affordances** we needed. Software design almost always works this way: the first two or three times we try to extend something, we discover changes that would make those tasks easier. We should do less of this as time goes by: if we are still doing large-scale refactoring the tenth time we use something, we should rethink our entire design.

19.5   Summary

Figure 19.4 summarizes the ideas introduced in this chapter. Note that the small bubble labelled "graph algorithm" could be expanded to a shelf full of books.

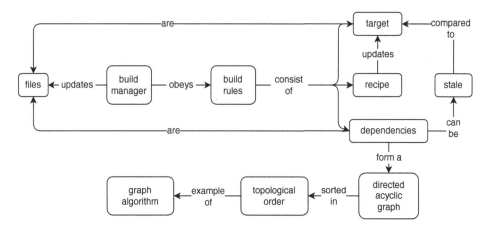

Figure 19.4: Concept map.

19.6 Exercises

Stable Sorting

Recent versions of Python guarantee that the entries in a dict preserve the order in which they were added, but do not make any such guarantee for sets. Explain why this makes it hard to test things that use sets.

Checking Schema

Rewrite the configuration validator to use JSON Schema[6] via the associated Python module[7].

Handling Failure

1. Modify the build manager so that a configuration file can specify whether its rule should succeed or fail. (This isn't particularly useful in real life, but it helps with testing.)

2. Modify it so that if a rule fails, other buildable targets are still built (but anything that depends directly or indirectly on the target whose rule failed is *not* built).

3. Write tests to check that this change works correctly.

Merging Files

1. Modify the build manager so that it can read multiple build files and execute their combined rules.

2. What does your solution do if two or more files specify rules for the same target?

---

[6]https://json-schema.org/
[7]https://python-jsonschema.readthedocs.io/

Using Hashes

1. Write a program called `build_init.py` that calculates a hash for every file mentioned in the build configuration and stores the hash along with the file's name in `build_hash.json`.

2. Modify the build manager to compare the current hashes of files with those stored in `build_hash.json` to determine what is out of date, and to update `build_hash.json` each time it runs.

Dry Run

A **dry run** of a build shows the rules that would be executed but doesn't actually execute them. Modify the build system in this chapter so that it can do dry runs.

Phony Targets

A **phony target** is one that doesn't correspond to a file. Developers often put phony targets in build files to give themselves an easy way to re-run tests, check code style, and so on. Modify the build system in this target so that users can mark targets as phony.

Multiple Build Files

1. Modify the tool built in this chapter so that one build file can import definitions and dependencies from another.

2. How does your system prevent circular dependencies?

20

A Package Manager

- Software packages often have multiple versions, which are usually identified by multi-part semantic version numbers.

- A package manager must find a mutually-compatible set of dependencies in order to install a package.

- Finding a compatible set of packages is equivalent to searching a multi-dimensional space.

- The work required to find a compatible set of packages can grow exponentially with the number of packages.

- Eliminating partially-formed combinations of packages can reduce the work required to find a compatible set.

- An automated theorem prover can determine if a set of logical propositions can be made consistent with each other.

- Most package managers use some kind of theorem prover to find compatible sets of packages to install.

Terms defined: **accumulator**, **backward-compatible**, **Boolean value**, **combinatorial explosion**, **cross product**, **model**, **patch**, **Recursive Enumeration pattern**, **scoring function**, **search space**, **semantic versioning**

Inspired by the Comprehensive TeX Archive Network (CTAN[1]), most languages have an online archive from which people can download packages, such as Python's PyPI[2]. Each package typically has a name, one or more versions, and a list of dependencies (which are also versioned). In order to install a package, we need to figure out exactly what versions of its dependencies to install: if A and B require different versions of C, we might not be able to use A and B together.

This chapter explores how to find a workable installation or prove that there isn't one. It is based in part on this tutorial[3] by Maël Nison[4] and on Andreas Zeller's[5] lecture on academic prototyping[6]; interested readers might also enjoy Michael Reim's[7] history of Unix packaging[8].

---

[1] https://www.ctan.org/
[2] https://pypi.org/
[3] https://classic.yarnpkg.com/blog/2017/07/11/lets-dev-a-package-manager/
[4] https://arcanis.github.io/
[5] https://andreas-zeller.info/
[6] https://www.fuzzingbook.org/html/AcademicPrototyping.html
[7] https://elderlinux.org/
[8] https://eerielinux.wordpress.com/2017/08/15/the-history-of-nix-package-management/

20.1 Semantic Versioning

Most software projects use **semantic versioning** for software releases. Each version is three integers X.Y.Z, where X is the major version, Y is the minor version, and Z is the **patch**.

A package's authors increment its major version number when a change to the package breaks **backward compatibility**, i.e., if code built for the old version will fail or behave unpredictably with the new one. The minor version number is incremented when changes won't break any existing code, and the patch number is changed for bug fixes that don't add any new features.

The notation for specifying ranges of versions looks like arithmetic: >=1.2.3 means "any version from 1.2.3 onward", <4 means "any version before 4.anything", and 1.0-3.1 means "any version in the specified range (including patches)". Note that version 2.1 is greater than version 1.99: no matter how large a minor version number becomes, it never spills over into the major version number.

It isn't hard to compare simple semantic version identifiers, but handling the whole standard[9] is almost as tricky as handling dates and times correctly. Our examples therefore number versions with plain integers; we recommend the semantic-version[10] package for working with the real thing.

20.2 Exhaustive Search

To avoid messing around with parsers, we store the manifest of available packages as JSON:

```
{
  "A": {
    "3": {"B": ["3", "2"], "C": ["2"]},
    "2": {"B": ["2"],      "C": ["2", "1"]},
    "1": {"B": ["1"]}
  },
  "B": {
    "3": {"C": ["2"]},
    "2": {"C": ["1"]},
    "1": {"C": ["1"]}
  },
  "C": {
    "2": [],
    "1": []
  }
}
```

The keys in the main dictionary identify packages (which we've called A, B, and C for simplicity). Each package has a dictionary whose keys are version numbers, and each version has a dictionary showing which versions of which other packages are dependencies (Figure 20.1). It's a complex data structure, but all of the detail is necessary.

---

[9]https://semver.org/
[10]https://pypi.org/project/semantic-version/

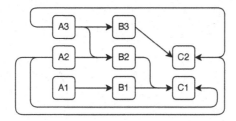

Figure 20.1: Structure of version dependency manifest.

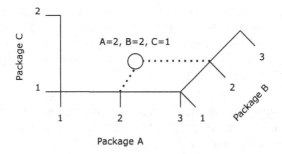

Figure 20.2: Finding allowable combinations of package versions.

Comments

We have been advising you since Chapter 5 not to design your own data format, but if you do, please include a single standard way for people to add comments. YAML has this, but JSON and CSV don't.

Imagine that each package we need is an axis on a multi-dimensional grid (Figure 20.2), so each point on the grid is a possible combination of package versions. We can exclude regions of this grid using the constraints on the package versions; the points that are left represent legal combinations.

How much work is it to check all of these possibilities? Our example has $3{\times}3{\times}2 = 18$ combinations. If we were to add another package to the mix with two versions, the **search space** would double; add another, and it would double again, which means that if each package has approximately c version and there are N packages, the work grows as $O(c^N)$. This exponential behavior is called **combinatorial explosion**, and it makes brute-force solutions impractical even for small problems. We will implement it as a starting point (and to give us something to test more complicated solutions against), but then we will need to find a more efficient approach.

Reproducibility

There may not be a strong reason to prefer one mutually-compatible set of packages over another, but a package manager should resolve the ambiguity the same way every time. It might not be what everyone wants, but at least they will be unhappy for the same reasons everywhere. This is why pip list (and similar commands for other

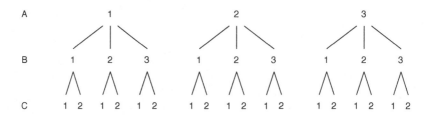

Figure 20.3: Generating all possible combinations of items.

> package managers) produce a listing of the exact versions of packages that have been
> installed: a spec written by a developer that lists allowed ranges of versions specifies
> what we *want*, while the listing created by the package manager specifies exactly what
> we *got*. If we want to reproduce someone else's setup for debugging purposes, we
> should install what is described in the latter file.

Our brute-force program generates all possible combinations of package versions, then
eliminates ones that aren't compatible with the manifest. Its main body is just those steps
in order with a few `print` statements to show the results:

```
def main():
    manifest = json.load(sys.stdin)
    possible = make_possibilities(manifest)
    print(f"{len(possible)} possibilities")
    allowed = [p for p in possible if compatible(manifest, p)]
    print(f"{len(allowed)} allowed")
    for a in allowed:
        print(a)
```

To generate the possibilities, we create a list of the available versions of each package,
then use Python's `itertools`[11] module to generate the **cross product** that contains all
possible combinations of items (Figure 20.3):

```
def make_possibilities(manifest):
    available = []
    for package, versions in manifest.items():
        available.append([(package, v) for v in versions])
    return list(itertools.product(*available))
```

To check a candidate against the manifest, we compare every entry X against every
other entry Y:

1. If X and Y are the same package, we keep looking. We need this rule because we're
   comparing every entry against every entry, which means we're comparing package versions to themselves. We could avoid this redundant check by writing a slightly smarter
   loop, but there's no point optimizing a horribly inefficient algorithm.

2. If package X's requirements say nothing about package Y, we keep searching. This rule
   handles the case of X not caring about Y, but it's also the reason we need to compare
   all against all, since Y might care about X.

3. Finally, if X does depend on Y, but this particular version of X doesn't list this particular
   version of Y as a dependency, we can rule out this combination.

---
[11] https://docs.python.org/3/library/itertools.html

4. If we haven't ruled out a candidate after doing all these checks, we add it to the list of allowed configurations.

Sure enough, these rules find 3 valid combinations among our 18 possibilities:

```
def compatible(manifest, combination):
    for package_i, version_i in combination:
        lookup_i = manifest[package_i][version_i]
        for package_j, version_j in combination:
            if package_i == package_j:
                continue
            if package_j not in lookup_i:
                continue
            if version_j not in lookup_i[package_j]:
                return False
    return True
```

```
18 possibilities
3 allowed
(('A', '3'), ('B', '3'), ('C', '2'))
(('A', '2'), ('B', '2'), ('C', '1'))
(('A', '1'), ('B', '1'), ('C', '1'))
```

20.3 Generating Possibilities Manually

Our brute-force code uses `itertools.product` to generate all possible combinations of several lists of items. To see how it works, let's rewrite `make_possibilities` to use a function of our own:

```
def make_possibilities(manifest):
    available = []
    for package, versions in manifest.items():
        available.append([(package, v) for v in versions])

    accum = []
    _make_possible(available, [], accum)
    return accum
```

The first half creates the same list of lists as before, where each sub-list is the available versions of a single package. It then creates an empty **accumulator** to collect all the combinations and calls a recursive function called `_make_possible` to fill it in.

Each call to `_make_possible` handles one package's worth of work (Figure 20.4). If the package is X, the function loops over the available versions of X, adds that version to the combination in progress, and calls itself with the remaining lists of versions. If there aren't any more lists to loop over, the recursive calls must have included exactly one version of each package, so the combination is appended to the accumulator.

```
def _make_possible(remaining, current, accum):
    if not remaining:
        accum.append(current)
    else:
        head, tail = remaining[0], remaining[1:]
        for h in head:
            _make_possible(tail, current + [h], accum)
```

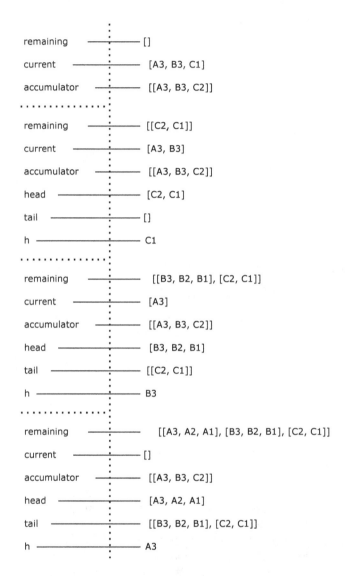

remaining ———— []
current ———— [A3, B3, C1]
accumulator ———— [[A3, B3, C2]]

remaining ———— [[C2, C1]]
current ———— [A3, B3]
accumulator ———— [[A3, B3, C2]]
head ———— [C2, C1]
tail ———— []
h ———— C1

remaining ———— [[B3, B2, B1], [C2, C1]]
current ———— [A3]
accumulator ———— [[A3, B3, C2]]
head ———— [B3, B2, B1]
tail ———— [[C2, C1]]
h ———— B3

remaining ———— [[A3, A2, A1], [B3, B2, B1], [C2, C1]]
current ———— []
accumulator ———— [[A3, B3, C2]]
head ———— [A3, A2, A1]
tail ———— [[B3, B2, B1], [C2, C1]]
h ———— A3

Figure 20.4: Generating all possible combinations of items recursively.

```
18 possibilities
3 allowed
[('A', '3'), ('B', '3'), ('C', '2')]
[('A', '2'), ('B', '2'), ('C', '1')]
[('A', '1'), ('B', '1'), ('C', '1')]
```

_make_possible uses recursion instead of nested loops because we don't know how many loops to write. If we knew the manifest only contained three packages, we would write a triply-nested loop to generate combinations, but if there were four, we would need a quadruply-nested loop, and so on. This **Recursive Enumeration** design pattern uses one recursive function call per loop so that we automatically get exactly as many loops as we need.

20.4 Incremental Search

Generating an exponentiality of combinations and then throwing most of them away is inefficient. Instead, we can modify the recursive generator to stop if a partially-generated combination of packages isn't legal. Combining generation and checking made the code more complicated, but as we'll see, it leads to some significant improvements.

The main function for our modified program is similar to its predecessor. After loading the manifest, we generate a list of all package names. Unlike our earlier code, the entries in this list don't include versions because we're going to be checking those as we go:

```
def main():
    manifest = json.load(sys.stdin)
    packages = list(manifest.keys())
    if len(sys.argv) > 1:
        packages.reverse()

    accum = []
    count = find(manifest, packages, accum, [], 0)

    print(f"count {count}")
    for a in accum:
        print(a)
```

Notice that we reverse the list of packages before starting our search if the user provides an extra command-line argument. We'll use this to see how ordering affects efficiency.

Our find function now has five parameters:

1. The manifest that tells us what's compatible with what.

2. The names of the packages we haven't considered yet.

3. An accumulator to hold all the valid combinations we've found so far.

4. The partially-completed combination we're going to extend next.

5. A count of the number of combinations we've considered so far, which we will use as a measure of efficiency.

```
def find(manifest, remaining, accum, current, count):
    count += 1
    if not remaining:
        accum.append(current)
    else:
        head, tail = remaining[0], remaining[1:]
        for version in manifest[head]:
            candidate = current + [(head, version)]
            if compatible(manifest, candidate):
                count = find(
                    manifest, tail, accum, candidate, count
                )
    return count
```

The algorithm combines the generation and checking we've already written:

1. If there are no packages left to consider—i.e., if `remaining` is an empty list—then what we've built so far in `current` must be valid, so we append it to `accumulator`.

2. Otherwise, we put the next package to consider in `head` and all the remaining packages in `tail`. We then check each version of the `head` package in turn. If adding it to the current collection of packages wouldn't cause a problem, we continue searching with that version in place.

How much work does incremental checking save us? Using the same test case as before, we only create 11 candidates instead of 18, so we've reduced our search by about a third:

```
python incremental.py < triple.json
```

```
count 11
[('A', '3'), ('B', '3'), ('C', '2')]
[('A', '2'), ('B', '2'), ('C', '1')]
[('A', '1'), ('B', '1'), ('C', '1')]
```

If we reverse the order in which we search, though, we only generate half as many candidates as before:

```
python incremental.py reversed < triple.json
```

```
count 9
[('C', '2'), ('B', '3'), ('A', '3')]
[('C', '1'), ('B', '2'), ('A', '2')]
[('C', '1'), ('B', '1'), ('A', '1')]
```

20.5   Using a Theorem Prover

Cutting the amount of work we have to do is good: can we do better? The answer is yes, but the algorithms involved are complicated and the jargon almost impenetrable. To give you a taste of how they work, we will solve our example problem using the Z3 theorem prover[12].

---
[12]https://en.wikipedia.org/wiki/Z3_Theorem_Prover

Installing packages and proving theorems may not seem to have a lot to do with each other, but an automated theorem prover's purpose is to determine how to make a set of logical propositions consistent with each other, or to prove that doing so is impossible. If we frame our problem as, "Is there a choice of package versions that satisfies all the inter-package dependencies at once?", then a theorem prover is exactly what we need.

To start, let's import a few things from z3 and create three **Boolean variables**:

```
from z3 import Bool, Implies, Not, Solver, sat, unsat

A = Bool("A")
B = Bool("B")
C = Bool("C")
```

Our three variables don't have values yet—they're not either true or false. Instead, each one represents all the possible states a Boolean could be in. If we had asked z3 to create one of its special integers, it would have given us something that initially encompassed all possible integer values.

Instead of assigning values to A, B, and C, we specify constraints on them, then ask z3 whether it's possible to find a set of values, or **model**, that satisfies all those constraints at once. For example, we can ask whether it's possible for A to equal B and B to equal C at the same time. The answer is "yes", and the solution the solver finds is to make them all `False`:

```
solver = Solver()
solver.add(A == B)
solver.add(B == C)
report("A == B & B == C", solver.check())
```

```
A == B & B == C: sat
A False
B False
C False
```

What if we say that A and B must be equal, but B and C must be unequal? In this case, the solver finds a solution in which A and B are `True` but C is `False`:

```
solver = Solver()
solver.add(A == B)
solver.add(B != C)
report("A == B & B != C", solver.check())
```

```
A == B & B != C: sat
A True
B True
C False
```

Finally, what if we require A to equal B and B to equal C but A and C to be unequal? No assignment of values to the three variables can satisfy all three constraints at once, and the solver duly tells us that:

```
solver = Solver()
solver.add(A == B)
solver.add(B == C)
solver.add(A != C)
report("A == B & B == C & B != C", solver.check())
```

```
A == B & B == C & B != C: unsat
```

Returning to package management, we can represent the versions from our running example like this:

```
A1 = Bool("A.1")
A2 = Bool("A.2")
A3 = Bool("A.3")

B1 = Bool("B.1")
B2 = Bool("B.2")
B3 = Bool("B.3")

C1 = Bool("C.1")
C2 = Bool("C.2")
```

We then tell the solver that we want one of the available versions of package A:

```
solver = Solver()
solver.add(Or(A1, A2, A3))
```

and that the three versions of package A are mutually exclusive:

```
solver.add(Implies(A1, Not(Or(A2, A3))))
solver.add(Implies(A2, Not(Or(A1, A3))))
solver.add(Implies(A3, Not(Or(A1, A2))))
```

We need equivalent statements for packages B and C; we'll explore in the exercises how to generate all of these from a package manifest.

Finally, we add the inter-package dependencies and search for a result:

```
solver.add(Implies(A3, And(Or(B3, B2), C2)))
solver.add(Implies(A2, And(B2, Or(C2, C1))))
solver.add(Implies(A1, B1))
solver.add(Implies(B3, C2))
solver.add(Implies(B2, C1))
solver.add(Implies(B1, C1))

print("result", solver.check(), solver.model())
```

```
result sat [B.3 = True,
 A.1 = False,
 C.2 = True,
 C.1 = False,
 B.2 = False,
 A.3 = True,
 A.2 = False,
 B.1 = False]
```

The output tells us that the combination of A.3, B.3, and C.2 will satisfy our constraints.

We saw earlier, though, that there are three solutions to our constraints. One way to find the others is to ask the solver to solve the problem again with the initial solution ruled out. We can repeat the process many times, adding "not the latest solution" to the constraints each time until the problem becomes unsolvable:

```
everything = [A1, A2, A3, B1, B2, B3, C1, C2]
while solver.check() == sat:
    model = solver.model()
    print([var for var in model.decls() if model[var]])
    settings = [var == model[var] for var in everything]
    cond = Not(And(*settings))
    solver.add(cond)
```

```
[B.3, C.2, A.3]
[C.1, B.2, A.2]
[A.1, C.1, B.1]
```

20.6 Summary

Figure 20.5 summarizes the key ideas introduced in this chapter. The most important thing to take away is that modern theorem provers can solve many more problems than most programmers realize. While formulating problems in ways that theorem provers understand can be challenging, solving those problems ourselves is usually much harder.

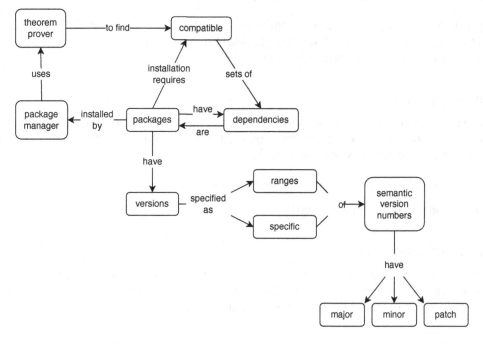

Figure 20.5: Concepts for package manager.

20.7 Exercises

Comparing Semantic Versions

Write a function that takes an array of semantic version specifiers and sorts them in ascending order. Remember that 2.1 is greater than 1.99.

Parsing Semantic Versions

Write a parser for a subset of the semantic versioning specification[13].

Using Scoring Functions

Many different combinations of package versions can be mutually compatible. One way to decide which actual combination to install is to create a **scoring function** that measures how good or bad a particular combination is. For example, a function could measure the "distance" between two versions as:

- 100 times the difference in major version numbers;

- 10 times the difference in minor version numbers if the major numbers agree; and

- the difference in the patch numbers if both major and minor numbers agree.

Implement this function and use it to measure the total distance between the set of packages found by the solver and the set containing the most recent version of each package. Does it actually solve the original problem?

Regular Releases

Some packages release new versions regularly, e.g., Version 2023.1 is released on March 1 of 2023, Version 2023.2 is released on September 1 of that year, version 2024.1 is released on March 1 of the following year, and so on.

1. How does this make package management easier?

2. How does it make it more difficult?

Searching Least First

Rewrite the constraint solver so that it searches packages by looking at those with the fewest available versions first. Does this reduce the amount of work done for the small examples in this chapter? Does it reduce the amount of work done for larger examples?

Using Exclusions

1. Modify the constraint solver so that it uses a list of package exclusions instead of a list of package requirements, i.e., its input tells it that version 1.2 of package Red can *not* work with versions 3.1 and 3.2 of package Green (which implies that Red 1.2 can work with any other versions of Green).

2. Explain why package managers aren't built this way.

Generating Constraints

Write a function that reads a JSON manifest describing package compatibilities and generates the constraints needed by the Z3 theorem prover.

---

[13]https://semver.org/

Buildability

1. Convert the build dependencies from one of the examples in Chapter 19 to a set of constraints for Z3 and use the solution to find a legal build order.

2. Modify the constraints to introduce a circular dependency and check that the solver correctly determines that there is no legal build order.

21

Transferring Files

- Every computer on a network has a unique IP address.

- The Domain Name System (DNS) translates human-readable names into IP addresses.

- Programs send and receive messages through numbered sockets.

- The program that receives a message is responsible for interpreting the bytes in the message.

- To test programs that rely on the network, replace the network with a mock object that simulates message transmission and receipt.

Terms defined: **client, deadlock, Domain Name System, Internet Protocol, IP address, port, server, socket, test fidelity, Transmission Control Protocol**

The Internet is simpler than most people realize (as well as being more complex than anyone could possibly comprehend). Most systems still follow the rules they did 30 years ago; in particular, most web servers still handle the same kinds of messages in the same way.

A typical web application is made up of **clients** and **servers**. A client program initiates communication by sending a message and waiting for a response; a server, on the other hand, waits for requests and then replies to them. There are typically many more clients than servers: for example, there may be hundreds or thousands of browsers fetching pages from this book's website right now, but there is only one server handling those requests.

This chapter shows how to build a simple low-level network program to move files from one machine to another. Chapter 22 will extend this to show how to build programs that communicate using HTTP. A central concern in both chapters is how to test such programs; while *who* sends *what* messages *when* changes from application to application, the testing techniques largely remain the same.

21.1 Using TCP/IP

Almost every program on the web uses a family of communication standards called **Internet Protocol** (IP). The one that concerns us is the **Transmission Control Protocol** (TCP/IP), which makes communication between computers look like reading and writing files. Programs using IP communicate through **sockets** (Figure 21.1). Each socket is one end of a point-to-point communication channel, just like a phone is one end of a phone call. A socket consists of an **IP address** that identifies a particular machine and a **port** on that machine.

The IP address consists of four 8-bit numbers, which are usually written as `93.184.216.34`; the **Domain Name System** (DNS) matches these numbers to symbolic names like `example.com` that are easier for human beings to remember. A port is a number

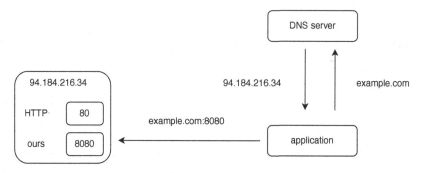

Figure 21.1: How sockets, IP addresses, and DNS work together.

in the range 0-65535 that uniquely identifies the socket on the host machine. (If an IP address is like a company's phone number, then a port number is like an extension.) Ports 0-1023 are reserved for well-known TCP/IP applications like web servers; custom applications should use the remaining ports (and should allow users to decide *which* port, since there's always the chance that two different people will pick 1234 or 6789).

A basic socket client looks like this:

```python
import socket

CHUNK_SIZE = 1024
SERVER_ADDRESS = ("localhost", 8080)

message = "message text"

sock = socket.socket(socket.AF_INET, socket.SOCK_STREAM)
sock.connect(SERVER_ADDRESS)
sock.sendall(bytes(message, "utf-8"))
print(f"client sent {len(message)} bytes")

received = sock.recv(CHUNK_SIZE)
received_str = str(received, "utf-8")
print(f"client received {len(received)} bytes: '{received_str}'")
```

We call it "basic" rather than "simple" because there's a lot going on here. From top to bottom:

1. We import some modules and define two constants. The first, SERVER_ADDRESS, consists of a host identifier and a port. (The string "localhost" means "the current machine".) The second, CHUNK_SIZE, will determine the maximum number of bytes in the messages we send and receive.

2. We use socket.socket to create a new socket. The values AF_INET and SOCK_STREAM specify the protocols we're using; we'll always use those in our examples, so we won't go into detail about alternatives.

3. We connect to the server, send our message as a bunch of bytes with sock.sendall, and print a message saying the data's been sent.

4. We then read up to a kilobyte from the socket with sock.recv. If we were expecting longer messages, we'd keep reading from the socket until there was no more data.

5. Finally, we print another message.

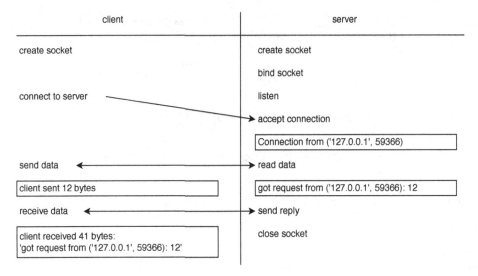

Figure 21.2: Steps and messages in client-server interaction.

The corresponding server has just as much low-level detail:

```python
import socket

CHUNK_SIZE = 1024

def handler():
    host, port = socket.gethostbyname("localhost"), 8080
    server_socket = socket.socket()
    server_socket.bind((host, port))

    server_socket.listen(1)
    conn, address = server_socket.accept()
    print(f"Connection from {address}")

    data = str(conn.recv(CHUNK_SIZE), "utf-8")
    msg = f"got request from {address}: {len(data)}"
    print(msg)

    conn.send(bytes(msg, "utf-8"))
    conn.close()
```

This code claims a socket, listens until it receives a single connection request, reads up to a kilobyte of data, prints a message, and replies to the client. Figure 21.2 shows the order of operations and messages when we run the client and server in separate terminal windows.

There's a *lot* going on here, so most people who have to program at this level use Python's socketserver[1] module, which provides two things: a class called TCPServer that manages incoming connections and another class called BaseRequestHandler that does everything *except* process the incoming data. In order to do that, we derive a class of our own from BaseRequestHandler that provides a handle method (Figure 21.3). Every time TCPServer gets a new connection, it creates a new object of our class and calls that object's handle method.

---
[1] https://docs.python.org/3/library/socketserver.html

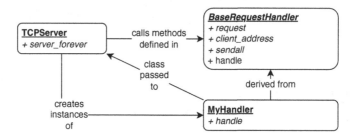

Figure 21.3: Classes used in a basic TCP server.

Using `TCPServer` and `BaseRequestHandler` as starting points, our server is:

```
import socketserver

CHUNK_SIZE = 1024
SERVER_ADDRESS = ("localhost", 8080)

class MyHandler(socketserver.BaseRequestHandler):
    def handle(self):
        data = self.request.recv(CHUNK_SIZE)
        cli = self.client_address[0]
        msg = f"got request from {cli}: {len(data)}"
        print(msg)
        self.request.sendall(bytes(msg, "utf-8"))

if __name__ == "__main__":
    server = socketserver.TCPServer(SERVER_ADDRESS, MyHandler)
    server.serve_forever()
```

These two classes use a different design than what we've seen before. Instead of creating one class for programmers to extend, the `socketserver` module puts the low-level details in `TCPServer`, which can be used as-is, and asks users to create a plug-in class from `BaseRequestHandler` for the server to use. This approach isn't intrinsically better or worse than the "derive and override" approach we've seen before; they're just two more tools in a software designer's toolbox.

21.2 Chunking

Our latest server reads data exactly once using `self.request.recv(CHUNK_SIZE)` with `CHUNK_SIZE` set to 1024. If the client sends more than a kilobyte of data, our server will ignore it. This can result in **deadlock**: the server is trying to send a reply while the client is trying to send the rest of the message, and since neither is listening, neither can move forward. Increasing the size of the memory buffer used to store the incoming message won't make this problem go away: the client (or a malicious attacker) could always send more data than we have allowed for.

Instead, we need to modify the server so that it keeps reading data until there is nothing left to read. Each time the `handle` method shown below goes around the loop, it tries to read another kilobyte. If it gets that much, it appends it to `data` and tries again. If it gets less than a kilobyte, we have reached the end of the transmission and can return the result:

```
class FileHandler(socketserver.BaseRequestHandler):
    def handle(self):
        print("server about to start receiving")
        data = bytes()
        while True:
            latest = self.request.recv(CHUNK_SIZE)
            print(f"...server received {len(latest)} bytes")
            data += latest
            if len(latest) < CHUNK_SIZE:
                print(f"...server breaking")
                break
        print(f"server finished received, about to reply")
        self.request.sendall(bytes(f"{len(data)}", "utf-8"))
```

We can modify the client to send data in chunks as well, but we handle this a little differently. Each call to `conn.send` in the function below tries to send all of the remaining data. The value returned by the function call tells us how many bytes were actually sent. If that number gets us to the end of the data we're sending, the function can exit the loop. If not, it adds the number of bytes sent to `total` so that it knows where to start sending the next time around:

```
def send_file(conn, filename):
    with open(filename, "rb") as reader:
        data = reader.read()
    print(f"client sending {len(data)} bytes")
    total = 0
    while total < len(data):
        sent = conn.send(data[total:])
        print(f"...client sent {sent} bytes")
        if sent == 0:
            break
        total += sent
        print(f"...client total now {total} bytes")
    return total
```

While we're here, we might as well write a function to create a socket:

```
def make_socket(host, port):
    conn = socket.socket(socket.AF_INET, socket.SOCK_STREAM)
    conn.connect((host, port))
    return conn
```

and another to wait for the acknowledgment from the server:

```
def receive_ack(conn):
    received = conn.recv(CHUNK_SIZE)
    return int(str(received, "utf-8"))
```

The main program is then:

```
def main(host, port, filename):
    conn = make_socket(host, port)
    bytes_sent = send_file(conn, filename)
    print(f"client main sent {bytes_sent} bytes")
    bytes_received = receive_ack(conn)
    print(f"client main received {bytes_received} bytes")
    print(bytes_sent == bytes_received)
```

When we run the client and server, the client prints:

```
client sending 1236 bytes
...client sent 1236 bytes
...client total now 1236 bytes
client main sent 1236 bytes
client main received 1236 bytes
True
```

and the server prints

```
server about to start receiving
...server received 1024 bytes
...server received 212 bytes
...server breaking
server finished received, about to reply
```

21.3 Testing

Testing single-process command-line applications is hard enough. To test a client-server application like the one above, we have to start the server, wait for it to be ready, then run the client, and then shut down the server if it hasn't shut down by itself. It's easy to do this interactively, but automating it is difficult because there's no way to tell how long to wait before trying to talk to the server and no easy way to shut the server down.

A partial solution is to use a mock object (Chapter 9) in place of a real network connection so that we can test each part of the application independently. To start, let's refactor our server's `handle` method so that it calls `self.debug` instead of printing directly:

```
class LoggingHandler(socketserver.BaseRequestHandler):
    def handle(self):
        self.debug("server about to start receiving")
        data = bytes()
        while True:
            latest = self.request.recv(BLOCK_SIZE)
            self.debug(f"...server received {len(latest)} bytes")
            data += latest
            if len(latest) < BLOCK_SIZE:
                self.debug(f"...server breaking")
                break
        self.debug(f"server finished received, about to reply")
        self.request.sendall(bytes(f"{len(data)}", "utf-8"))
```

The `debug` method takes any number of arguments and passes them to `print`:

```
def debug(self, *args):
    print(*args)
```

The `handle` method in this class relies on the `self.request` object created by the framework to send and receive data. We can create a testable server by deriving a class from `LoggingHandler` that inherits the `handle` method (which we want to test) but creates a mock request object and overrides the `debug` method so it doesn't print logging messages:

```
class MockHandler(LoggingHandler):
    def __init__(self, message):
        self.request = MockRequest(message)
```

```
def debug(self, *args):
    pass
```

Notice that we *don't* call the constructor of `LoggingHandler` in the constructor of `MockHandler`. If we did, we would trigger a call to the constructor of `BaseRequestHandler`, which would then be upset because we haven't defined a host or a port.

The class we use to create our mock `request` object needs three things:

1. A constructor that records the data we're going to pretend to have received over a socket and does whatever other setup is needed.

2. A `recv` method with the same signature as the real object's `recv` method.

3. A `sendall` method whose signature matches that of the real thing as well.

The whole class is:

```
class MockRequest:
    def __init__(self, message):
        self._message = message
        self._position = 0
        self._sent = []

    def recv(self, max_bytes):
        assert self._position <= len(self._message)
        top = min(len(self._message), self._position + BLOCK_SIZE)
        result = self._message[self._position:top]
        self._position = top
        return result

    def sendall(self, outgoing):
        self._sent.append(outgoing)
```

With it, we can now write unit tests like this:

```
def test_short():
    msg = bytes("message", "utf-8")
    handler = MockHandler(msg)
    handler.handle()
    assert handler.request._sent == [bytes(f"{len(msg)}", "utf-8")]
```

The key to our approach is the notion of **fidelity**: how close is what we test to what we use in production? In an ideal world they are exactly the same, but in cases like this it makes sense to sacrifice a little fidelity for testability's sake.

21.4 Summary

Figure 21.4 summarizes the idea introduces in this chapter. While understanding how to send data over a network is important, knowing how to test programs that interact with the outside world is just as important.

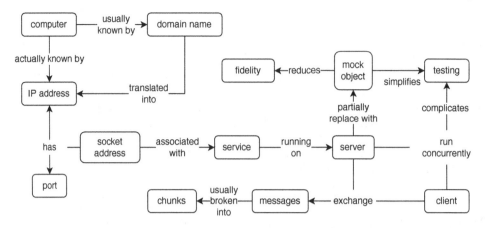

Figure 21.4: File transfer concept map.

21.5 Exercises

Chunk Sizes

What happens if the client tries to send zero bytes to the server? What happens if it sends exactly CHUNK_SIZE bytes or CHUNK_SIZE+1 bytes?

Efficiency

Suppose a client sends N chunks of data to a server. The current implementation will copy the first chunk $N-1$ times, the second chunk $N-2$ times, and so on, so that the total copying work is $O(N^2)$. Modify the server so that it collects chunks in a list and concatenates them at the end instead.

Saving and Listing Files

1. Modify the protocol used by this chapter's client and server so that the client sends the file's name, a newline, and then the file's contents, and the server saves the file under that name.

2. Modify the protocol again so that the client can send the word dir followed by a newline and no other data and the server will send back a list of the files in its current working directory.

A Socket Client Class

Build a socketclient class that works like the socketserver class but sends data instead of handling requests. How useful is it in practice?

22

Serving Web Pages

- The HyperText Transfer Protocol (HTTP) specifies one way to interact via messages over sockets.

- A minimal HTTP request has a method, a URL, and a protocol version.

- A complete HTTP request may also have headers and a body.

- An HTTP response has a status code, a status phrase, and optionally some headers and a body.

- HTTP is a stateless protocol: the application is responsible for remembering things between requests.

Terms defined: **body (of HTTP request or response)**, **header (of HTTP request or response)**, **HTTP**, **HTTP method**, **HTTP protocol version**, **HTTP request**, **HTTP response**, **HTTP status code**, **path resolution**, **query parameter**, **throw low, catch high**, **Universal Resource Locator**

Copying files from one machine to another is useful (Chapter 21), but we want to do more. What we *don't* want to do is create a new protocol for every application, any more than we create new file formats (Chapter 5).

The **HyperText Transfer Protocol** (HTTP) defines a way for programs to exchange data over the web. It is deliberately simple: the client sends a **request** specifying what it wants over a socket, and the server sends a **response** containing some data. Servers can construct responses however they want: they can copy files from disk, generate HTML dynamically, or do anything else a programmer can think of.

This chapter shows how to build a simple web server that understands the basics of HTTP and how to test programs of this kind. What we will build is much simpler than Apache[1], nginx[2], or other industrial-strength servers, but all the key ideas will be there.

22.1 Protocol

An HTTP request is just text: any program that wants to can create one or parse one. An absolutely minimal HTTP request has just the name of a **method**, a **URL**, and a **protocol version** on a single line separated by spaces:

```
GET /index.html HTTP/1.1
```

The HTTP method is almost always either GET (to fetch information) or POST (to submit form data or upload files). The URL specifies what the client wants: it is often a path to a file on disk, such as /index.html, but (and this is the crucial part) it's completely up to the

---

[1] https://httpd.apache.org/
[2] https://nginx.org/

server to decide what to do with it. The HTTP version is usually "HTTP/1.0" or "HTTP/1.1"; the differences between the two don't matter to us.

Most real requests have a few extra lines called **headers**, which are key-value pairs like the ones shown below:

```
GET /index.html HTTP/1.1
Accept: text/html
Accept-Language: en, fr
If-Modified-Since: 16-May-2023
```

Unlike the keys in hash tables, keys may appear any number of times in HTTP headers, so that (for example) a request can specify that it's willing to accept several types of content.

Finally, the **body** of the request is any extra data associated with it, such as form data or uploaded files. There must be a blank line between the last header and the start of the body to signal the end of the headers, and if there is a body, the request must have a header called Content-Length that tells the server how many bytes are in the body.

An HTTP response is formatted like an HTTP request. Its first line has the protocol followed by a **status code** and a status phrase, such as "200 OK" or "404 Not Found". There are then some headers (including Content-Length if the reply has a body), a blank line, and the body:

```
HTTP/1.1 200 OK
Date: Thu, 16 June 2023 12:28:53 GMT
Content-Type: text/html
Content-Length: 53

<html>
<body>
<h1>Hello, World!</h1>
</body>
</html>
```

Constructing HTTP requests is tedious, so most people use a library to do the repetitive work. The most popular one in Python is the requests[3] module, and works like this:

```
import requests

response = requests.get("http://third-bit.com/test.html")
print("status code:", response.status_code)
print("content length:", response.headers["content-length"])
print(response.text)
```

```
status code: 200
content length: 103
<html>
  <head>
    <title>Test Page</title>
  </head>
  <body>
    <p>test page</p>
  </body>
</html>
```

request.get sends an HTTP GET request to a server and returns an object containing the response (Figure 22.1). That object's status_code member is the response's status code; its content_length member is the number of bytes in the response data, and text

---
[3]https://requests.readthedocs.io/

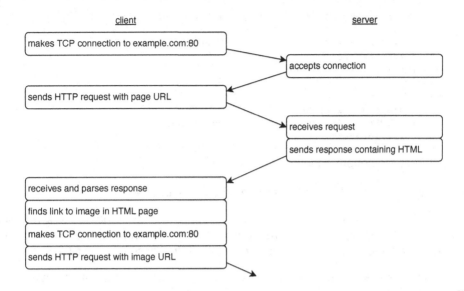

Figure 22.1: Lifecycle of an HTTP request and response.

is the actual data—in this case, an HTML page that we can analyze or render. Keep in mind that `requests` isn't doing anything magical: it is just formatting some text, opening a socket connection (Chapter 21), sending that text through the connection, and then reading a response. We will implement some of this ourselves in the exercises.

22.2   Hello, Web

We're now ready to write a simple HTTP server that will:

1. wait for someone to connect and send an HTTP request;

2. parse that request;

3. figure out what to send back; and

4. reply with an HTML page.

Steps 1, 2, and 4 are the same from one application to another, so the Python standard library has a module called `http.server`[4] to do most of the work. Here's the entire server:

```
from http.server import BaseHTTPRequestHandler, HTTPServer

PAGE = """<html><body><p>test page</p></body></html>"""

class RequestHandler(BaseHTTPRequestHandler):
    def do_GET(self):
        content = bytes(PAGE, "utf-8")
        self.send_response(200)
        self.send_header(
```

---

[4]https://docs.python.org/3/library/http.server.html

```
                "Content-Type", "text/html; charset=utf-8"
        )
        self.send_header("Content-Length", str(len(content)))
        self.end_headers()
        self.wfile.write(content)
if __name__ == "__main__":
    server_address = ("localhost", 8080)
    server = HTTPServer(server_address, RequestHandler)
    server.serve_forever()
```

Let's start at the bottom and work our way up.

1. `server_address` specifies the hostname and port of the server.

2. The `HTTPServer` class takes care of parsing requests and sending back responses. When we construct it, we give it the server address and the name of the class we've written that handles requests the way we want—in this case, `RequestHandler`.

3. Finally, we call the server's `serve_forever` method, which runs until it crashes or we stop it with Ctrl-C.

   So what does `RequestHandler` do?

1. When the server receives a `GET` request, it looks in the request handler for a method called `do_GET`. (If it gets a `POST`, it looks for `do_POST` and so on.)

2. `do_GET` converts the text of the page we want to send back from characters to bytes— we'll talk about this below.

3. It then sends a response code (200), a couple of headers to say what the content type is and how many bytes the receiver should expect, and a blank line (produced by the `end_headers` method).

4. Finally, `do_GET` sends the content of the response by calling `self.wfile.write`. `self.wfile` is something that looks and acts like a write-only file, but is actually sending bytes to the socket connection.

   If we run this program from the command line, it doesn't display anything:

```
python basic_http_server.py
```

but if we then go to `http://localhost:8080` with our browser we see this:

```
Hello, web!
```

and this in our shell:

```
127.0.0.1 - - [16/Sep/2022 06:34:59] "GET / HTTP/1.1" 200 -
127.0.0.1 - - [16/Sep/2022 06:35:00] "GET /favicon.ico HTTP/1.1" 200 -
```

The first line is straightforward: since we didn't ask for a particular file, our browser has asked for '/' (the root directory of whatever the server is serving). The second line appears because our browser automatically sends a second request for an image file called `/favicon.ico`, which it will display as an icon in the address bar if it exists.

22.3 Serving Files

Serving the same page for every request isn't particularly useful, so let's rewrite our simple server to return files. The basic logic looks like this:

```
class RequestHandler(BaseHTTPRequestHandler):
    def do_GET(self):
        try:
            url_path = self.path.lstrip("/")
            full_path = Path.cwd().joinpath(url_path)
            if not full_path.exists():
                raise ServerException(f"{self.path} not found")
            elif full_path.is_file():
                self.handle_file(self.path, full_path)
            else:
                raise ServerException(f"{self.path} unknown")
        except Exception as msg:
            self.handle_error(msg)
```

We first turn the path in the URL into a local file path by removing the leading /. Translating filenames this way is called **path resolution**, and in doing it, we assume that all the files we're supposed to serve live in or below the directory in which the server is running. If the resolved path corresponds to a file, we send it back to the client; if not, we generate and send an error message.

It might seem simpler to rewrite do_GET to use if/else instead of try/except, but doing the latter has an advantage: we can handle errors that occur inside methods we're calling (like handle_file) in the same place and in the same way as we handle errors that occur here. This approach is sometimes called **throw low, catch high**, which means that errors should be flagged in many places but handled in a few places high up in the code. The method that handles files is an example of this:

```
def handle_file(self, given_path, full_path):
    try:
        with open(full_path, 'rb') as reader:
            content = reader.read()
        self.send_content(content, HTTPStatus.OK)
    except IOError:
        raise ServerException(f"Cannot read {given_path}")
```

If there's an error at any point in the processing cycle, we send a page with an error message *and* an error status code. The former gives human users something to read, while the latter gives software a meaningful value in a predictable place:

```
def handle_error(self, msg):
    content = ERROR_PAGE.format(path=self.path, msg=msg)
    content = bytes(content, "utf-8")
    self.send_content(content, HTTPStatus.NOT_FOUND)
```

The error page is just HTML with some placeholders for the path and message:

```
ERROR_PAGE = """\
<html>
  <head><title>Error accessing {path}</title></head>
  <body>
    <h1>Error accessing {path}: {msg}</h1>
  </body>
</html>
"""
```

The code that actually sends the response is similar to what we've seen before:

```
def send_content(self, content, status):
    self.send_response(int(status))
    self.send_header("Content-Type", "text/html; charset=utf-8")
    self.send_header("Content-Length", str(len(content)))
    self.end_headers()
    self.wfile.write(content)
```

This server works, but only for a very forgiving definition of "works". We are careful not to show clients the actual paths to files on the server in our error messages, but if someone asked for `http://localhost:8080/../../passwords.txt`, this server will happily look two levels up from the directory where it's running and try to return that file. The server machine's passwords probably aren't stored there, but with enough ..'s and some patience, an attacker could poke around large parts of our filesystem. We will tackle this in the exercises.

Another problem is that `send_content` always tells clients that it is returning an HTML file with the `Content-Type` header. It should instead look at the extension on the file's name and set the content type appropriately, e.g., return `image/png` for a PNG-formatted image.

One thing the server is doing right is character encoding. The `send_content` method expects `content` to be a `bytes` object, not a string, because the HTTP protocol requires the content length to be the number of bytes. The server reads files in binary mode by using `"rb"` instead of just `"r"` when it opens files in `handle_file`, converts the internally-generated error page from characters to bytes using the UTF-8 encoding and specifies `charset=utf-8` as part of the content type.

22.4   Testing

As with the server in Chapter 21, we can work backward from a test we want to be able to write to create a testable server. We would like to create a file, simulate an HTTP GET request, and check that the status, headers, and content are correct. Figure 22.2 shows the final inheritance hierarchy:

- `BaseHTTPRequestHandler` comes from the Python standard library.

- `MockRequestHandler` defines replacements for its method.

- `ApplicationRequestHandler` contains our server's logic.

- `RequestHandler` combines our application code with Python's request handler.

- `MockHandler` combines it with our mock request handler.

It's a lot of work to test a single GET request, but we can re-use `MockRequestHandler` to test the application-specific code for other servers. Most libraries don't provide helper classes like this to support testing, but programmers appreciate those that do.

`MockRequestHandler` is just a few lines of code, though it would be longer if our application relied on more methods from the library class we're replacing:

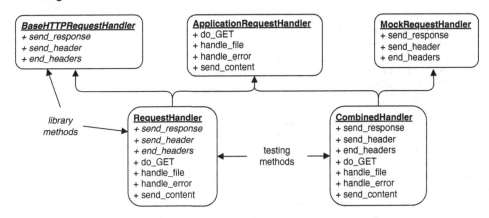

Figure 22.2: Class hierarchy for a testable server.

```
from io import BytesIO

class MockRequestHandler:
    def __init__(self, path):
        self.path = path
        self.status = None
        self.headers = {}
        self.wfile = BytesIO()

    def send_response(self, status):
        self.status = status

    def send_header(self, key, value):
        if key not in self.headers:
            self.headers[key] = []
        self.headers[key].append(value)

    def end_headers(self):
        pass
```

The application-specific class contains the code we've already seen:

```
class ApplicationRequestHandler:
    def do_GET(self):
        try:
            url_path = self.path.lstrip("/")
            full_path = Path.cwd().joinpath(url_path)
            if not full_path.exists():
                raise ServerException(f"'{self.path}' not found")
            elif full_path.is_file():
                self.handle_file(self.path, full_path)
            else:
                raise ServerException(f"Unknown object '{self.path}'")
        except Exception as msg:
            self.handle_error(msg)

    # ...etc...
```

MockHandler handles the simulated request and also stores the values that the client
would receive:

```
def test_existing_path(fs):
    content_str = "actual"
    content_bytes = bytes(content_str, "utf-8")
    fs.create_file("/actual.txt", contents=content_str)
    handler = MockHandler("/actual.txt")
    handler.do_GET()
    assert handler.status == int(HTTPStatus.OK)
    assert handler.headers["Content-Type"] == \
        ["text/html; charset=utf-8"]
    assert handler.headers["Content-Length"] == \
        [str(len(content_bytes))]
    assert handler.wfile.getvalue() == content_bytes
```

The main body of our runnable server combines the two classes to create what it needs:

```
if __name__ == '__main__':
    class RequestHandler(
            BaseHTTPRequestHandler,
            ApplicationRequestHandler
    ):
        pass

    serverAddress = ('', 8080)
    server = HTTPServer(serverAddress, RequestHandler)
    server.serve_forever()
```

Our tests, on the other hand, create a server with mocked methods:

```
class MockHandler(
        MockRequestHandler,
        ApplicationRequestHandler
):
    pass
```

22.5   Summary

Figure 22.3 summarizes the ideas introduced in this chapter. Given the impact the World-Wide Web has had, newcomers are often surprised by how simple of HTTP actually is.

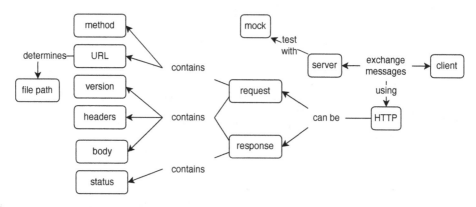

Figure 22.3: HTTP concept map.

22.6 Exercises

Parsing HTTP Requests

Write a function that takes a list of lines of text as input and parses them as if they were an HTTP request. The result should be a dictionary with the request's method, URL, protocol version, and headers.

Query Parameters

A URL can contain **query parameters**. Read the documentation for the `urlparse`[5] module and then modify the file server example so that a URL containing a query parameter `bytes=N` (for a positive integer N) returns the first N bytes of the requested file.

Better Path Resolution

Modify the file server so that:

1. it must be given the absolute path to a directory as a command-line argument when started; and

2. it only serves files in or below that directory (so that paths containing . . and other tricks can't be used to retrieve arbitrary files).

Better Content Types

Read the documentation for the `mimetypes`[6] module and then modify the file server to return the correct content type for files that aren't HTML (such as images).

Uploading Files

Modify the file server to handle POST requests.

1. The URL must specify the name of the file being uploaded.

2. The body of the request must be the bytes of the file.

3. All uploaded files are saved in a single directory, i.e., upload paths cannot contain directory components.

Checking Content Length

Modify the file server so that:

1. if the client sends more content than indicated in the `Content-Length` header, the extra bytes are read but ignored; and

2. if the client sends less content, the server doesn't wait indefinitely for the missing bytes.

   What status code should the server return to the client in each case?

---

[5]https://docs.python.org/3/library/urllib.parse.html
[6]https://docs.python.org/3/library/mimetypes.html

Directory Listing

1. Modify the file server so that if the path portion of the URL identifies a directory, the server returns a plain text list of the directory's contents.

2. Write tests for this using the `pyfakefs`[7] module.

Dynamic Results

Modify the file server so that if the client requests the "file" `/time`, the server returns an HTML page that reports the current time on the server's machine.

Templated Results

Modify the file server to:

1. turn the query parameters in the URL into a dictionary;

2. use that dictionary to fill in a template page (Chapter 12); and

3. return the resulting HTML page to the client.

---

[7]https://pytest-pyfakefs.readthedocs.io/

23

A File Viewer

- The curses module manages text terminals in a platform-independent way.

- Write debugging information to a log file when the screen is not available.

- We can use a callable object in place of a function to satisfy an API's requirements.

- Test programs using synthetic data.

- Using delayed construction and/or factory methods can make code easier to evolve.

- Refactor code before attempting to add new features.

- Separate the logic for managing data from the logic for displaying it.

Terms defined: **buffer (of text)**, **delayed construction**, **enumeration**, **factory method**, **log file**, **synthetic data**, **viewport**

Before they need version control tools or interpreters, programmers need a way to edit text files. Even simple editors like Notepad and Nano[1] do a lot of things: moving a cursor, inserting and deleting characters, and more. This is too much to fit into one lesson, so this chapter builds a tool for viewing files, which Chapter 24 extends to create an editor with undo and redo. Our example is inspired by this tutorial[2] written by Wasim Lorgat[3].

23.1 Curses

Our starting point is the curses[4] module, which handles interaction with text terminals on several different operating systems in a uniform way. A very simple curses-based program looks like this:

```
import curses

def main(stdscr):
    while True:
        key = stdscr.getkey()

if __name__ == "__main__":
    curses.wrapper(main)
```

curses.wrapper takes a function with a single parameter as input, does some setup, and then calls that function with an object that acts as an interface to the screen. (It is called stdscr, for "standard screen", by analogy with standard input stdin and standard

---

[1] https://www.nano-editor.org/
[2] https://wasimlorgat.com/posts/editor.html
[3] https://wasimlorgat.com/
[4] https://docs.python.org/3/library/curses.html

output stdout.) Our function `main` is just an infinite loop that consumes keystrokes but does nothing with them. When we run the program, it clears the screen and waits for the user to interrupt it by typing Ctrl-C.

We'd like to see what the user is typing, but since the program has taken over the screen, `print` statements won't be of use. Running this program inside a single-stepping debugger is challenging for the same reason, so for the moment we will cheat and create a **log file** for the program to write to:

```
LOG = None

def open_log(filename):
    global LOG
    LOG = open(filename, "w")

def log(*args):
    print(*args, file=LOG)
```

With this in hand, we can rewrite our program to take the name of the log file as its sole command-line argument and print messages to that file to show the keys that are being pressed. We can also modify the program so that when the user presses `q`, the program exits cleanly:

```
def main(stdscr):
    while True:
        key = stdscr.getkey()
        util.log(repr(key))
        if key.lower() == "q":
            return

if __name__ == "__main__":
    util.open_log(sys.argv[1])
    curses.wrapper(main)
```

Notice that we print the representation of the characters using `repr` so that (for example) a newline character shows up in the file as `'\n'` rather than as a blank line.

We are now ready to actually show some text. Given a list of strings, the revised `main` function below will repeatedly:

1. clear the screen,

2. display each line of text in the correct location,

3. wait for a keystroke, and

4. exit if the key is a `q`.

```
def main(stdscr, lines):
    while True:
        stdscr.erase()
        for (y, line) in enumerate(lines):
            stdscr.addstr(y, 0, line)
        key = stdscr.getkey()
        if key.lower() == "q":
            return
```

Two things about this function need to be kept in mind. First, as explained in Chapter 14, screens put (0, 0) in the upper left rather than the lower left, and increasing values of Y move down rather than up. To make things even more confusing, curses uses (row, column) coordinates, so we have to remember to write (y, x) instead of (x, y).

The other oddity in this function is that it erases the entire screen each time the user presses a key. Doing this is unnecessary in most cases—if the user's action doesn't modify the text being shown, there's no need to redraw it—but keeping track of which actions do and don't require redraw would require extra code (and extra debugging). For now, we'll do the simple, inefficient thing.

Here's how we run our revised main function:

```
if __name__ == "__main__":
    num_lines, logfile = int(sys.argv[1]), sys.argv[2]
    lines = make_lines(num_lines)
    open_log(logfile)
    curses.wrapper(lambda stdscr: main(stdscr, lines))
```

From top to bottom, we make a list of strings to display, open the log file, and then use lambda to make an anonymous function that takes a single screen object as input (which curses.wrapper requires) and immediately calls main with the two arguments that *it* requires.

A real text viewer would display the contents of a file, but for development we will just make up a regular pattern of text:

```
from string import ascii_lowercase

def make_lines(num_lines):
    result = []
    for i in range(num_lines):
        ch = ascii_lowercase[i % len(ascii_lowercase)]
        result.append(ch + "".join(str(j % 10) for j in range(i)))
    return result
```

If we ask for five lines, the pattern is:

```
a
b0
c01
d012
e0123
```

These lines are a very (very) simple example of **synthetic data**, i.e., data that is made up for testing purposes. If the viewer doesn't work for this text it probably won't work on actual files, and the patterns in the synthetic data will help us spot mistakes in the display.

23.2 Windowing

Our file viewer works, but only for small examples. If we ask it to display 100 lines, or anything else that is larger than our screen, it falls over with the message _curses.error: addwstr() returned ERR because it is trying to draw outside screen. The solution is to create a Window class that knows how big the screen is and only displays lines (or parts of lines) that fit inside it:

```
class Window:
    def __init__(self, screen):
        self._screen = screen
```

```
def draw(self, lines):
    self._screen.erase()
    for (y, line) in enumerate(lines):
        if 0 <= y < curses.LINES:
            self._screen.addstr(y, 0, line[:curses.COLS])
```

Our main function is then:

```
def main(stdscr, lines):
    window = Window(stdscr)
    window.draw(lines)
    while True:
        key = stdscr.getkey()
        if key.lower() == "q":
            return
```

Notice that main creates the window object. We can't create it earlier and pass it into main as we do with lines because the constructor for Window needs the screen object, which doesn't exist until curses.wrapper calls main. This is an example of **delayed construction** and is going to constrain the rest of our design (Figure 23.1).

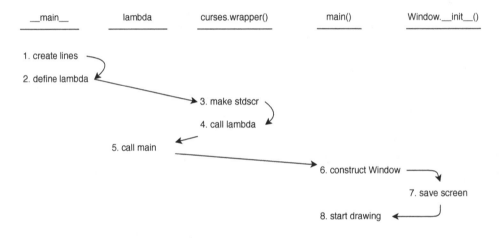

Figure 23.1: Order of operations in delayed construction.

Nothing says we have to make our window exactly the same size as the terminal that is displaying it. In fact, testing will be a lot simpler if we can create windows of arbitrary size (so long as they aren't *larger* than the terminal). This version of Window takes an extra parameter size which is either None (meaning "use the full terminal") or a (rows, columns) pair specifying the size we want:

```
class Window:
    def __init__(self, screen, size):
        self._screen = screen
        if size is None:
            self._nrow = curses.LINES
            self._ncol = curses.COLS
        else:
            self._nrow, self._ncol = size

    def draw(self, lines):
        self._screen.erase()
```

```
        for (y, line) in enumerate(lines):
            if 0 <= y < self._nrow:
                self._screen.addstr(y, 0, line[:self._ncol])
```

We're going to have a lot of two-dimensional (row, column) coordinates in this program, a pair _of_constants to be more readable than 0 and 1 or R and C. (We should really create an **enumeration**, but a pair of constants is good enough for now.)

```
ROW = 0
COL = 1
```

```
class Window:
    def draw(self, lines):
        self._screen.erase()
        for (y, line) in enumerate(lines):
            if 0 <= y < self._size[ROW]:
                self._screen.addstr(y, 0, line[:self._size[COL]])
```

23.3 Moving

Our program no longer crashes when given large input to display, but we can't see any of the text outside the window. To fix that, we need to teach the application to scroll. let's create another class to keep track of the position of a cursor:

```
class Cursor:
    def __init__(self):
        self._pos = [0, 0]

    def pos(self):
        return tuple(self._pos)

    def up(self): self._pos[ROW] -= 1

    def down(self): self._pos[ROW] += 1

    def left(self): self._pos[COL] -= 1

    def right(self): self._pos[COL] += 1
```

The cursor keeps track of its current (row, column) position in a list, but Cursor.pos returns the location as a separate tuple so that other code can't modify it. In general, nothing outside an object should be able to change the data structures that object uses to keep track of its state; otherwise, it's very easy for the internal state to become inconsistent in difficult-to-debug ways.

Now that we have a way to keep track of where the cursor is, we can tell curses to draw the cursor in the right location each time it renders the screen:

```
def main(stdscr, size, lines):
    window = Window(stdscr, size)
    cursor = Cursor()
    while True:
        window.draw(lines)
        stdscr.move(*cursor.pos())
        key = stdscr.getkey()
```

```
        if key == "KEY_UP": cursor.up()
        elif key == "KEY_DOWN": cursor.down()
        elif key == "KEY_LEFT": cursor.left()
        elif key == "KEY_RIGHT": cursor.right()
        elif key.lower() == "q":
            return
```

As this code shows, the screen's `getkey` method returns the names of the arrow keys. And since `stdscr.move` takes two arguments but `cursor.pos` returns a two-element tuple, we spread the latter with * to satisfy the former.

When we run this program and start pressing the arrow keys, the cursor does indeed move. In fact, we can move it to the right of the text, or below the bottom line of the text if there are fewer lines of text than rows in our window. What's worse, if we move the cursor off the left or top edges of the screen our program crashes with the message `_curses.error:` `wmove() returned ERR`. And we still can't see all the lines in a long "file": the text doesn't scroll down when we go to the bottom.

We need to constrain the cursor's movement so that it stays inside the text (not just the window), while simultaneously moving the text up or down when appropriate. Before tackling those problems, we will reorganize the code to give ourselves a better starting point.

23.4 Refactoring

Our first change is to write a class to represent the application as a whole; our program will then create one instance of this class, which will own the window and cursor. The trick to making this work is to take advantage of one of the protocols introduced in Chapter 9: if an object has a method named `__call__`, that method will be invoked when the object is "called" as if it were a function:

```
class Pretend:
    def __init__(self, increment):
        self._increment = increment

    def __call__(self, value):
        return value + self._increment

p = Pretend(3)
result = p(10)
print(result)
```

```
13
```

Since the `MainApp` class below defines `__call__`, `curses.wrapper` believes we have given it the single-parameter function it needs:

```
class MainApp:
    def __init__(self, size, lines):
        self._size = size
        self._lines = lines

    def __call__(self, screen):
        self._setup(screen)
        self._run()
```

```
def _setup(self, screen):
    self._screen = screen
    self._window = Window(self._screen, self._size)
    self._cursor = Cursor()
```

The `__call__` method calls `_setup` to create and store the objects the application needs, then `_run` to handle interaction. The latter is:

```
def _run(self):
    while True:
        self._window.draw(self._lines)
        self._screen.move(*self._cursor.pos())
        key = self._screen.getkey()
        if key == "KEY_UP": self._cursor.up()
        elif key == "KEY_DOWN": self._cursor.down()
        elif key == "KEY_LEFT": self._cursor.left()
        elif key == "KEY_RIGHT": self._cursor.right()
        elif key.lower() == "q":
            return
```

Finally, we pull the startup code into a function `start` so that we can use it in future versions of this code:

```
def start():
    num_lines, logfile = int(sys.argv[1]), sys.argv[2]
    size = None
    if len(sys.argv) > 3:
        size = (int(sys.argv[3]), int(sys.argv[4]))
    lines = make_lines(num_lines)
    open_log(logfile)
    return size, lines
```

and then launch our application like this:

```
if __name__ == "__main__":
    size, lines = start()
    app = MainApp(size, lines)
    curses.wrapper(app)
```

Next, we refactor `_run` to handle keystrokes using dynamic dispatch instead of a long chain of `if`/`elif` statement:

```
TRANSLATE = {
    "\x18": "CONTROL_X"
}

def _interact(self):
    key = self._screen.getkey()
    key = self.TRANSLATE.get(key, key)
    name = f"_do_{key}"
    if hasattr(self, name):
        getattr(self, name)()

def _do_CONTROL_X(self):
    self._running = False

def _do_KEY_UP(self):
    self._cursor.up()
```

A little experimentation showed that while the `curses` module uses names like "KEY_DOWN" for arrow keys, it returns actual control codes for key combinations like Ctrl-X. The `TRANSLATE` dictionary turns these into human-readable names that we can glue together with _do_ to make a method name; we got the hexadecimal value "\x18" by logging keystrokes to a file and then looking at its contents. We could probably have found this value in some documentation somewhere if we had looked hard enough, but a ten-second experiment seemed simpler.

With `_interact` in place, we can rewrite `_run` to be just five lines long:

```
class DispatchApp(MainApp):
    def __init__(self, size, lines):
        super().__init__(size, lines)
        self._running = True

    def _run(self):
        while self._running:
            self._window.draw(self._lines)
            self._screen.move(*self._cursor.pos())
            self._interact()
```

It now relies on a member variable called _running to keep the loop going. We could have had each key handler method return `True` or `False` to signal whether to keep going or not, but we found out the hard way that it's very easy to forget to do this, since almost every handler method's result is going to be the same.

Inheritance

`DispatchApp` inherits from our first `MainApp` so that we can recycle the initialization code we wrote for the latter. To make this happen, `DispatchApp.__init__` upcalls to `MainApp.__init__` using `super().__init__`. We probably wouldn't create multiple classes in a real program, but doing this simplifies exposition when teaching. In order to make this work cleanly, we did have to move some code around as later examples showed us that we should have divided things up differently in earlier examples.

This is normal. Nobody has perfect foresight; if we haven't built a particular kind of application several times, we can't anticipate all of the affordances we might need, so going back and refactoring old code to make new code easier to write is perfectly natural. If we need to refactor every time we want to add something new, though, we should probably rethink our design entirely.

We now have classes to represent the application, the window, and the cursor, but we are still storing the text to display as a naked list of lines. Let's wrap it up in a class:

```
class Buffer:
    def __init__(self, lines):
        self._lines = lines[:]

    def lines(self):
        return self._lines
```

This **text buffer** class doesn't do much yet, but will later keep track of the viewable region. Again, we make a copy of `lines` rather than using the list the caller gives us so that other code can't change the buffer's internals. The corresponding change to the application class is:

```
class BufferApp(DispatchApp):
    def __init__(self, size, lines):
        super().__init__(size, lines)

    def _setup(self, screen):
        self._screen = screen
        self._make_window()
        self._make_buffer()
        self._make_cursor()

    def _make_window(self):
        self._window = Window(self._screen, self._size)

    def _make_buffer(self):
        self._buffer = Buffer(self._lines)

    def _make_cursor(self):
        self._cursor = Cursor()
```

Factory Methods

We want to re-use as much of `BufferApp` as possible in upcoming versions of our file
viewer. If `setup` calls the constructors of specific classes to create the window, buffer,
and cursor objects, we will have to rewrite the entire method each time we change the
classes we use for those things. Putting constructor calls in **factory methods** makes
the code longer but allows us to override them one by one. We didn't do this when
we were first writing these examples; instead, as described in the previous callout, we
went back and refactored earlier classes to make later ones easier.

23.5 Clipping

We are now ready to keep the cursor inside both the text and the screen. The `ClipCursor`
class below takes the buffer as a constructor argument so that it can ask how many rows
there are and how big each one is, but its `up`, `down`, `left`, and `right` methods have exactly
the same signatures as the corresponding methods in the original `Cursor` class. As a result,
while we have to change the code that *creates* a cursor, we won't have to make any changes
to the code that *uses* the cursor:

```
class ClipCursor(Cursor):
    def __init__(self, buffer):
        super().__init__()
        self._buffer = buffer

    def up(self):
        self._pos[ROW] = max(self._pos[ROW]-1, 0)

    def down(self):
        self._pos[ROW] = min(self._pos[ROW]+1, self._buffer.nrow()-1)

    def left(self):
        self._pos[COL] = max(self._pos[COL]-1, 0)
```

```
def right(self):
    self._pos[COL] = min(
        self._pos[COL]+1,
        self._buffer.ncol(self._pos[ROW])-1
    )
```

The logic in the movement methods in `ClipCursor` is relatively straightforward. If the user wants to go up, don't let the cursor go above line 0. If the user wants to go down, on the other hand, don't let the cursor go below the last line, and so on. These methods rely on the buffer being able to report the number of rows it has and the number of columns in a particular row, so we define a new `ClipBuffer` class that provides those, and then override the `_make_buffer` and `_make_cursor` methods in the application class to construct the appropriate objects *without* changing the kind of window we are creating:

```
class ClipBuffer(Buffer):
    def nrow(self):
        return len(self._lines)

    def ncol(self, row):
        return len(self._lines[row])

class ClipApp(BufferApp):
    def _make_buffer(self):
        self._buffer = ClipBuffer(self._lines)

    def _make_cursor(self):
        self._cursor = ClipCursor(self._buffer)
```

When we run this program, we are no longer able to move the cursor outside the window or outside the displayed text—unless, that is, we go to the end of a long line and then move up to a shorter one. The problem is that `up` and `down` only change the cursor's idea of the row it is on; they don't check that the column position is still inside the text. The fix is simple:

```
class ClipCursorFixed(ClipCursor):
    def up(self):
        super().up()
        self._fix()

    def down(self):
        super().down()
        self._fix()

    def _fix(self):
        self._pos[COL] = min(
            self._pos[COL],
            (self._buffer.ncol(self._pos[ROW])-1))
```

One sign of a good design is that there is one (hopefully obvious) place to make a change in order to fix a bug or add a feature. By that measure, we seem to be on the right track.

23.6   Viewport

We are finally ready to scroll the text vertically so that all of the lines can be seen no matter how small the window is. (We will leave horizontal scrolling as an exercise.) A full-featured editor would introduce another class, often called a **viewport**, to track the currently-visible portion of the buffer. To keep things simple, we will add two member variables to the buffer instead to keep track of the top-most visible line and the height of the window:

```
class ViewportBuffer(ClipBuffer):
    def __init__(self, lines):
        super().__init__(lines)
        self._top = 0
        self._height = None

    def lines(self):
        return self._lines[self._top:self._top + self._height]

    def set_height(self, height):
        self._height = height

    def _bottom(self):
        return self._top + self._height
```

The most important change in the buffer is that `lines` returns the visible portion of the text rather than all of it. Another change is that the buffer initializes `_height` to `None` and requires someone to set it to a real value later because the application's `_setup` method creates the cursor, buffer, and window independently. If we were building a single class rather than layering tutorial classes on top of each other, we would probably go back and change `_setup` to remove the need for this.

Our buffer also gains two more methods. The first transforms the cursor's position from buffer coordinates to screen coordinates:

```
def transform(self, pos):
    result = (pos[ROW] - self._top, pos[COL])
    return result
```

The second method moves `_top` up or down when we reach the edge of the display:

```
def scroll(self, row, col):
    old = self._top
    if (row == self._top - 1) and self._top > 0:
        self._top -= 1
    elif (row == self._bottom()) and \
        (self._bottom() < self.nrow()):
        self._top += 1
```

As before, we derive a new application class to create the right kind of buffer object. We also override `_run` to scroll the buffer after each interaction with the user:

```
class ViewportApp(ClipAppFixed):
    def _make_buffer(self):
        self._buffer = ViewportBuffer(self._lines)

    def _make_cursor(self):
        self._cursor = ViewportCursor(self._buffer, self._window)

    def _run(self):
        self._buffer.set_height(self._window.size()[ROW])
        while self._running:
            self._window.draw(self._buffer.lines())
            screen_pos = self._buffer.transform(self._cursor.pos())
            self._screen.move(*screen_pos)
            self._interact()
            self._buffer.scroll(*self._cursor.pos())
```

Notice that the `ViewportApp` class creates a `ViewportCursor`. When we were testing the program, we discovered that we had introduced a bug: the cursor could go outside the window again if the line it was currently on was wider than the window. The solution is to add another check to `_fix` and to ensure that left and right movement constrain the cursor's position in the same way as vertical movement:

```python
class ViewportCursor(ClipCursorFixed):
    def __init__(self, buffer, window):
        super().__init__(buffer)
        self._window = window

    def left(self):
        super().left()
        self._fix()

    def right(self):
        super().right()
        self._fix()

    def _fix(self):
        self._pos[COL] = min(
            self._pos[COL],
            self._buffer.ncol(self._pos[ROW]) - 1,
            self._window.size()[COL] - 1
        )
```

23.7 Summary

Figure 23.2 summarizes the ideas introduced in this chapter. Keeping track of several sets of coordinates is a lot of bookkeeping; one of the big attractions of frameworks like Textualize[5] is how much of this they do for us.

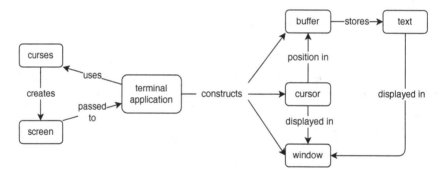

Figure 23.2: Concept map.

---

[5]https://www.textualize.io/

23.8 Exercises

Using `global`

1. Why does `open_log` need the line `global LOG`? What happens if it is removed?

2. Why doesn't the `log` function need this statement?

Horizontal Scrolling

Modify the application to scroll horizontally as well as vertically.

Explain the Bug

Replace the `ViewportCursor` class in the final version of the code with the earlier `ClipCursorFixed` class, then explain the bug `ViewportCursor` was created to fix.

Line Numbers

Modify the file viewer to show line numbers on the left side of the text.

Inheritance

Figure 23.3 shows the classes we created in this tutorial. Summarize the changes in each.

	main	window	cursor	buffer	app
first_curses.py	main				
logging_curses.py	main				
show_lines.py	main				
use_window.py	main	Window			
size_window.py	main	Window			
cursor_const.py	main	Window			
move_cursor.py	main		Cursor		
main_app.py					MainApp
dispatch_app.py					DispatchApp
buffer_class.py				Buffer	BufferApp
clip_cursor.py			ClipCursor	ClipBuffer	ClipApp
clip_fixed.py			ClipCursorFixed		ClipAppFixed
viewport.py			ViewportCursor	ViewportBuffer	ViewportApp

Figure 23.3: Class definitions and inheritance in lesson.

Sizing

The `Window` classes defined in this chapter accept user input to determine the size of the drawable area, using `curses.LINES` and `curses.COLS` by default. If a user provides sizes which are larger than the available area and tries to draw into that area, `curses` raises an error. Modify the code so that it doesn't.

24

Undo and Redo

- Replace user interface components with mock objects to simplify testing.

- Record actions and state to check behavior these mock objects.

- Use objects to represent actions to record history and enable undo.

- Recording state is easier but more expensive than recording changes.

Terms defined: **abstract base class**, **Command pattern**, **headless application**

Viewing text files is useful, but we'd like to be able to edit them as well. This chapter therefore modifies the file viewer of Chapter 23 so that we can add and delete text. And since people make mistakes, we will also implement undo, which will introduce another commonly-used design pattern.

24.1 Getting Started

Our file viewer has four classes:

- A `Window` can draw lines and report its size.

- A `Buffer` stores lines of text, keeps track of a viewport, and transforms buffer coordinates to screen coordinates.

- A `Cursor` knows its position in the buffer and can move up, down, left, and right.

- The `App` makes a window, a buffer, and a cursor, then maps keys to actions.

To make unit testing simpler, we start by adding one more class: a replacement for the screen object provided by the `curses`[1] module. This class stores the current state of the display in a rectangular grid so that our tests can check it easily. It also takes a list of keystrokes as input to simulate interaction with the user:

```
class HeadlessScreen:
    def __init__(self, size, keystrokes):
        self._size = size
        self._keys = keystrokes
        self._i_key = 0
        self.erase()

    def getkey(self):
        if self._i_key == len(self._keys):
            key = "CONTROL_X"
        else:
```

---

[1] https://docs.python.org/3/library/curses.html

```
            key = self._keys[self._i_key]
            self._i_key += 1
        return key

    def addstr(self, row, col, text):
        assert 0 <= row < self._size[ROW]
        assert col == 0
        assert len(text) <= self._size[COL]
        self._display[row] = text + self._display[row][len(text):]
```

GUI applications that don't display anything are often called **headless** applications. Giving our simulated keystrokes to the screen seems odd—it would make more sense for App to have a method that gets keystrokes—but it's the simplest way to fit everything in beside the classes we already have.

Clean Exit

Notice that when the screen runs out of simulated keystrokes it produces CONTROL_X, meaning "exit the application". We need this to break out of the keystroke-processing loop in the application, and no, we didn't think of this up front.

To finish this change, we also need to define a HeadlessWindow that takes a desired screen size and passes it to the screen:

```
class HeadlessWindow(Window):
    def __init__(self, screen, size):
        assert size is not None and len(size) == 2
        super().__init__(screen, size)
```

Finally, our new application class records keystrokes, the cursor position, and the screen contents for testing:

```
class HeadlessApp(App):
    def __init__(self, size, lines):
        super().__init__(size, lines)
        self._log = []

    def get_log(self):
        return self._log

    def _add_log(self, key):
        self._log.append((key, self._cursor.pos(), self._screen.display()))

    def _make_window(self):
        self._window = HeadlessWindow(self._screen, self._size)
```

We can now write tests like this:

```
def test_scroll_down():
    size = (2, 2)
    lines = ["abc", "def", "ghi"]
    keys = ["KEY_DOWN"] * 3
    screen = HeadlessScreen(size, keys)
    app = HeadlessApp(size, lines)
    app(screen)
    assert app.get_log()[-1] == ("CONTROL_X", (2, 0), ["de", "gh"])
```

24.2   Insertion and Deletion

We are now ready to implement insertion and deletion. The first step is to add methods to the buffer class that update a line of text:

```
class InsertDeleteBuffer(Buffer):
    def insert(self, pos, char):
        assert 0 <= pos[ROW] < self.nrow()
        assert 0 <= pos[COL] <= self.ncol(pos[ROW])
        line = self._lines[pos[ROW]]
        line = line[:pos[COL]] + char + line[pos[COL]:]
        self._lines[pos[ROW]] = line

    def delete(self, pos):
        assert 0 <= pos[ROW] < self.nrow()
        assert 0 <= pos[COL] < self.ncol(pos[ROW])
        line = self._lines[pos[ROW]]
        line = line[:pos[COL]] + line[pos[COL] + 1:]
        self._lines[pos[ROW]] = line
```

Notice that we delete the character *under* the cursor, not the one to the left of the cursor: this is delete-in-place rather than backspace-delete. Notice also that we have done a little defensive programming by checking that the coordinates given for the operation make sense.

The window, cursor, and screen don't need to change to support insertion and deletion, but the application class needs several updates. The first is to define the set of characters that can be inserted, which for our example will be letters and digits, and to create a buffer of the appropriate kind:

```
class InsertDeleteApp(HeadlessApp):
    INSERTABLE = set(string.ascii_letters + string.digits)

    def _make_buffer(self):
        self._buffer = InsertDeleteBuffer(self._lines)
```

We also need to create handlers for insertion and deletion:

```
def _do_DELETE(self):
    self._buffer.delete(self._cursor.pos())

def _do_INSERT(self, key):
    self._buffer.insert(self._cursor.pos(), key)
```

Finally, since we don't want to have to add one handler for each insertable character, let's write a _get_key method that returns a pair of values. The first indicates the "family" of the key, while the second is the actual key. If the family is None, the key is a special key with its own handler; otherwise, we look up the handler for the key's family:

```
def _get_key(self):
    key = self._screen.getkey()
    if key in self.INSERTABLE:
        return "INSERT", key
    else:
        return None, key

def _interact(self):
    family, key = self._get_key()
    if family is None:
```

```
        name = f"_do_{key}"
        if hasattr(self, name):
            getattr(self, name)()
    else:
        name = f"_do_{family}"
        if hasattr(self, name):
            getattr(self, name)(key)
    self._add_log(key)
```

We're going to write a lot of tests for this application, so let's write a helper function to create a fixture, run the application, and return it:

```
def make_fixture(keys, size, lines):
    screen = HeadlessScreen(size, keys)
    app = InsertDeleteApp(size, lines)
    app(screen)
    return app
```

Our tests are now straightforward to set up and check:

```
def test_delete_middle():
    app = make_fixture(["KEY_RIGHT", "DELETE"], (1, 3), ["abc"])
    assert app.get_log()[-1] == ("CONTROL_X", (0, 1), ["ac_"])
```

> **Edge Case**
>
> One of our tests uncovers the fact that our application crashes if we try to delete a character when the buffer is empty:
>
> ```
> def test_delete_when_impossible():
>     try:
>         make_fixture(["DELETE"], (1, 1), [""])
>     except AssertionError:
>         pass
> ```
>
> Our focus is implementing undo, so we will leave fixing this for an exercise.

24.3 Going Backward

In order to undo things we have to:

1. keep track of *actions* and reverse them, or

2. keep track of *state* and restore it.

Recording actions can be trickier to implement but requires less space than saving the entire state of the application after each change, so that's what most systems do. The starting point is to append a record of every action to a log:

```
class HistoryApp(InsertDeleteApp):
    def __init__(self, size, keystrokes):
        super().__init__(size, keystrokes)
        self._history = []
```

```
def get_history(self):
    return self._history

def _do_DELETE(self):
    row, col = self._cursor.pos()
    char = self._buffer.char((row, col))
    self._history.append(("delete", (row, col), char))
    self._buffer.delete(self._cursor.pos())
```

But what about undoing cursor movement? If we add a character, move to another location, and then undo, shouldn't the cursor go back to where it was before deleting the character? And how are we going to interpret these log records? Will we need a second dispatch method with its own handlers?

The common solution to these problems is to use the **Command** design pattern. This pattern turns verbs into nouns, i.e., each action is represented as an object with methods to go forward and backward. Our actions all derive from an **abstract base class** so that they can be used interchangeably. That base class is:

```
class Action:
    def __init__(self, app):
        self._app = app

    def do(self):
        raise NotImplementedError(f"{self.__class__.__name__}: do")

    def undo(self):
        raise NotImplementedError(f"{self.__class__.__name__}: undo")
```

The child classes for insertion and deletion are:

```
class Insert(Action):
    def __init__(self, app, pos, char):
        super().__init__(app)
        self._pos = pos
        self._char = char

    def do(self):
        self._app._buffer.insert(self._pos, self._char)

    def undo(self):
        self._app._buffer.delete(self._pos)
```

```
class Delete(Action):
    def __init__(self, app, pos):
        super().__init__(app)
        self._pos = pos
        self._char = self._app._buffer.char(pos)

    def do(self):
        self._app._buffer.delete(self._pos)

    def undo(self):
        self._app._buffer.insert(self._pos, self._char)
```

We could implement one class for each direction of cursor movement, but instead choose to create a single class:

```
class Move(Action):
    def __init__(self, app, direction):
        super().__init__(app)
        self._direction = direction
        self._old = self._app._cursor.pos()
        self._new = None

    def do(self):
        self._app._cursor.act(self._direction)
        self._new = self._app._cursor.pos()

    def undo(self):
        self._app._cursor.move_to(self._old)
```

This class records the new cursor position as well as the old one to make debugging easier. It depends on adding two new methods to `Cursor` to move in a particular direction by name (e.g., "right" or "left") and to move to a particular location:

```
def act(self, direction):
    assert hasattr(self, direction)
    getattr(self, direction)()

def move_to(self, pos):
    self._pos = pos
    self._fix()
```

Our application's `_interact` method changes too. Instead of relying on keystroke handler methods to do things, it expects them to create action objects (Figure 24.1). These objects are appended to the application's history, and then asked to do whatever they do:

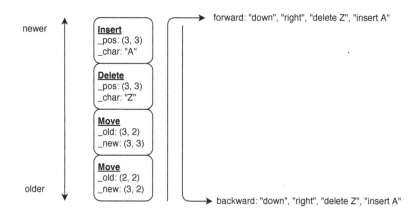

Figure 24.1: Representing actions as objects in the Command design pattern.

```
def _interact(self):
    family, key = self._get_key()
    name = f"_do_{family}" if family else f"_do_{key}"
    if not hasattr(self, name):
        return
    action = getattr(self, name)(key)
    self._history.append(action)
    action.do()
    self._add_log(key)
```

Note that we have modified all the handler methods to take the keystroke as an input argument so that we don't have to distinguish between cases where it's needed and cases where it isn't. This simplifies the code a little at the expense of introducing unused parameters into the handlers for special keys like cursor movement.

Finally, each handler method now builds an object and returns it:

```
def _do_DELETE(self, key):
    return Delete(self, self._cursor.pos())

def _do_INSERT(self, key):
    return Insert(self, self._cursor.pos(), key)

def _do_KEY_UP(self, key):
    return Move(self, "up")
```

With all these changes in place, our application *almost* works. We add an _do_UNDO handler that pops the most recent action from the history and calls its undo method. When we test this, though, we wind up in an infinite loop because we are appending the action to the history before doing the action, so we are essentially undoing our undo forever. The solution is to modify the base class Action to have a .save method that tells the application whether or not to save this action. The default implementation returns True, but we override it in Undo to return False:

```
class Undo(Action):
    def do(self):
        action = self._app._history.pop()
        action.undo()

    def save(self):
        return False

    def __str__(self):
        return f"Undo({self._app._history[-1]})"
```

Note that popping the most recent action off the history stack only works once we modify the application's _interact method so that it only saves actions that ought to be saved:

```
class UndoableApp(ActionApp):
    def _interact(self):
        family, key = self._get_key()
        name = f"_do_{family}" if family else f"_do_{key}"
        if not hasattr(self, name):
            return
        action = getattr(self, name)(key)
        action.do()
        if action.save():
            self._history.append(action)
        self._add_log(key)
```

We can now write tests like this to check that we can insert a character, undo the action, and get back the screen we originally had:

```
def test_insert_undo():
    app = make_fixture(["z", "UNDO"])
    assert get_screen(app) == ["ab", "cd"]
```

24.4 Summary

Figure 24.2 summarizes the concepts introduced in this chapter. Real text editors (even simple ones) obviously have many more features, but we have now seen most of the key ideas.

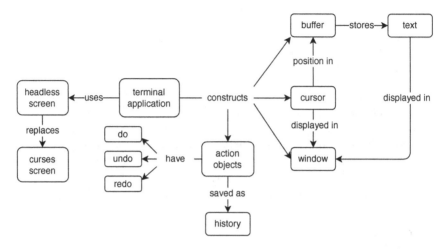

Figure 24.2: Concept map.

24.5 Exercises

Combining Movement

Modify the application so that successive movement operations are combined into a single undo step.

Forgetting Moves

Most editors do not save cursor movements in their undo history. Modify the code in this chapter so that undo only works on changes to the content being edited.

Limiting History

Modify the application so that only the most recent hundred operations can be undone.

Breaking Lines

Modify the code so that pressing the Enter key inserts a new line or breaks the current line in two. What information do you have to store to make this operation undoable?

Redoing Operations

Implement a "redo" command that re-executes an operation that has been undone. How does redo differ from undoing an undo? Does it make sense to redo an action that wasn't done?

Repeating Operations

1. Implement a command to repeat the most recent operation.

2. How should repeated operations be represented in the application's history?

Saving Operations

Use the ideas of Chapter 16 to save operations to a file and reload them so that users can resume editing sessions.

25

A Virtual Machine

- Every computer has a processor with a particular instruction set, some registers, and memory.

- Instructions are just numbers but may be represented as assembly code.

- Instructions may refer to registers, memory, both, or neither.

- A processor usually executes instructions in order but may jump to another location based on whether a conditional is true or false.

Terms defined: **Application Binary Interface**, **assembler**, **assembly code**, **bytecode**, **conditional jump**, **disassembler**, **instruction pointer**, **instruction set**, **label (of address in memory)**, **op code**, **register (in hardware)**, **virtual machine**, **word (of memory)**

The interpreter in Chapter 7 relied on Python to do most of the actual work. The standard version of Python is implemented in C and relies on C's operators to add numbers, index arrays, and so on, but C is compiled to instructions for a particular processor. Each operation in the little language of Chapter 7 is therefore expanded by several layers of software to become something that hardware can actually run. To show how that lower layer works, this chapter builds a simulator of a small computer. If you want to dive deeper into programming at this level, have a look at the game Human Resource Machine[1].

25.1   Architecture

Our **virtual machine** (VM) simulates a computer with three parts (Figure 25.1):

1. The **instruction pointer** (IP) holds the memory address of the next instruction to execute. It is automatically initialized to point at address 0, so that is where every program must start. This requirement is part of our VM's **Application Binary Interface** (ABI).

2. Four **registers** named R0 to R3 that instructions can access directly. There are no memory-to-memory operations in our VM: everything happens in or through registers.

3. 256 **words** of memory, each of which can store a single value. Both the program and its data live in this single block of memory; we chose the size 256 so that the address of each word will fit in a single byte.

Our processor's **instruction set** defines what it can do. Instructions are just numbers, but we will write them in a simple text format called **assembly code** that gives those number human-readable names.

---

[1] https://tomorrowcorporation.com/humanresourcemachine

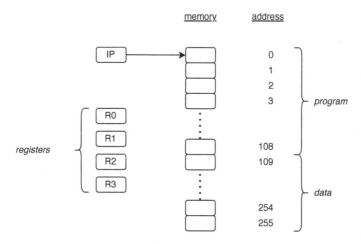

Figure 25.1: Architecture of the virtual machine.

Name	Code	Format	Action	Example	Equivalent
hlt	1	--	Halt program	hlt	sys.exit(0)
ldc	2	rv	Load constant	ldc R0 99	R0 = 99
ldr	3	rr	Load register	ldr R0 R1	R0 = memory[R1]
cpy	4	rr	Copy register	cpy R0 R1	R0 = R1
str	5	rr	Store register	str R0 R1	memory[R1] = R0
add	6	rr	Add	add R0 R1	R0 = R0 + R1
sub	7	rr	Subtract	sub R0 R1	R0 = R0 - R1
beq	8	rv	Branch if equal	beq R0 99	if (R0==0) IP = 99
bne	9	rv	Branch if not equal	bne R0 99	if (R0!=0) IP = 99
prr	10	r-	Print register	prr R0	print(R0)
prm	11	r-	Print memory	prm R0	print(memory[R0])

Table 25.1: Virtual machine op codes.

The instructions for our VM are 3 bytes long. The **op code** fits in one byte, and each instruction may include zero, one, or two single-byte operands. (Instructions are sometimes called **bytecode**, since they're packed into bytes, but so is everything else in a computer.)

Each operand is a register identifier, a constant, or an address, which is just a constant that identifies a location in memory. Since constants have to fit in one byte, this means that the largest number we can represent directly is 256. Table 25.1 uses the letters r and v to indicate instruction format, where r indicates a register identifier and v indicates a constant value.

To start building our virtual machine, we put the VM's details in a file that can be loaded by other modules:

```
NUM_REG = 4   # number of registers
RAM_LEN = 256  # number of words in RAM

OPS = {
    "hlt": {"code": 0x1, "fmt": "--"},  # Halt program
    "ldc": {"code": 0x2, "fmt": "rv"},  # Load value
    "ldr": {"code": 0x3, "fmt": "rr"},  # Load register
    "cpy": {"code": 0x4, "fmt": "rr"},  # Copy register
    "str": {"code": 0x5, "fmt": "rr"},  # Store register
```

```
    "add": {"code": 0x6, "fmt": "rr"},   # Add
    "sub": {"code": 0x7, "fmt": "rr"},   # Subtract
    "beq": {"code": 0x8, "fmt": "rv"},   # Branch if equal
    "bne": {"code": 0x9, "fmt": "rv"},   # Branch if not equal
    "prr": {"code": 0xA, "fmt": "r-"},   # Print register
    "prm": {"code": 0xB, "fmt": "r-"},   # Print memory
}

OP_MASK  = 0xFF  # select a single byte
OP_SHIFT = 8   # shift up by one byte
OP_WIDTH = 6   # op width in characters when printing
```

There isn't a name for this design pattern, but putting all the constants that define a system in one file instead of scattering them across multiple files makes them easier to find as well as ensuring consistency.

25.2 Execution

We start by defining a class with an instruction pointer, some registers, and some memory along with a prompt for output. A program is just an array of numbers representing instructions. To load a program into our VM, we copy those numbers into memory and reset the instruction pointer and registers:

```
class VirtualMachine:
    def __init__(self):
        self.initialize([])
        self.prompt = ">>"

    def initialize(self, program):
        assert len(program) <= RAM_LEN, "Program too long"
        self.ram = [
            program[i] if (i < len(program)) else 0
            for i in range(RAM_LEN)
        ]
        self.ip = 0
        self.reg = [0] * NUM_REG
```

Notice that the VM's constructor calls `initialize` with an empty array (i.e., a program with no instructions) to do initial setup. If an object has a method to reset or reinitialize itself, having its constructor use that method is a way to avoid duplicating code.

To execute the next instruction, the VM gets the value in memory that the instruction pointer currently refers to and moves the instruction pointer on by one address. It then uses bitwise operations (Chapter 17) to extract the op code and operands from the instruction (Figure 25.2).

```
def fetch(self):
    instruction = self.ram[self.ip]
    self.ip += 1
    op = instruction & OP_MASK
    instruction >>= OP_SHIFT
    arg0 = instruction & OP_MASK
    instruction >>= OP_SHIFT
    arg1 = instruction & OP_MASK
    return [op, arg0, arg1]
```

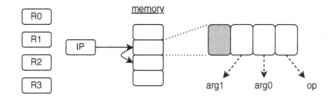

Figure 25.2: Using bitwise operations to unpack instructions.

We always unpack two operands regardless of whether the instructions have them or not, since this is what most hardware implementations would do.

Processor Design

Some processors do have variable-length instructions, but they make the hardware more complicated and therefore slower. To decide whether these costs are worth paying, engineers rely on simulation and profiling (Chapter 15). Backward compatibility is also an issue: if earlier processors supported variable-length instructions, later ones must somehow do so as well in order to run old programs.

The next step is to add a `run` method to our VM that fetches instructions and executes them until told to stop:

```
def run(self):
    running = True
    while running:
        op, arg0, arg1 = self.fetch()
        if op == OPS["hlt"]["code"]:
            running = False
        elif op == OPS["ldc"]["code"]:
            self.reg[arg0] = arg1
        elif op == OPS["ldr"]["code"]:
            self.reg[arg0] = self.ram[self.reg[arg1]]
        elif op == OPS["cpy"]["code"]:
            self.reg[arg0] = self.reg[arg1]
        else:
            assert False, f"Unknown op {op:06x}"
```

Let's look more closely at three of these instructions. The first, `str`, stores the value of one register in the address held by another register:

```
elif op == OPS["str"]["code"]:
    self.ram[self.reg[arg1]] = self.reg[arg0]
```

Adding the value in one register to the value in another register is simpler:

```
elif op == OPS["add"]["code"]:
    self.reg[arg0] += self.reg[arg1]
```

as is jumping to a fixed address if the value in a register is zero. This **conditional jump** instruction is how we implement `if`:

```
elif op == OPS["beq"]["code"]:
    if self.reg[arg0] == 0:
        self.ip = arg1
```

25.3 Assembly Code

We could write out numerical op codes by hand just as early programmers[2] did. However, it is much easier to use an **assembler**, which is just a small compiler for a language that very closely represents actual machine instructions.

Each command in our assembly languages matches an instruction in the VM. Here's an assembly language program to print the value stored in R1 and then halt:

```
# Print initial contents of R1.
prr R1
hlt
```

Its numeric representation (in hexadecimal) is:

```
00010a
000001
```

One thing the assembly language has that the instruction set doesn't is **labels** on addresses in memory. The label loop doesn't take up any space; instead, it tells the assembler to give the address of the next instruction a name so that we can refer to @loop in jump instructions. For example, this program prints the numbers from 0 to 2 (Figure 25.3):

```
# Count up to 3.              000002
# - R0: loop index.           030102
# - R1: loop limit.           00000a
ldc R0 0                      010202
ldc R1 3                      020006
loop:                         010204
prr R0                        000207
ldc R2 1                      020209
add R0 R2                     000001
cpy R2 R1
sub R2 R0
bne R2 @loop
hlt
```

Let's trace this program's execution (Figure 25.4):

1. R0 holds the current loop index.

2. R1 holds the loop's upper bound (in this case 3).

3. The loop prints the value of R0 (one instruction).

4. The program adds 1 to R0. This takes two instructions because we can only add register-to-register.

5. It checks to see if we should loop again, which takes three instructions.

6. If the program *doesn't* jump back, it halts.

---

[2]http://eniacprogrammers.org/

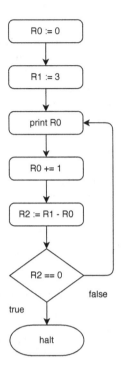

Figure 25.3: Flowchart of assembly language program to count up from 0 to 2.

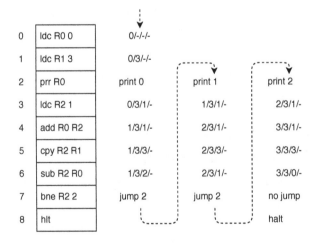

Figure 25.4: Tracing registers and memory values for a simple counting program.

The implementation of the assembler mirrors the simplicity of assembly language. The main method gets interesting lines, finds the addresses of labels, and turns each remaining line into an instruction:

```
class Assembler:
    def assemble(self, lines):
        lines = self._get_lines(lines)
        labels = self._find_labels(lines)
        instructions = [
            ln for ln in lines if not self._is_label(ln)
        ]
        compiled = [
            self._compile(instr, labels) for instr in instructions
        ]
        program = self._to_text(compiled)
        return program
```

To find labels, we go through the lines one by one and either save the label *or* increment the current address (because labels don't take up space):

```
def _find_labels(self, lines):
    result = {}
    loc = 0
    for ln in lines:
        if self._is_label(ln):
            label = ln[:-1].strip()
            assert label not in result, f"Duplicated {label}"
            result[label] = loc
        else:
            loc += 1
    return result

def _is_label(self, line):
    return line.endswith(":")
```

To compile a single instruction we break the line into pieces, look up the format for the operands, and pack the values:

```
def _compile(self, instruction, labels):
    tokens = instruction.split()
    op, args = tokens[0], tokens[1:]
    fmt, code = OPS[op]["fmt"], OPS[op]["code"]

    if fmt == "--":
        return self._combine(code)

    elif fmt == "r-":
        return self._combine(self._reg(args[0]), code)

    elif fmt == "rr":
        return self._combine(
            self._reg(args[1]), self._reg(args[0]), code
        )

    elif fmt == "rv":
        return self._combine(
            self._val(args[1], labels),
            self._reg(args[0]), code
        )
```

To convert a value, we either look up the label's address (if the value starts with @) or convert the value to a number:

```
def _val(self, token, labels):
    if token[0] != "@":
        return int(token)
    lbl = token[1:]
    assert lbl in labels, f"Unknown label '{token}'"
    return labels[lbl]
```

Combining op codes and operands into a single value is the reverse of the unpacking done by the virtual machine:

```
def _combine(self, *args):
    assert len(args) > 0, "Cannot combine no arguments"
    result = 0
    for a in args:
        result <<= OP_SHIFT
        result |= a
    return result
```

As a test, this program counts up to 3:

```
# Count up to 3.
# - R0: loop index.
# - R1: loop limit.
ldc R0 0
ldc R1 3
loop:
prr R0
ldc R2 1
add R0 R2
cpy R2 R1
sub R2 R0
bne R2 @loop
hlt
```

```
>> 0
>> 1
>> 2
R000000 = 000003
R000001 = 000003
R000002 = 000000
R000003 = 000000
000000:    000002  030102  00000a  010202
000004:    020006  010204  000207  020209
000008:    000001  000000  000000  000000
```

25.4 Arrays

It's tedious to write programs when each value needs a unique name. We can do a lot more once we have arrays, so let's add those to our assembler. We don't have to make any changes to the virtual machine, which doesn't care if we think of a bunch of numbers as individuals or elements of an array, but we do need a way to create arrays and refer to them.

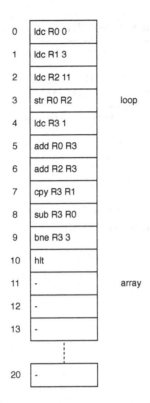

0	ldc R0 0	
1	ldc R1 3	
2	ldc R2 11	
3	str R0 R2	loop
4	ldc R3 1	
5	add R0 R3	
6	add R2 R3	
7	cpy R3 R1	
8	sub R3 R0	
9	bne R3 3	
10	hlt	
11	-	array
12	-	
13	-	
20	-	

Figure 25.5: Allocating storage for arrays in the virtual machine.

We will allocate storage for arrays at the end of the program by using .data on a line of its own to mark the start of the data section and then label: number to give a region a name and allocate some storage space (Figure 25.5).

This enhancement only requires a few changes to the assembler. First, we need to split the lines into instructions and data allocations:

```
DIVIDER = ".data"

def assemble(self, lines):
    lines = self._get_lines(lines)
    to_compile, to_allocate = self._split(lines)

    labels = self._find_labels(lines)
    instructions = [ln for ln in to_compile if not self._is_label(ln)]

    base_of_data = len(instructions)
    self._add_allocations(base_of_data, labels, to_allocate)

    compiled = [self._compile(instr, labels) for instr in instructions]
    program = self._to_text(compiled)
    return program

def _split(self, lines):
    try:
        split = lines.index(self.DIVIDER)
        return lines[0:split], lines[split + 1:]
    except ValueError:
        return lines, []
```

Second, we need to figure out where each allocation lies and create a label accordingly:

```python
def _add_allocations(self, base_of_data, labels, to_allocate):
    for alloc in to_allocate:
        fields = [a.strip() for a in alloc.split(":")]
        assert len(fields) == 2, f"Invalid allocation directive '{alloc}'"
        lbl, num_words_text = fields
        assert lbl not in labels, f"Duplicate label '{lbl}' in allocation"
        num_words = int(num_words_text)
        assert (base_of_data + num_words) < RAM_LEN, \
            f"Allocation '{lbl}' requires too much memory"
        labels[lbl] = base_of_data
        base_of_data += num_words
```

And that's it: no other changes are needed to either compilation or execution. To test it, let's fill an array with the numbers from 0 to 3:

```
# Count up to 3.
# - R0: loop index.
# - R1: loop limit.
# - R2: array index.
# - R3: temporary.
ldc R0 0
ldc R1 3
ldc R2 @array
loop:
str R0 R2
ldc R3 1
add R0 R3
add R2 R3
cpy R3 R1
sub R3 R0
bne R3 @loop
hlt
.data
array: 10
```

```
R000000 = 000003
R000001 = 000003
R000002 = 00000e
R000003 = 000000
000000:     000002    030102    0b0202    020005
000004:     010302    030006    030206    010304
000008:     000307    030309    000001    000000
00000c:     000001    000002    000000    000000
```

25.5 Summary

Figure 25.6 summarizes the new ideas in this chapter. Real processors and the VMs for languages like Python are more complex, but experience shows that keeping things simple makes it much easier to make them fast and reliable.

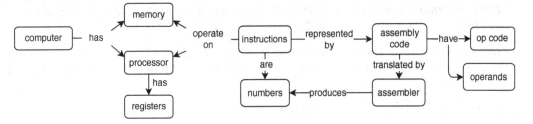

Figure 25.6: Concept map for virtual machine and assembler.

25.6 Exercises

Swapping Values

Write an assembly language program that swaps the values in R1 and R2 without affecting the values in other registers.

Reversing an Array

Write an assembly language program that starts with:

- the base address of an array in one word

- the length of the array N in the next word

- N values immediately thereafter

and that reverses the array in place.

Increment and Decrement

1. Add instructions inc and dec that add one to the value of a register and subtract one from the value of a register respectively.

2. Rewrite the examples to use these instructions. How much shorter do they make the programs? Do they make it easier to read?

Using Long Addresses

1. Modify the virtual machine so that the ldr and str instructions contain 16-bit addresses rather than 8-bit addresses and increase the virtual machine's memory to 64K words to match.

2. How does this complicate instruction interpretation?

Operating on Strings

The C programming language stored character strings as non-zero bytes terminated by a byte containing zero.

1. Write a program that starts with the base address of a string in R1 and finishes with the length of the string (not including the terminator) in the same register.

2. Write a program that starts with the base address of a string in R1 and the base address of some other block of memory in R2 and copies the string to that new location (including the terminator).

3. What happens in each case if the terminator is missing?

Call and Return

1. Add another register to the virtual machine called SP (for "stack pointer") that is automatically initialized to the *last* address in memory.

2. Add an instruction psh (short for "push") that copies a value from a register to the address stored in SP and then subtracts one from SP.

3. Add an instruction pop (short for "pop") that adds one to SP and then copies a value from that address into a register.

4. Using these instructions, write a subroutine that evaluates 2x+1 for every value in an array.

Disassembling Instructions

A **disassembler** turns machine instructions into assembly code. Write a disassembler for the instruction set used by our virtual machine. (Since the labels for addresses are not stored in machine instructions, disassemblers typically generate labels like @L001 and @L002.)

Linking Multiple Files

1. Modify the assembler to handle .include filename directives.

2. What does your modified assembler do about duplicate label names? How does it prevent infinite includes (i.e., A.as includes B.as which includes A.as again)?

Providing System Calls

Modify the virtual machine so that developers can add "system calls" to it.

1. On startup, the virtual machine loads an array of functions defined in a file called syscalls.py.

2. The sys instruction takes a one-byte constant argument. It looks up the corresponding function and calls it with the values of R0-R3 as arguments and places the result in R0.

Unit Testing

1. Write unit tests for the assembler.

2. Once they are working, write unit tests for the virtual machine.

26

A Debugger

- Interactive programs can be tested by simulating input and recording output.

- Testing interactive programs is easier if their inputs and outputs can easily be replaced with mock objects.

- Debuggers usually implement breakpoints by temporarily replacing actual instructions with special ones.

- Using lookup tables for function or method dispatch makes programs easier to extend.

Terms defined: **breakpoint, clear (a breakpoint), conditional breakpoint, debugger, disassemble, reverse lookup, watchpoint**

We have finally come to another of the questions that sparked this book: how does a **debugger** work? Debuggers are as much a part of good programmers' lives as version control but are taught far less often (in part, we believe, because it's harder to create homework questions for them). This chapter builds a simple single-stepping debugger for the virtual machine of Chapter 25 and shows how we can test interactive applications. If you would like to go further and (much) deeper, please have a look at Sy Brand's[1] tutorial[2].

26.1 One Step at a Time

Before we start work, let's consolidate and reorganize the code in our virtual machine. The methods all work as they did before, but we've made a few changes to allow for future growth. The first is to pass an output stream to the constructor, which by default will be `sys.stdout`:

```
def __init__(self, writer=sys.stdout):
    """Set up memory."""
    self.writer = writer
    self.initialize([])
```

We then replace every `print` statement with a call to new method called `write`. For example, the "print register" instruction calls `self.write`:

```
elif op == OPS["prr"]["code"]:
    self.assert_is_register(arg0)
    self.write(f"{self.reg[arg0]:06x}")
```

For now, `write` just prints things to whatever output stream the virtual machine (VM) was given:

---

[1] https://blog.tartanllama.xyz/
[2] https://blog.tartanllama.xyz/writing-a-linux-debugger-setup/

```
def write(self, *args):
    msg = "".join(args) + "\n"
    self.writer.write(msg)
```

Our virtual machine now loads a program and runs it to completion, so it's either running or finished. We want to add a third state for single-step execution, so let's start by adding an enumeration to `architecture.py`:

```
class VMState(Enum):
    """Virtual machine states."""
    FINISHED = 0
    STEPPING = 1
    RUNNING = 2
```

We could use strings to keep track of states, but as soon as there are more than two there are likely to be many, and having them spelled out makes it easier for the next person to find out what they can be.

We are now in a better position to move forward, so we derive a new class from our refactored VM:

```
class VirtualMachineStep(VirtualMachineBase):
```

(Again, if we were writing this code under normal circumstances, we would enhance the existing class, but since we want to keep several versions around for teaching, we derive and extend.)

The old `run` method kept going until the program finished. The new `run` method is necessarily more complicated. The VM is initially in the STEPPING state (because if we start it in the RUNNING state, we would never have an opportunity to interact with it to change its state). As long as the program isn't finished, we fetch, decode, and execute the next instruction as usual, but we stop after each one if we're single-stepping:

```
def run(self):
    self.state = VMState.STEPPING
    while True:
        if self.state == VMState.STEPPING:
            self.interact(self.ip)
        if self.state == VMState.FINISHED:
            break
        instruction = self.ram[self.ip]
        self.ip += 1
        op, arg0, arg1 = self.decode(instruction)
        self.execute(op, arg0, arg1)
```

The interaction method needs to handle several cases:

1. The user enters an empty line (i.e., presses return), in which case it loops around and waits for something else.

2. The user asks to **disassemble** the current instruction or show the contents of memory, in which case it does that and loops around.

3. The user wants to quit, so `interact` changes the VM's state to FINISHED.

4. The user wants to run the rest of the program without stopping, so `interact` changes VM's state to RUNNING.

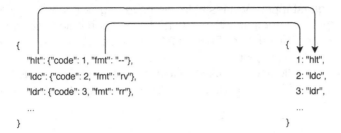

Figure 26.1: Building a consistent lookup table.

5. The user wants to execute a single step, in which case the method breaks out of the loop without changing the VM's state. `run` will then see that the VM is still in single-stepping mode and will execute a single instruction.

The method that disassembles an instruction to show us what we're about to do checks a **reverse lookup table** to create a printable representation of an instruction and its operands:

```
def disassemble(self, addr, instruction):
    op, arg0, arg1 = self.decode(instruction)
    assert op in OPS_LOOKUP, f"Unknown op code {op} at {addr}"
    return f"{OPS_LOOKUP[op]} | {arg0} | {arg1}"
```

We build the reverse lookup table from the OPS table in `architecture.py` so that it's always in sync with the table we're using to construct operations (Figure 26.1):

```
OPS_LOOKUP = {value["code"]: key for key, value in OPS.items()}
```

If we wrote the reverse lookup table ourselves, sooner or later we'd forget to update it when updating the forward lookup table.

But there's a more important change in this new virtual machine. It doesn't use Python's built-in `input` function to get input from the user—or rather, it does, but only by default. The constructor for our single-stepping VM is:

```
def __init__(self, reader=input, writer=sys.stdout):
    super().__init__(writer)
    self.reader = reader
```

and its `read` method is:

```
def read(self, prompt):
    return self.reader(prompt).strip()
```

As with the `write` method introduced in the previous section, adding this wrapper method will help us with testing, which is our next topic.

26.2 Testing

Our debugger is an interactive application that waits for input from the user, does something that may or may not print output, then waits again. The waiting is a problem for tools like pytest[3], which expect the function being tested to run to completion after being launched.

---

[3]https://docs.pytest.org/

To make our single-stepping VM testable, we have to give it input when it wants some and capture its output for later inspection. We had a similar problem when testing the web server of Chapter 21 and the editor of Chapter 24, and our solution is similar: we will replace `input` and `print` with mock objects.

As shown earlier, our VM uses an object with a `write` method to produce output. We can define a class which provides this method but saves messages in a list for later inspection instead of printing them:

```
class Writer:
    def __init__(self):
        self.seen = []

    def write(self, *args):
        self.seen.extend(args)
```

Similarly, our VM gets input from a function that takes a prompt as an argument and returns whatever the user typed. We can define a class with a `__call__` method which acts like such a function but which returns strings from a list instead of waiting for the user:

```
class Reader:
    def __init__(self, *args):
        self.commands = args
        self.index = 0

    def __call__(self, prompt):
        assert self.index < len(self.commands)
        self.index += 1
        return self.commands[self.index - 1]
```

With these in hand, we can write a helper function that compiles a program, creates a virtual machine, and runs it with a mock reader and a mock writer:

```
def execute(source, reader, writer):
    program = Assembler().assemble(source.split("\n"), False)
    vm = VM(reader, writer)
    vm.initialize(program)
    vm.run()
```

We can now write tests, like this one for the "disassemble" command:

```
def test_disassemble():
    source = """
hlt
"""
    reader = Reader("d", "q")
    writer = Writer()
    execute(source, reader, writer)
    assert writer.seen == ["hlt | 0 | 0\n"]
```

Line by line, it:

1. Creates the program to test (which in this case consists of a single `hlt` instruction).

2. Creates a `Reader` that will supply the commands `"d"` (for "disassemble") and `"q"` (for "quit") in that order.

3. Creates a `Writer` to capture the program's output.

4. Runs the program in a fresh VM with that reader and writer.

5. Checks that the output captured in the writer is correct.

Defining two classes and a helper function to test a one-line program may seem like a lot of work, but we're not testing the one-line program or the VM—we're testing the debugger. For example, the close below:

1. Defines a multiline string that loads 55 into R0, prints it, and then loads 65 into the same register to print before halting.

2. Creates a `Reader` that issues three "s" (single-step) commands and a "q" (quit) command. Note that this isn't enough to reach the second print command.

3. Executes the program.

4. Checks that the `Writer` has only recorded one line of output, not two.

```
def test_print_two_values():
    source = """
    ldc R0 55
    prr R0
    ldc R0 65
    prr R0
    hlt
    """
    reader = Reader("s", "s", "s", "q")
    writer = Writer()
    execute(source, reader, writer)
    assert writer.seen == [
        "000037\n"
    ]
```

This test actually uncovered a bug in an earlier version of the debugger in which it would always execute one more instruction when told to quit. Interactive testing might have spotted that, but it could easily reappear; this test will warn us if it does.

Our `Reader` and `Writer` aren't good for much beyond testing our VM, but there are other tools that can simulate input and output for a wider range of applications. Expect[4] (which can be used through Python's `pexpect`[5] module) is often used to script command-line applications as well as to test them. Selenium[6] and Cypress[7] do the same for browser-based applications: programmers can use them to simulate mouse clicks, window resizing, and other events, then check the contents of the page that the application produces in response. They are all more difficult to set up and use than a simple test that 1+1 is 2, but that's because the things they do are genuinely complex. Designing applications with testing in mind—for example, routing all input and output through a single method each—helps reduce that complexity.

26.3   Extensibility

We are going to add one more big feature to our debugger, but before we do, let's do some refactoring. First, we move every interactive operation into a method of its own that does

---

[4]https://en.wikipedia.org/wiki/Expect
[5]https://pexpect.readthedocs.io/
[6]https://www.selenium.dev/
[7]https://www.cypress.io/

something and then returns `True` if the debugger is supposed to stay in interactive mode
and `False` if interaction is over. The method for showing the contents of memory is:

```
def _do_memory(self, addr):
    self.show()
    return True
```

while the one for advancing one step is:

```
def _do_step(self, addr):
    self.state = VMState.STEPPING
    return False
```

and so on. Once that's done, we modify `interact` to choose operations from a lookup table
called `self.handlers`. Its keys are the commands typed by the user, and its values are the
operation methods we just created:

```
def interact(self, addr):
    prompt = "".join(sorted({key[0] for key in self.handlers}))
    interacting = True
    while interacting:
        try:
            command = self.read(f"{addr:06x} [{prompt}]> ")
            if not command:
                continue
            elif command not in self.handlers:
                self.write(f"Unknown command {command}")
            else:
                interacting = self.handlers[command](self.ip)
        except EOFError:
            self.state = VMState.FINISHED
            interacting = False
```

Finally, we extend the virtual machine's constructor to build the required lookup table.
For convenience, we register the methods under both single-letter keys and longer command names:

```
def __init__(self, reader=input, writer=sys.stdout):
    super().__init__(reader, writer)
    self.handlers = {
        "d": self._do_disassemble,
        "dis": self._do_disassemble,
        "i": self._do_ip,
        "ip": self._do_ip,
        "m": self._do_memory,
        "memory": self._do_memory,
        "q": self._do_quit,
        "quit": self._do_quit,
        "r": self._do_run,
        "run": self._do_run,
        "s": self._do_step,
        "step": self._do_step,
    }
```

As in previous chapters, creating a lookup table like this makes the class easier to
extend. If we want to add another command (which we will do in the next section) we just
add a method to perform the operation and register it in the lookup table. So long as new
commands don't need anything more than the address of the current instruction, we never
need to modify `interact` again.

26.4 Breakpoints

Suppose we suspect there's a bug in our program that only occurs after several thousand lines of code have been executed. We would have to be pretty desperate to single-step through all of that even once, much less dozens of times as we're exploring new ideas or trying new fixes. Instead, we want to set a **breakpoint** to tell the computer to stop at a particular location and drop us into the debugger. We might even use a **conditional breakpoint** that would only stop if, for example, the variable x was zero at that point, but we'll leave that for the exercises.

The easiest way to implement breakpoints would be to have the VM store their addresses in a set. We would then modify run to check that set each time it was supposed to fetch a new instruction, and stop if it was at one of those addresses (Figure 26.2).

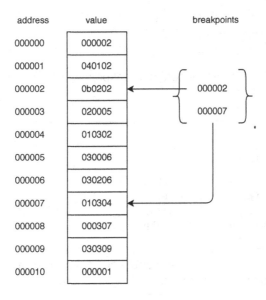

Figure 26.2: Storing breakpoints beside the program.

An alternative design is to add a new instruction to our architecture called brk. When the user sets a breakpoint at some address, we replace the instruction at that address with a breakpoint instruction and store the original instruction in a lookup table. If the user later **clears** the breakpoint, we copy the original instruction back into place, and if the VM encounters a breakpoint instruction while it is running, it drops into interactive mode (Figure 26.3).

Putting breakpoints inline is more complicated than storing them beside the program, but it is how debuggers for low-level languages like C actually work. It also makes the virtual machine more efficient: instead of spending a few (actual) instructions checking a breakpoint table every time we execute an instruction, we only pay a price when we actually encounter a breakpoint. The difference isn't important in our little toy, but little savings like this add up quickly in a real interpreter for a language like Python or JavaScript.

The first step in implementing breakpoints is to add two more commands to the lookup table we created in the previous section:

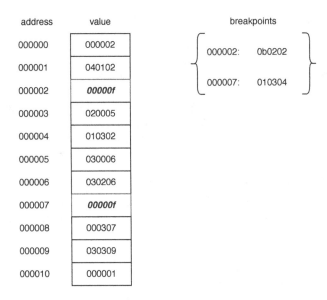

Figure 26.3: Inserting breakpoints into a program.

```
def __init__(self):
    super().__init__()
    self.breaks = {}
    self.handlers |= {
        "b": self._do_add_breakpoint,
        "break": self._do_add_breakpoint,
        "c": self._do_clear_breakpoint,
        "clear": self._do_clear_breakpoint,
    }
```

To add a breakpoint, we copy the instruction at the given address into the dictionary self.breaks and replace it with a breakpoint instruction:

```
def _do_add_breakpoint(self, addr):
    if self.ram[addr] == OPS["brk"]["code"]:
        return True
    self.breaks[addr] = self.ram[addr]
    self.ram[addr] = OPS["brk"]["code"]
    return True
```

Notice that if there's already a breakpoint in place, we don't do anything. We also return True to tell interact to wait for another command from the user.

Clearing a breakpoint is just as easy:

```
def _do_clear_breakpoint(self, addr):
    if self.ram[addr] != OPS["brk"]["code"]:
        return True
    self.ram[addr] = self.breaks[addr]
    del self.breaks[addr]
    return True
```

We also update show to display any breakpoints that have been set:

```
def show(self):
    super().show()
```

```
if self.breaks:
    self.write("-" * 6)
    for key, instruction in self.breaks.items():
        self.write(f"{key:06x}: {self.disassemble(key, instruction)}")
```

The implementation first calls the parent's show method to display what we've seen so far before adding more information. Extending methods by upcalling this way saves typing and ensures that changes in the parent class automatically show up in the child class.

The final step is to change run so that the VM actually stops at a breakpoint:

```
def run(self):
    self.state = VMState.STEPPING
    while self.state != VMState.FINISHED:
        instruction = self.ram[self.ip]
        op, arg0, arg1 = self.decode(instruction)

        if op == OPS["brk"]["code"]:
            original = self.breaks[self.ip]
            op, arg0, arg1 = self.decode(original)
            self.interact(self.ip)
            self.ip += 1
            self.execute(op, arg0, arg1)

        else:
            if self.state == VMState.STEPPING:
                self.interact(self.ip)
            self.ip += 1
            self.execute(op, arg0, arg1)
```

The logic here is relatively straightforward. If the instruction is a breakpoint, the VM uses the original instruction from the breakpoint lookup table, then gives the user a chance to interact before executing that original instruction. Otherwise, the VM interacts with the user if it is in single-stepping mode and then carries on as before.

We can test our new-and-improved VM using the tools developed earlier in this chapter, but even before we do that, the changes to run tell us that we should rethink some of our design. Using a lookup table for interactive commands allowed us to add commands without modifying interact; another lookup table would enable us to add new instructions without having to modify run. We will explore this in the exercises.

26.5   Summary

Figure 26.4 summarizes the key ideas in this chapter.

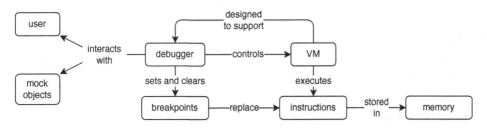

Figure 26.4: Concepts for debugger.

26.6   Exercises

Show Memory Range

Modify the debugger so that if the user provides a single address to the `"memory"` command, the debugger shows the value at that address. If the user provides two addresses, on the other hand, the debugger shows all the memory between those addresses.

1. How did this change the way command lookup and execution work?

2. Is your solution general enough to handle likely future changes without rewriting?

Breakpoint Addresses

Modify the debugger so that if the user provides a single address to the `"break"` or `"clear"` command, it sets or clears the breakpoint at that address. Did this feature require any changes beyond those made for the previous exercise?

Command Completion

Modify the debugger to recognize commands based on any number of distinct leading characters. For example, any of `"m"`, `"me"`, `"mem"`, and so on should trigger the `_do_memory` method. Programmers should *not* have to specify all these options themselves; instead, they should be able to specify the full command name and the method it corresponds to, and the VM's constructor should take care of the rest.

Conditional Breakpoints

Modify the debugger so that users can specify conditions for breakpoints, i.e., can specify that the VM should only stop at a location if R0 contains zero or if the value at a particular location in memory is greater than 3. (This exercise is potentially very large; you may restrict the kinds of conditions the user can set to make the problem more tractable, or explore ways of using `eval` to support the general case.)

Watchpoints

Modify the debugger and VM so that the user can create **watchpoints**, i.e., can specify that the debugger should halt the VM when the value at a particular address changes. For example, if the user specifies a watchpoint for address 0x0010, then the VM automatically halts whenever a new value is stored at that location.

Instruction Lookup

Modify the virtual machine so that `execute` looks up instructions in a table in the same way as debugger commands.

Changing Memory

Modify the debugger so that users can change the values in registers or at particular addresses in memory while the program is running.

Displaying Source

1. Modify the debugger so that when the debugger is displaying memory, it shows the assembly code instructions corresponding to particular addresses as well as the numeric codes.

2. How can the debugger distinguish between locations that contain instructions and locations that contain data?

Interleaving Testing

Modify the testing tools developed in this chapter so that users can specify input and output as they would naturally occur, i.e., can specify one or more commands, then the output expected from those commands, then some more input and the corresponding output, and so on.

Pattern Matching in Tests

1. Tools like Expect[8] allow programmers to match output with regular expressions. Modify the testing tools developed in this chapter to do that as well.

2. When is this useful? When is it potentially dangerous?

---

[8]https://en.wikipedia.org/wiki/Expect

27

Conclusion

Consider the bicycle: more specifically, the De Rosa SK Pininfarina (Figure 27.1). I think it's beautiful, but I wouldn't call it art, because being beautiful isn't its primary purpose. It was created to be useful; the fact that it can also be appreciated aesthetically is an intentional bonus.

Figure 27.1: De Rosa SK Pininfarina bicycle.

English doesn't have a word for things like this, but there are lots of other examples. Architecture and typography have deep roots, and starting in the early 20th century, people like Christopher Dresser[1], Jo Sinel[2], and Raymond Loewy[3] established industrial design around the idea that mass-produced artifacts were worthy of serious analysis from an aesthetic as well as a utilitarian point of view.

Now think about your favorite piece of software. We have long accepted that its interface can and should be critiqued in the same way as a power drill:

- Does it do what it's supposed to?

- Is it pleasurable to use?

---

[1] https://en.wikipedia.org/wiki/Christopher_Dresser
[2] https://en.wikipedia.org/wiki/Joseph_Claude_Sinel
[3] https://en.wikipedia.org/wiki/Raymond_Loewy

What's missing is the third leg of the industrial design tripod:

• Did its design facilitate its manufacture and maintenance?

At a deeper level, what's *really* missing is a shared vocabulary and a suite of canonical examples that would give us a basis for critiquing software in the way that we can a train or a sofa. We use words like "elegant" when referring to Unix's pipe-and-filter model, but when asked to explain, we run out of meaning long before any reasonably intelligent industrial designer runs out of things to say about the design of a toenail clipper. Will the materials hold up under constant use? Can it be assembled at a reasonable cost? Will people understand how to use it without having to wade through a manual? Will it please the eye when it's sitting on the counter? Training in industrial design gives weight to all of these separately and together, and gives students the tools they need to distinguish the good from the bad.

In retrospect, this is what [Oram2007; Brown2011; Brown2012] were groping toward. If we had decided 50 years ago to call programming "industrial design for software" rather than "software engineering", our conversations might be intellectually richer today. I hope this book will help us get there. I hope that some day we'll be able to talk to each other about the beauty of software because it *is* beautiful and we deserve to have ways to say that. Until then:

Start where you are.
Use what you have.
Help who you can.

A

Bibliography

[Aniche2022] Maurício Aniche. *Effective Software Testing: A developer's guide*. Manning, 2022. ISBN: 978-1633439931.

[Armstrong2013] Tavish Armstrong, ed. *The Performance of Open Source Applications*. Lulu, 2013. ISBN: 978-1304488787.

[Bentley1982] Jon Louis Bentley. *Writing Efficient Programs*. Prentice-Hall PTR, 1982. ISBN: 978-0139702440.

[Brand1995] Stewart Brand. *How Buildings Learn: What Happens After They're Built*. Penguin USA, 1995. ISBN: 978-0140139969.

[Brown2016] Amy Brown and Michael DiBernardo, eds. *500 Lines or Less: Experienced Programmers Solve Interesting Problems*. Lulu, 2016. ISBN: 978-1329871274.

[Brown2011] Amy Brown and Greg Wilson, eds. *The Architecture of Open Source Applications: Elegance, Evolution, and a Few Fearless Hacks*. Lulu, 2011. ISBN: 978-1257638017.

[Brown2012] Amy Brown and Greg Wilson, eds. *The Architecture of Open Source Applications: Structure, Scale, and a Few More Fearless Hacks*. Lulu, 2012. ISBN: 978-0201103427.

[Fowler2018] Martin Fowler. *Refactoring: Improving the Design of Existing Code*. Addison-Wesley Professional, 2018. ISBN: 978-0134757599.

[Fucci2016] Davide Fucci, Giuseppe Scanniello, Simone Romano, Martin Shepperd, Boyce Sigweni, Fernando Uyaguari, Burak Turhan, Natalia Juristo, and Markku Oivo. "An external replication on the effects of test-driven development using a multi-site blind analysis approach". In: *Proc. ESEM'16*. ACM, Sept. 2016. DOI: 10.1145/2961111.2962592. URL: https://doi.org/10.1145/2961111.2962592.

[Gamma1994] Erich Gamma, Richard Helm, Ralph Johnson, and John Vlissides. *Design Patterns: Elements of Reusable Object-Oriented Software*. Addison-Wesley Professional, 1994. ISBN: 978-0201633610.

[Goldberg1991] David Goldberg. "What every computer scientist should know about floating-point arithmetic". In: *ACM Computing Surveys* 23.1 (Mar. 1991). DOI: 10.1145/103162.103163.

[Hermans2021] Felienne Hermans. *The Programmer's Brain: What Every Programmer Needs to Know About Cognition*. Manning, 2021. ISBN: 9781617298677.

[Kamin1990] Samuel N. Kamin. *Programming Languages: An Interpreter-Based Approach*. Addison-Wesley, 1990. ISBN: 978-0201068245.

[Kerievsky2004] Joshua Kerievsky. *Refactoring to Patterns*. Addison-Wesley Professional, 2004. ISBN: 978-0321213358.

[Kernighan1983] Brian W. Kernighan and Rob Pike. *The Unix Programming Environment*. Prentice-Hall, 1983. ISBN: 978-0139376818.

[Kernighan1979] Brian W. Kernighan and P. J. Plauger. *The Elements of Programming Style.* McGraw-Hill, 1979. ISBN: 978-0070342071.

[Kernighan1981] Brian W. Kernighan and P. J. Plauger. *Software Tools in Pascal.* Addison-Wesley Professional, 1981. ISBN: 978-0201103427.

[Kernighan1988] Brian W. Kernighan and Dennis M. Ritchie. *The C Programming Language.* Prentice-Hall, 1988. ISBN: 978-0131103627.

[Kohavi2020] Ron Kohavi, Diane Tang, and Ya Xu. *Trustworthy Online Controlled Experiments: A Practical Guide to A/B Testing.* Cambridge University Press, 2020. ISBN: 978-1108724265.

[Meszaros2007] Gerard Meszaros. *xUnit Test Patterns: Refactoring Test Code.* Addison-Wesley, 2007. ISBN: 978-0131495050.

[Nystrom2021] Robert Nystrom. *Crafting Interpreters.* Genever Benning, 2021. ISBN: 978-0990582939.

[Oram2007] Andy Oram and Greg Wilson, eds. *Beautiful Code: Leading Programmers Explain How They Think.* O'Reilly, 2007. ISBN: 978-0596510046.

[Patterson2017] David A. Patterson and John L. Hennessy. *Computer Organization and Design: The Hardware/Software Interface.* Morgan Kaufmann, 2017. ISBN: 978-0128122754.

[Petre2016] Marian Petre and André van der Hoek. *Software Design Decoded: 66 Ways Experts Think.* MIT Press, 2016. ISBN: 978-0262035187.

[Schon1984] Donald A. Schon. *The Reflective Practitioner: How Professionals Think in Action.* Basic Books, 1984. ISBN: 978-0465068784.

[Tichy2010] Walter Tichy. "The Evidence for Design Patterns". In: *Making Software: What Really Works, and Why We Believe It.* Ed. by Andy Oram and Greg Wilson. 2010. ISBN: 978-0596808327.

[Wilson2019] Greg Wilson. *Teaching Tech Together.* Chapman & Hall/CRC Press, 2019. ISBN: 978-0367352974.

[Wilson2022a] Greg Wilson. *Software Design by Example: A Tool-Based Introduction with JavaScript.* CRC Press/Taylor & Francis, 2022. ISBN: 978-1032399676.

[Wilson2022b] Greg Wilson. "Twelve quick tips for software design". In: *PLOS Computational Biology* 18.2 (Feb. 2022). DOI: `10.1371/journal.pcbi.1009809`.

[Wirth1976] Niklaus Wirth. *Algorithms + Data Structures = Programs.* Prentice-Hall, 1976. ISBN: 978-0-13-022418-7.

[Zeller2023] Andreas Zeller, Rahul Gopinath, Marcel Böhme, Gordon Fraser, and Christian Holler. *The Fuzzing Book.* Viewed 2023-01-07. CISPA Helmholtz Center for Information Security, 2023. URL: `https://www.fuzzingbook.org/`.

B

Bonus Material

Each chapter in this book is designed to be teachable in one classroom hour. This appendix presents material that extends core ideas but would break that **attention budget**.

B.1   Using Function Attributes

This material extends Chapter 6.

Since functions are objects, they can have attributes. The function `dir` (short for "directory") returns a list of their names:

```
def example():
    "Docstring for example."
    print("in example")

print(dir(example))
```

```
['__annotations__', '__builtins__', '__call__', '__class__', \
 '__closure__', '__code__', '__defaults__', '__delattr__', \
 '__dict__', '__dir__', '__doc__', '__eq__', '__format__', '__ge__', \
 '__get__', '__getattribute__', '__getstate__', '__globals__', \
 '__gt__', '__hash__', '__init__', '__init_subclass__', \
 '__kwdefaults__', '__le__', '__lt__', '__module__', '__name__', \
 '__ne__', '__new__', '__qualname__', '__reduce__', '__reduce_ex__', \
 '__repr__', '__setattr__', '__sizeof__', '__str__', \
 '__subclasshook__']
```

Most programmers never need to use most of these, but `__name__` holds the function's original name and `__doc__` holds its docstring:

```
print("docstring:", example.__doc__)
print("name:", example.__name__)
```

```
docstring: Docstring for example.
name: example
```

We can modify the test runner of Chapter 6 to use the function's `__name__` attribute in reports instead of the key in the `globals` dictionary:

```
def run_tests(prefix):
    for (name, func) in globals().items():
        if name.startswith(prefix):
            try:
                func()
                print(func.__name__, "passed")
            except AssertionError:
                print(func.__name__, "failed")
            except Exception:
```

```
                    print(func.__name__, "had error")

run_tests("test_")
```

```
test_sign_negative passed
test_sign_positive passed
test_sign_zero failed
test_sign_error had error
```

More usefully, we can say that if a test function's docstring contains the string "test:skip" then we should skip the test, while "test:fail" means we expect this test to fail. Let's rewrite our tests to show this off:

```
TEST_FAIL = "test:fail"
TEST_SKIP = "test:skip"

def test_sign_negative():
    "test:skip"
    assert sign(-3) == -1

def test_sign_positive():
    assert sign(19) == 1

def test_sign_zero():
    "test:fail"
    assert sign(0) == 0

def test_sign_error():
    """Expect an error."""                                    •
    assert sgn(1) == 1
```

and then modify `run_tests` to look for these strings and act accordingly:

```
def run_tests(prefix):
    all_names = [n for n in globals() if n.startswith(prefix)]
    for name in all_names:
        func = globals()[name]
        try:
            if func.__doc__ and TEST_SKIP in func.__doc__:
                print(f"skip: {name}")
            else:
                func()
                print(f"pass: {name}")
        except AssertionError as e:
            if TEST_FAIL in func.__doc__:
                print(f"pass (expected failure): {name}")
            else:
                print(f"fail: {name} {str(e)}")
        except Exception as e:
            doc = f"/{func.__doc__}" if func.__doc__ else ""
            print(f"error: {name}{doc} {str(e)}")

run_tests("test_")
```

The output is now:

```
skip: test_sign_negative
pass: test_sign_positive
pass (expected failure): test_sign_zero
error: test_sign_error/Expect an error. name 'sgn' is not defined
```

Instead of (ab)using docstrings like this, we can instead add our own attributes to functions. Let's say that if a function has an attribute called `skip` with the value `True` then the function is to be skipped, while if it has an attribute called `fail` whose value is `True` then the test is expected to fail. Our tests become:

```
def test_sign_negative():
    assert sign(-3) == -1
test_sign_negative.skip = True

def test_sign_positive():
    assert sign(19) == 1

def test_sign_zero():
    assert sign(0) == 0
test_sign_zero.fail = True

def test_sign_error():
    assert sgn(1) == 1
```

We can write a helper function called `classify` to classify tests. Note that it uses `hasattr` to check if an attribute is present before trying to get its value:

```
def classify(func):
    if hasattr(func, "skip") and func.skip:
        return "skip"
    if hasattr(func, "fail") and func.fail:
        return "fail"
    return "run"
```

Finally, our test runner becomes:

```
def run_tests(prefix):
    all_names = [n for n in globals() if n.startswith(prefix)]
    for name in all_names:
        func = globals()[name]
        kind = classify(func)
        try:
            if kind == "skip":
                print(f"skip: {name}")
            else:
                func()
                print(f"pass: {name}")
        except AssertionError as e:
            if kind == "fail":
                print(f"pass (expected failure): {name}")
            else:
                print(f"fail: {name} {str(e)}")
        except Exception as e:
            print(f"error: {name} {str(e)}")

run_tests("test_")
```

B.2   Lazy Evaluation

This material extends Chapter 7.

One way to evaluate a design is to ask how extensible it is. The answer for our interpreter is now, "Pretty easily." For example, we can add a `comment` "operation" that does nothing and returns `None` simply by writing `do_comment` function:

```
def do_comment(env, args):
    """Ignore instructions.
    ["comment" "text"] => None
    """
    return None
```

An `if` statement is a bit more complex. If its first argument is true, it evaluates and returns its second argument (the "if" branch). Otherwise, it evaluates and returns its second argument (the "else" branch):

```
def do_if(env, args):
    """Make a choice: only one sub-expression is evaluated.
    ["if" C A B] => A if C else B
    """
    assert len(args) == 3
    cond = do(env, args[0])
    choice = args[1] if cond else args[2]
    return do(env, choice)
```

As we said in Chapter 8, this is called lazy evaluation to distinguish it from the more usual eager evaluation that evaluates everything up front. `do_if` only evaluates what it absolutely needs to; most languages do this so that we can safely write things like:

```
if x != 0:
    return 1/x
else:
    return None
```

If the language always evaluated both branches, then the code shown above would fail whenever x was zero, even though it's supposed to handle that case. In this case it might seem obvious what the language should do, but most languages use lazy evaluation for `and` and `or` as well so that expressions like:

```
thing and thing.part
```

will produce `None` if `thing` is `None` and `reference.part` if it isn't.

B.3   Extension

This material extends Chapter 13.

It's easy to check a single style rule by extending `NodeVisitor`, but what if we want to check dozens of rules? Traversing the AST dozens of times would be inefficient. And what if we want people to be able to add their own rules? Inheritance is the wrong tool for this: if several people each create their own `NodeVisitor` with a `visit_Name` method, we'd have

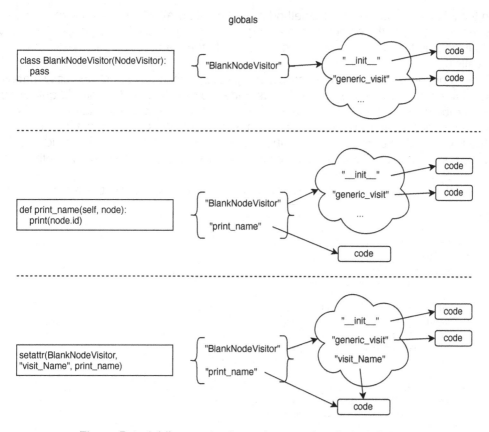

Figure B.1: Adding methods to classes after their definition.

to inherit from all those classes and then have the new class's `visit_Name` call up to all of its parents' equivalent methods.

One way around this is to **inject** methods into classes after they have been defined. The code fragment below creates a new class called `BlankNodeVisitor` that doesn't add anything to `NodeVisitor`, then uses `setattr` to add a method to it after it has been defined (Figure B.1):

```
class BlankNodeVisitor(ast.NodeVisitor):
    pass

def print_name(self, node):
    print(node.id)

setattr(BlankNodeVisitor, "visit_Name", print_name)
```

This trick works because classes and objects are just specialized dictionaries (for some large value of "just"). If we create an object of `BlankNodeVisitor` and call its `visit` method:

```
with open(sys.argv[1], "r") as reader:
    source = reader.read()
tree = ast.parse(source)
finder = BlankNodeVisitor()
finder.visit(tree)
```

then the inherited `generic_visit` method does what it always does. When it encounters a `Name` node, it looks in the object for something called `visit_Name`. Since it doesn't find anything, it looks in the object's class for something with that name, finds our injected method, and calls it.

With a bit more work, we could have our injected method save and then call whatever `visit_Name` method was there when it was added to the class, but we would quickly run into a problem. As we've seen in earlier examples, the methods that handle nodes are responsible for deciding whether and when to recurse into those nodes' children. If we pile method on top of one another, then either each one is going to trigger recursion (so we recurse many times) or there will have to be some way for each one to signal whether it did that so that other methods don't.

To avoid this complication, most systems use a different approach. Consider this class:

```python
Handler = namedtuple("Handler", ["func", "data"])

class RegisterNodeVisitor(ast.NodeVisitor):
    def __init__(self):
        super().__init__()
        self.handlers = {}

    def add_handler(self, nodeType, func, data=None):
        handler = Handler(func, data)
        if nodeType not in self.handlers:
            self.handlers[nodeType] = []
        self.handlers[nodeType].append(handler)

    def visit_Name(self, node):
        for handler in self.handlers.get(ast.Name, []):
            handler.func(node, handler.data)
```

The `add_handler` method takes three parameters: the type of node a callback function is meant to handle, the function itself, and an optional extra piece of data to pass to the function along with an AST node. It saves the handler function and the data in a lookup table indexed by the type of node the function is meant to handle. Each of the methods inherited from `NodeVisitor` then looks up handlers for its node type and runs them.

So what do handlers look like? Each one is a function that takes a node and some data as input and does whatever it's supposed to do:

```python
def count_names(node, counter):
    counter[node.id] += 1
```

Setting up the visitor is a bit more complicated, since we have to create and register the handler:

```python
with open(sys.argv[1], "r") as reader:
    source = reader.read()
tree = ast.parse(source)

finder = RegisterNodeVisitor()
counter = Counter()
finder.add_handler(ast.Name, count_names, counter)

finder.visit(tree)
print(counter)
```

However, we can now register as many handlers as we want for each kind of node.

B.4   Tracing Inheritance

This material extends Chapter 13.

In order to keep track of the code we wrote for this book, we built a tool that reports which methods are defined or redefined in which classes. To show how it works, this file that defines four classes, each of which defines or redefines some methods:

```
class Parent:
    def red(self):
        pass

    def green(self):
        pass


class LeftChild(Parent):
    def green(self):
        pass

    def blue(self):
        pass


class RightChild(Parent):
    def red(self):
        pass

    def blue(self):
        pass


class GrandChild(LeftChild):
    def red(self):
        pass

    def blue(self):
        pass

    def orange(self):
        pass
```

As in Chapter 13, our class's constructor creates a stack to keep track of where we are. It also creates a couple of dictionaries to keep track of how classes inherit from each other and the methods each class defines:

```
class FindClassesAndMethods(ast.NodeVisitor):
    def __init__(self):
        super().__init__()
        self.stack = []
        self.parents = {}
        self.methods = {}
```

When we encounter a new class definition, we push its name on the stack, record its parents, and create an empty set to hold its methods:

```
def visit_ClassDef(self, node):
    class_name = node.name
```

```
assert class_name not in self.methods
self.stack.append(class_name)
self.methods[class_name] = set()
self.parents[class_name] = {p.id for p in node.bases}
self.generic_visit(node)
self.stack.pop()
```

When we encounter a function definition, the first thing we do is check the stack. If it's empty, we're looking at a top-level function rather than a method, so there's nothing for us to do. (We actually should recurse through the function's children, since it's possible to define classes inside functions, but we'll leave as an exercise.) If this function definition is inside a class, on the other hand, we add its name to our records:

```
def visit_FunctionDef(self, node):
    if not self.stack:
        return
    class_name = self.stack[-1]
    assert class_name in self.methods
    method_name = node.name
    assert method_name not in self.methods[class_name]
    self.methods[class_name].add(method_name)
```

Once we're done searching the AST, we print out a table of the classes and methods we've seen (Table B.1). We could make this display easier to read—for example, we could sort the classes from parent to child and display methods in the order they were first defined—but none of that requires us to inspect the AST.

	GrandChild	LeftChild	Parent	RightChild
blue	X	X		X
green		X	X	
orange	X			
red	X		X	X

Table B.1: Inheritance and methods.

B.5   Inspecting Functions

This material extends Chapter 15.

The implementation of dataframe filtering in Chapter 15 was somewhat brittle. A better implementation of filtering would make use of the fact that Python's `inspect`[1] module lets us examine objects in memory. In particular, `inspect.signature` can tell us what parameters a function takes:

```
import inspect

def example(first, second):
    pass

sig = inspect.signature(example)
```

---

[1] https://docs.python.org/3/library/inspect.html

```
print("signature:", sig)
print("type:", type(sig))
print("names:", sig.parameters)
print("parameters:", list(sig.parameters.keys()))
```

```
signature: (first, second)
type: <class 'inspect.Signature'>
names: OrderedDict([('first', <Parameter "first">), ('second', \
<Parameter "second">)])
parameters: ['first', 'second']
```

If, for example, the user wants to compare the red and blue columns of a dataframe, they can give us a function that has two parameters called red and blue. We can then use those parameter names to figure out which columns we need from the dataframe.

B.6   User-Defined Classes

This material extends Chapter 16.

The persistence framework of Chapter 16 only handles built-in data types, but can easily be extended to handle user-defined classes as well. To start, we refactor the code so that the save method doesn't get any larger:

```
class SaveExtend(SaveAlias):
    def __init__(self, writer):
        super().__init__(writer)

    def save(self, thing):
        if self._aliased(thing):
            return
        if self._builtin(thing):
            return
        assert False, f"Don't know how to handle {thing}"
```

The method to handle built-in types is:

```
def _builtin(self, thing):
    typename = type(thing).__name__
    method = f"_{typename}"
    if not hasattr(self, method):
        return False
    self.seen.add(id(thing))
    getattr(self, method)(thing)
    return True
```

and the one that handles aliases is:

```
def _aliased(self, thing):
    thing_id = id(thing)
    if thing_id not in self.seen:
        return False
    self._write("alias", thing_id, "")
    return True
```

None of this code is new: we've just moved things into methods to make each piece easier to understand.

So how does a class indicate that it can be saved and loaded by our framework? Our options are:

1. Require it to inherit from a base class that we provide so that we can use `isinstance` to check if an object is persistable. This approach is used in strictly-typed languages like Java, but method #2 below is considered more **Pythonic**.

2. Require it to implement a method with a specific name and signature without deriving from a particular base class. This approach is called **duck typing**: if it walks like a duck and quacks like a duck, it's a duck. Since option #1 would require users to write this method anyway, it's the one we'll choose.

3. Require users to register a **helper class** that knows how to save and load objects of the class we're interested in. This approach is also commonly used in strictly-typed languages as a way of adding persistence after the fact without disrupting the class hierarchy.

To implement option #2, we specify that if a class has a method called `to_dict`, we will call that to get the object's contents as a dictionary and then persist that dictionary. Before doing that, though, we will save a line indicating that this dictionary should be used to reconstruct an object of a particular class:

```
def _extension(self, thing):
    if not hasattr(thing, "to_dict"):
        return False
    self._write("@extension", id(thing), thing.__class__.__name__)
    self.save(thing.to_dict())
    return True
```

Loading user-defined classes requires more work because we have to map class names back to actual classes. (We could also use introspection to find *all* the classes in the program and build a lookup table of the ones with the right method.) We start by modifying the loader's constructor to take zero or more extension classes as arguments and then build a name-to-class lookup table from them:

```
class LoadExtend(LoadAlias):
    def __init__(self, reader, *extensions):
        super().__init__(reader)
        self.seen = {}
        self.extensions = {e.__name__: e for e in extensions}
```

The `load` method then looks for aliases, built-in types, and extensions in that order. Instead of using a chain of `if` statements we loop over the methods that handle these cases. If a method decides that it can handle the incoming data it returns a result; if it can't, it raises a `KeyError` exception, and if none of the methods handle a case we fail:

```
def load(self):
    key, ident, value = self._next()
    for method in (self._aliased, self._builtin, self._extension):
        try:
            return method(key, ident, value)
        except KeyError:
            pass
    assert False, f"Don't know how to handle {key} {ident} {value}"
```

The code to handle built-ins and aliases is copied from our previous work and modified to raise `KeyError`:

```
def _aliased(self, key, ident, value):
    if key != "alias":
        raise KeyError()
    assert ident in self.seen
    return self.seen[ident]

def _builtin(self, key, ident, value):
    method = f"_{key}"
    if not hasattr(self, method):
        raise KeyError()
    return getattr(self, method)(ident, value)
```

The method that handles extensions checks that the value on the line just read indicates an extension, then reads the dictionary containing the object's contents from the input stream and uses it to build an instance of the right class:

```
def _extension(self, key, ident, value):
    if (key != "@extension") or (value not in self.extensions):
        raise KeyError()
    cls = self.extensions[value]
    contents = self.load()
    return cls(**contents)
```

Here's a class that defines the required method:

```
class Parent:
    def __init__(self, name):
        self.name = name

    def to_dict(self):
        return {"name": self.name}
```

and here's a test to make sure everything works:

```
def test_extend_extension_class():
    fixture = Parent("subject")
    writer = StringIO()
    Save(writer).save(fixture)
    reader = StringIO(writer.getvalue())
    result = Load(reader, Parent).load()
    assert isinstance(result, Parent)
    assert result.name == fixture.name
```

What's in a Name?

The first version of these classes used the word "extension" rather than "@extension". That led to the most confusing bug in this whole chapter. When load reads a line, it runs self._builtin before running self._extension. If the first word on the line is "extension" (without the @) then self._builtin constructs the method name _extension, finds that method, and calls it as if we were loading an object of a built-in type: which we're not. Using @extension as the leading indicator leads to self._builtin checking for "_@extension" in the loader's attributes, which doesn't exist, so everything goes as it should.

B.7   Floating Point Numbers

This material extends Chapter 17.

The rules for storing floating point numbers make those for Unicode look simple. The root of the problem is that we cannot represent an infinite number of real values with a finite set of bit patterns. And no matter what values we represent, there will be an infinite number of values between each of them that we can't. The explanation that follows is simplified to keep it manageable; please read [Goldberg1991] for more detail.

Floating point numbers are represented by a sign, a **mantissa**, and an **exponent**. In a 32-bit word the IEEE 754 standard calls for 1 bit of sign, 23 bits for the mantissa, and 8 bits for the exponent. We will illustrate how it works using a much smaller representation: no sign, 3 bits for the mantissa, and 2 for the exponent. Figure B.2 shows the values this scheme can represent.

magnitude

	000	001	010	011	100	101	110	111
00	1	1	1	1	1	1	1	1
01	0	1	2	3	4	5	6	7
10	0	1	4	9	16	25	36	49
11	0	1	8	27	64	125	216	343

(exponent)

Figure B.2: Representing floating point numbers.

The IEEE standard avoids the redundancy in this representation by shifting things around. Even with that, though, formats like this can't represent a lot of values: for example, ours can store 8 and 10 but not 9. This is exactly like the problem hand calculators have with fractions like 1/3: in decimal, we have to round that to 0.3333 or 0.3334.

But if this scheme has no representation for 9 then $8 + 1$ must be stored as either 8 or 10. What should $8 + 1 + 1$ be? If we add from the left, $(8 + 1) + 1$ is $8 + 1$ is 8, but if we add from the right, $8 + (1 + 1)$ is $8 + 2$ is 10. Changing the order of operations makes the difference between right and wrong.

The authors of numerical libraries spend a lot of time worrying about things like this. In this case sorting the values and adding them from smallest to largest gives the best chance of getting the best possible answer. In other situations, like inverting a matrix, the rules are much more complicated.

Another observation about our number line is that while the values are unevenly spaced, the *relative* spacing between each set of values stays the same: the first group is separated by 1, then the separation becomes 2, then 4, and so on. This observation leads to a couple of useful definitions:

• The **absolute error** in an approximation is the absolute value of the difference between the approximation and the actual value.

• The **relative error** is the ratio of the absolute error to the absolute value we're approximating.

For example, being off by 1 in approximating 8+1 and 56+1 is the same absolute error, but the relative error is larger in the first case than in the second. Relative error is almost always more useful than absolute: it makes little sense to say that we're off by a hundredth when the value in question is a billionth.

One implication of this is that we should never compare floating point numbers with == or != because two numbers calculated in different ways will probably not have exactly the same bits. It's safe to use <, >=, and other orderings, though, since they don't depend on being the same down to the last bit.

If we do want to compare floating point numbers we can use something like the approx class[2] from pytest[3] which checks whether two numbers are within some tolerance of each other. A completely different approach is to use something like the fractions[4] module, which (as its name suggests) uses numerators and denominators to avoid some precision issues. This post[5] describes one clever use of the module.

B.8   Big and Little Endian

This material extends Chapter 17.

Suppose we want to store a 32-bit integer in memory. As Figure B.3 shows, we can order its four bytes in two different ways. **Little-endian** order stores the least significant bits of integer at the first (lowest) address in memory, while **big-endian** order stores the most significant bits first.

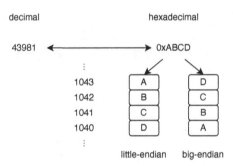

Figure B.3: Big-endian and little-endian byte order.

Modern Intel processors use little-endian order, but as this article[6] explains, some other processors (and most network protocols) use big-endian order. There are pros and cons to both, which we won't go into here. What you *do* need to know is that if you move data from one architecture to another, it's your responsibility to flip the bytes around, because the machine doesn't know what the bytes mean. This is such a pain that the struct[7] module

[2]https://docs.pytest.org/en/4.6.x/reference.html#pytest-approx
[3]https://docs.pytest.org/
[4]https://docs.python.org/3/library/fractions.html
[5]https://www.textualize.io/blog/7-things-ive-learned-building-a-modern-tui-framework/
[6]https://en.wikipedia.org/wiki/Endianness

and other libraries like it will do things for you if you ask it to. If you're using `struct`, the first character of a format string optionally indicates the byte order (Table B.2).

Character	Byte order	Size	Alignment
@	native	native	native
=	native	standard	none
<	little	endian	standard none
>	big	endian	standard none
!	network	standard	none

Table B.2: `struct` package endian indicators.

B.9   Generating Test Cases

This material extends Chapter 20.

Theorem provers like Z3 and PicoSAT[8] are far more powerful than most programmers realize. Borrowing an example from Andreas Zeller[9], we can use theorem provers to generate test cases. Suppose we have a function that classifies triangles as equilateral, scalene, or isosceles. We can set up some integer variables:

```
A = Int("A")
B = Int("B")
C = Int("C")
lengths = (A > 0, B > 0, C > 0)
```

and then ask it to create an equilateral triangle based solely on the definition:

```
equilateral = And(A == B, B == C, C == A)
solver = Solver()
solver.add(lengths)
solver.add(equilateral)
print("equilateral", solver.check(), solver.model())
```

```
equilateral sat [C = 1, B = 1, A = 1]
```

The same technique can generate a test case for scalene triangles:

```
scalene = And(A != B, B != C, C != A)
solver = Solver()
solver.add(lengths)
solver.add(scalene)
print("scalene", solver.check(), solver.model())
```

```
scalene sat [C = 3, A = 1, B = 2]
```

---

[7]https://docs.python.org/3/library/struct.html
[8]http://fmv.jku.at/picosat/
[9]https://andreas-zeller.info/

and isosceles triangles:

```
isosceles = Or(
    And(A == B, C != A),
    And(A == B, B != C),
    And(A != B, B == C)
)
solver = Solver()
solver.add(lengths)
solver.add(isosceles)
print("isosceles", solver.check(), solver.model())
```

```
isosceles sat [C = 2, A = 1, B = 2]
```

C

Syllabus

Introduction

- The complexity of a system increases more rapidly than its size.

- The best way to learn design is to study examples, and the best programs to use as examples are the ones programmers use every day.

- These lessons assume readers can write small programs and want to write larger ones, or are looking for material to use in software design classes that they teach.

- All of the content is free to read and re-use under open licenses, and all royalties from sales of this book will go to charity.

Objects and Classes

- Objects are useful without classes, but classes make them easier to understand.

- A well-designed class defines a contract that code using its instances can rely on.

- Objects that respect the same contract are polymorphic, i.e., they can be used interchangeably even if they do different specific things.

- Objects and classes can be thought of as dictionaries with stereotyped behavior.

- Most languages allow functions and methods to take a variable number of arguments.

- Inheritance can be implemented in several ways that differ in the order in which objects and classes are searched for methods.

Finding Duplicate Files

- A hash function creates a fixed-size value from an arbitrary sequence of bytes.

- Use big-oh notation to estimate the running time of algorithms.

- The output of a hash function is deterministic but not easy to predict.

- A good hash function's output is evenly distributed.

- A large cryptographic hash can be used to uniquely identify a file's contents.

Matching Patterns

- Use globs and regular expressions to match patterns in text.

- Use inheritance to make matchers composable and extensible.

- Simplify code by having objects delegate work to other objects.

- Use the Null Object pattern to eliminate special cases in code.

- Use standard refactorings to move code from one working state to another.

- Build and check the parts of your code you are least sure of first to find out if your design will work.

Parsing Text

- Parsing transforms text that's easy for people to read into objects that are easy for computers to work with.

- A grammar defines the textual patterns that a parser recognizes.

- Most parsers tokenize input text and then analyze the tokens.

- Most parsers need to implement some form of precedence to prioritize different patterns.

- Operations like addition and function call work just like user-defined functions.

- Programs can overload built-in operators by defining specially-named methods that are recognized by the compiler or interpreter.

Running Tests

- Functions are objects you can save in data structures or pass to other functions.

- Python stores local and global variables in dictionary-like structures.

- A unit test performs an operation on a fixture and passes, fails, or produces an error.

- A program can use introspection to find functions and other objects at runtime.

An Interpreter

- Compilers and interpreters are just programs.

- Basic arithmetic operations are just functions that have special notation.

- Programs can be represented as trees, which can be stored as nested lists.

- Interpreters recursively dispatch operations to functions that implement low-level steps.

- Programs store variables in stacked dictionaries called environments.

- One way to evaluate a program's design is to ask how extensible it is.

Functions and Closures

- When we define a function, our programming system saves instructions for later use.

- Since functions are just data, we can separate creation from naming.

- Most programming languages use eager evaluation, in which arguments are evaluated before a function is called.

- Programming languages can also use lazy evaluation, in which expressions are passed to functions for just-in-time evaluation.

- Every call to a function creates a new stack frame on the call stack.

- When a function looks up variables it checks its own stack frame and the global frame.

- A closure stores the variables referenced in a particular scope.

Protocols

- Temporarily replacing functions with mock objects can simplify testing.

- Mock objects can record their calls and/or return variable results.

- Python defines protocols so that code can be triggered by keywords in the language.

- Use the context manager protocol to ensure cleanup operations always execute.

- Use decorators to wrap functions after defining them.

- Use closures to create decorators that take extra parameters.

- Use the iterator protocol to make objects work with for loops.

A File Archiver

- Version control tools use hashing to uniquely identify each saved file.

- Each snapshot of a set of files is recorded in a manifest.

- Using a mock filesystem for testing is safer and faster than using the real thing.

- Operations involving multiple files may suffer from race conditions.

- Use a base class to specify what a component must be able to do and derive child classes to implement those operations.

An HTML Validator

- HTML consists of text and of elements represented by tags with attributes.

- HTML is represented in memory as a Document Object Model (DOM) tree.

- Trees are usually processed using recursion.

- The Visitor design pattern is often used to perform an action for each member of a data structure.

- We can summarize and check the structure of an HTML page by visiting each node and recording what we find there.

A Template Expander

- Static site generators create HTML pages from templates, directives, and data.

- A static site generator has the same core features as a programming language.

- Special-purpose mini-languages quickly become as complex as other languages.

- Static methods are a convenient way to group functions together.

A Code Linter

- A linter checks that a program conforms to a set of style and usage rules.

- Linters typically use the Visitor design pattern to find nodes of interest in an abstract syntax tree.

- Programs can modify a program's AST and then unparse it to create modified versions of the original program.

- Dynamic code modification is very powerful, but the technique can produce insecure and unmaintainable code.

Page Layout

- A layout engine places page elements based on their size and organization.

- Page elements are organized as a tree of basic blocks, rows, and columns.

- The layout engine calculates the position of each block based on its size and the position of its parent.

- Drawing blocks on top of each other is an easy way to render them.

- Use multiple inheritance and mixin classes to inject methods into classes.

Performance Profiling

- Create abstract classes to specify interfaces.

- Store two-dimensional data as rows or as columns.

- Use reflection to match data to function parameters.

- Measure performance to evaluate engineering tradeoffs.

Object Persistence

- A persistence framework saves and restores objects.

- Persistence must handle aliasing and circularity.

- Users should be able to extend persistence to handle objects of their own types.

- Software designs should be open for extension but closed for modification.

Binary Data

- Programs usually store integers using two's complement rather than sign and magnitude.

- Characters are usually encoded as bytes using either ASCII, UTF-8, or UTF-32.

- Programs can use bitwise operators to manipulate the bits representing data directly.

- Low-level compiled languages usually store raw values, while high-level interpreted languages use boxed values.

- Sets of values can be packed into contiguous byte arrays for efficient transmission and storage.

A Database

- Database stores records so that they can be accessed by key.

- Log-structured database appends new records to database and invalidates older versions of records.

- Classes are data structures that can be saved like any other data.

- The filesystem saves data in fixed-size pages.

- We can improve the efficiency of a database by saving records in blocks.

A Build Manager

- Build managers track dependencies between files and update files that are stale.

- Every build rule has a target, some dependencies, and a recipe for updating the target.

- Build rules form a directed graph which must not contain cycles.

- Pattern rules describe the dependencies and recipes for sets of similar files.

- Pattern rules can use automatic variables to specify targets and dependencies in recipes.

A Package Manager

- Software packages often have multiple versions, which are usually identified by multi-part semantic version numbers.

- A package manager must find a mutually-compatible set of dependencies in order to install a package.

- Finding a compatible set of packages is equivalent to searching a multi-dimensional space.

- The work required to find a compatible set of packages can grow exponentially with the number of packages.

- Eliminating partially-formed combinations of packages can reduce the work required to find a compatible set.

- An automated theorem prover can determine if a set of logical propositions can be made consistent with each other.

- Most package managers use some kind of theorem prover to find compatible sets of packages to install.

Transferring Files

- Every computer on a network has a unique IP address.

- The Domain Name System (DNS) translates human-readable names into IP addresses.

- Programs send and receive messages through numbered sockets.

- The program that receives a message is responsible for interpreting the bytes in the message.

- To test programs that rely on the network, replace the network with a mock object that simulates message transmission and receipt.

Serving Web Pages

- The HyperText Transfer Protocol (HTTP) specifies one way to interact via messages over sockets.

- A minimal HTTP request has a method, a URL, and a protocol version.

- A complete HTTP request may also have headers and a body.

- An HTTP response has a status code, a status phrase, and optionally some headers and a body.

- HTTP is a stateless protocol: the application is responsible for remembering things between requests.

A File Viewer

- The curses module manages text terminals in a platform-independent way.

- Write debugging information to a log file when the screen is not available.

- We can use a callable object in place of a function to satisfy an API's requirements.

- Test programs using synthetic data.

- Using delayed construction and/or factory methods can make code easier to evolve.

- Refactor code before attempting to add new features.

- Separate the logic for managing data from the logic for displaying it.

Undo and Redo

- Replace user interface components with mock objects to simplify testing.

- Record actions and state to check behavior these mock objects.

- Use objects to represent actions to record history and enable undo.

- Recording state is easier but more expensive than recording changes.

A Virtual Machine

- Every computer has a processor with a particular instruction set, some registers, and memory.

- Instructions are just numbers but may be represented as assembly code.

- Instructions may refer to registers, memory, both, or neither.

- A processor usually executes instructions in order but may jump to another location based on whether a conditional is true or false.

A Debugger

- Interactive programs can be tested by simulating input and recording output.

- Testing interactive programs is easier if their inputs and outputs can easily be replaced with mock objects.

- Debuggers usually implement breakpoints by temporarily replacing actual instructions with special ones.

- Using lookup tables for function or method dispatch makes programs easier to extend.

D

License

All of the written material is made available under the Creative Commons - Attribution - Non-Commercial 4.0 International license (CC-BY-NC-4.0), while the software is made available under the Hippocratic License.

D.1 Writing

This is a human-readable summary of (and not a substitute for) the license. For the full legal text of this license, please see https://creativecommons.org/licenses/by-nc/4.0/legalcode.

All of this site is made available under the terms of the Creative Commons Attribution - NonCommercial 4.0 license. You are free to:

- **Share** — copy and redistribute the material in any medium or format

- **Adapt** — remix, transform, and build upon the material

- The licensor cannot revoke these freedoms as long as you follow the license terms.

Under the following terms:

- **Attribution** — You must give appropriate credit, provide a link to the license, and indicate if changes were made. You may do so in any reasonable manner, but not in any way that suggests the licensor endorses you or your use.

- **NonCommercial** — You may not use the material for commercial purposes.

- **No additional restrictions** — You may not apply legal terms or technological measures that legally restrict others from doing anything the license permits.

Notices:

You do not have to comply with the license for elements of the material in the public domain or where your use is permitted by an applicable exception or limitation.

No warranties are given. The license may not give you all of the permissions necessary for your intended use. For example, other rights such as publicity, privacy, or moral rights may limit how you use the material.

D.2 Software

Licensor hereby grants permission by this license ("License"), free of charge, to any person or entity (the "Licensee") obtaining a copy of this software and associated documentation files (the "Software"), to deal in the Software without restriction, including without limitation the rights to use, copy, modify, merge, publish, distribute, sublicense, and/or sell copies of the Software, and to permit persons to whom the Software is furnished to do so, subject to the following conditions:

- The above copyright notice and this License or a subsequent version published on the Hippocratic License Website[1] shall be included in all copies or substantial portions of the Software. Licensee has the option of following the terms and conditions either of the above numbered version of this License or of any subsequent version published on the Hippocratic License Website.

- Compliance with Human Rights Laws and Human Rights Principles:

  1. Human Rights Laws. The Software shall not be used by any person or entity for any systems, activities, or other uses that violate any applicable laws, regulations, or rules that protect human, civil, labor, privacy, political, environmental, security, economic, due process, or similar rights (the "Human Rights Laws"). Where the Human Rights Laws of more than one jurisdiction are applicable to the use of the Software, the Human Rights Laws that are most protective of the individuals or groups harmed shall apply.

  2. Human Rights Principles. Licensee is advised to consult the articles of the United Nations Universal Declaration of Human Rights[2] and the United Nations Global Compact[3] that define recognized principles of international human rights (the "Human Rights Principles"). It is Licensor's express intent that all use of the Software be consistent with Human Rights Principles. If Licensor receives notification or otherwise learns of an alleged violation of any Human Rights Principles relating to Licensee's use of the Software, Licensor may in its discretion and without obligation (i) (a) notify Licensee of such allegation and (b) allow Licensee 90 days from notification under (i)(a) to investigate and respond to Licensor regarding the allegation and (ii) (a) after the earlier of 90 days from notification under (i)(a), or Licensee's response under (i)(b), notify Licensee of License termination and (b) allow Licensee an additional 90 days from notification under (ii)(a) to cease use of the Software.

  3. Indemnity. Licensee shall hold harmless and indemnify Licensor against all losses, damages, liabilities, deficiencies, claims, actions, judgments, settlements, interest, awards, penalties, fines, costs, or expenses of whatever kind, including Licensor's reasonable attorneys' fees, arising out of or relating to Licensee's non-compliance with this License or use of the Software in violation of Human Rights Laws or Human Rights Principles.

- Enforceability: If any portion or provision of this License is determined to be invalid, illegal, or unenforceable by a court of competent jurisdiction, then such invalidity, illegality, or unenforceability shall not affect any other term or provision of this License or invalidate or render unenforceable such term or provision in any other jurisdiction. Upon a determination that any term or provision is invalid, illegal, or unenforceable, to the extent permitted by applicable law, the court may modify this License to affect the original intent of the parties as closely as possible. The section headings are for convenience only and are not intended to affect the construction or interpretation of this License. Any rule of construction to the effect that ambiguities are to be resolved against the drafting party shall not apply in interpreting this License. The language in this License shall be interpreted as to its fair meaning and not strictly for or against any party.

---

[1] https://firstdonoharm.dev/
[2] https://www.un.org/en/universal-declaration-human-rights/
[3] https://www.unglobalcompact.org/what-is-gc/mission/principles

   THE SOFTWARE IS PROVIDED "AS IS", WITHOUT WARRANTY OF ANY KIND, EX-
PRESS OR IMPLIED, INCLUDING BUT NOT LIMITED TO THE WARRANTIES OF MER-
CHANTABILITY, FITNESS FOR A PARTICULAR PURPOSE AND NONINFRINGEMENT.
IN NO EVENT SHALL THE AUTHORS OR COPYRIGHT HOLDERS BE LIABLE FOR ANY
CLAIM, DAMAGES OR OTHER LIABILITY, WHETHER IN AN ACTION OF CONTRACT,
TORT OR OTHERWISE, ARISING FROM, OUT OF OR IN CONNECTION WITH THE
SOFTWARE OR THE USE OR OTHER DEALINGS IN THE SOFTWARE.

   The Hippocratic License is an Ethical Source license[4].

---

[4]https://ethicalsource.dev

E

Code of Conduct

In the interest of fostering an open and welcoming environment, we as contributors and maintainers pledge to making participation in our project and our community a harassment-free experience for everyone, regardless of age, body size, disability, ethnicity, gender identity and expression, level of experience, education, socioeconomic status, nationality, personal appearance, race, religion, or sexual identity and orientation.

E.1 Our Standards

Examples of behavior that contributes to creating a positive environment include:

- using welcoming and inclusive language,

- being respectful of differing viewpoints and experiences,

- gracefully accepting constructive criticism,

- focusing on what is best for the community, and

- showing empathy towards other community members.

  Examples of unacceptable behavior by participants include:

- the use of sexualized language or imagery and unwelcome sexual attention or advances,

- trolling, insulting/derogatory comments, and personal or political attacks,

- public or private harassment,

- publishing others' private information, such as a physical or electronic address, without explicit permission, and

- other conduct which could reasonably be considered inappropriate in a professional setting

E.2 Our Responsibilities

Project maintainers are responsible for clarifying the standards of acceptable behavior and are expected to take appropriate and fair corrective action in response to any instances of unacceptable behavior.

Project maintainers have the right and responsibility to remove, edit, or reject comments, commits, code, wiki edits, issues, and other contributions that are not aligned to this Code of Conduct, or to ban temporarily or permanently any contributor for other behaviors that they deem inappropriate, threatening, offensive, or harmful.

E.3 Scope

This Code of Conduct applies both within project spaces and in public spaces when an individual is representing the project or its community. Examples of representing a project or community include using an official project email address, posting via an official social media account, or acting as an appointed representative at an online or offline event. Representation of a project may be further defined and clarified by project maintainers.

E.4 Enforcement

Instances of abusive, harassing, or otherwise unacceptable behavior may be reported by emailing the project team. All complaints will be reviewed and investigated and will result in a response that is deemed necessary and appropriate to the circumstances. The project team is obligated to maintain confidentiality with regard to the reporter of an incident. Further details of specific enforcement policies may be posted separately.

Project maintainers who do not follow or enforce the Code of Conduct in good faith may face temporary or permanent repercussions as determined by other members of the project's leadership.

E.5 Attribution

This Code of Conduct is adapted from the Contributor Covenant[1] version 1.4.

---

[1] https://www.contributor-covenant.org/

F

Contributing

Contributions are very welcome; please contact us by email or by filing an issue on this site. All contributors must abide by our Code of Conduct.

F.1 Editing Content

1. Clone the GitHub repository at https://github.com/gvwilson/sdxpy[1].

2. Create a new Python virtual environment.

3. `pip install -r lib/mccole/requirements.txt`.

4. `pip install -r ./requirements.txt`.

5. `make` will show a list of available commands.

6. `make build` to regenerate HTML from Markdown.

   - The generated HTML can be found in `./docs`.
   - You must have draw.io[2] installed and on your path to regenerate diagrams.

7. `make serve` to regenerate HTML and preview it locally.

   - The preview appears at `http://localhost:4000/`.
   - Ark[3] will regenerate the HTML as the Markdown files are edited and saved.

8. To change a code example and its output:

   1. `cd ./src/chapter`.
   2. Edit the Python file(s) you wish to change.
   3. Run `make` in the chapter directory to rebuild the corresponding output files.

Please see `CONTRIBUTING.md` in the root directory of our GitHub repository[4] for a complete description of our formatting rules.

---

[1] https://github.com/gvwilson/sdxpy
[2] https://app.diagrams.net/
[3] https://www.dmulholl.com/docs/ark/main/
[4] https://github.com/gvwilson/sdxpy/

F.2   Making Decisions

This project uses Martha's Rules[5] for consensus decision making:

1. Before each meeting, anyone who wishes may sponsor a proposal by filing an issue in the GitHub repository tagged "comm-proposal". People must file proposals at least 24 hours before a meeting in order for them to be considered at that meeting, and they must include:

   - a one-line summary (the subject line of the issue)
   - the full text of the proposal
   - any required background information
   - pros and cons
   - possible alternatives

2. A quorum is established in a meeting if half or more of voting members are present.

3. Once a person has sponsored a proposal, they are responsible for it. The group may not discuss or vote on the issue unless the sponsor or their delegate is present. The sponsor is also responsible for presenting the item to the group.

4. After the sponsor presents the proposal, a "sense" vote is cast for the proposal before any discussion:

   - Who likes the proposal?
   - Who can live with the proposal?
   - Who is uncomfortable with the proposal?

5. If everyone likes or can live with the proposal, it passes immediately.

6. If most of the group is uncomfortable with the proposal, it is postponed for further rework by the sponsor.

7. Otherwise, members who are uncomfortable can briefly state their objections. A timer is then set for a brief discussion moderated by the facilitator. After 10 minutes or when no one has anything further to add (whichever comes first), the facilitator calls for a yes-or-no vote on the question: "Should we implement this decision over the stated objections?" If a majority votes "yes", the proposal is implemented. Otherwise, the proposal is returned to the sponsor for further work.

F.3   FAQ

Why is this book free to read online?

Because only a tiny minority of technical books make enough money to pay back the time required to create them, and because I would rather be able to fix errata than have people pirating out-of-date PDFs.

---

[5]https://journals.sagepub.com/doi/10.1177/088610998600100206

Why are the royalties going to charity?

The Red Door Family Shelter[6] and places like it have always been short of money and resources, and the COVID-19 pandemic only made matters worse. They do more good on the average Tuesday than most of us do in a year (or a lifetime); I'm glad to be able to help however I can.

What sort of feedback would be useful?

Everything is welcome, but what would help most is:

1. Fixes for mistakes in the code, the descriptions, or the formatting. All of the examples run and all of the tests pass, but that doesn't guarantee they're correct.

2. Reports of continuity errors, e.g., places where a concept is used before it is explained.

3. Suggestions for new diagrams, or for ways to improve existing ones.

4. New or clearer summary points for each chapter's syllabus.

5. More or better exercises. "This is too hard" or "this is unclear" helps as well.

Why don't the examples connect with each other?

It was tempting, but attempts to do this in the past have not gone well. First, it makes maintenance much more difficult because a change in an early chapter may have knock-on effects on several subsequent chapters. Second, it constrains what is taught and in what order: if the examples are independent of each other, instructors can pick and choose the pieces that are most relevant to their audience and goals.

How did you settle on these particular topics?

I started with a list of tools programmers use that can be implemented in the small (like version control systems and debuggers). I added a few things that programmers rely on (like page layout and object persistence), then went back and filled in gaps, which is why there are chapters on functions and closures, protocols, and binary data.

Will there be a sequel?

If enough people want to write chapters I would be happy to organize and edit a second volume. Some things I'd particularly like to see are:

- An object-relational mapper to show people how tools like SQLAlchemy[7] work.

- A discrete event simulator to show people how tools like SimPy[8] work.

- An issue-tracking system, mostly to show how workflow management and authentication work.

- Another build system that uses publish/subscribe instead of the top-down approach of Chapter 19.

---

[6]https://www.reddoorshelter.ca/
[7]https://www.sqlalchemy.org/
[8]https://simpy.readthedocs.io/

- A fuzz tester that uses some of the ideas from [Zeller2023].

- A package installer to complement the package manager of Chapter 20.

- A file compression tool like `zip`.

- A database that uses B-trees instead of a log for storage.

Why did you build your own production pipeline?

I've written or edited books with GitBook[9], Quarto[10], Jupyter Book[11], and other tools like them, and found them more frustrating than helpful. For example, the code samples in this book often show one or two methods from a class rather than the whole class; there is no straightforward way to achieve that with tools built on computational notebooks. That said, I'm sure the authors of those systems would find this book's tooling just as frustrating as I find theirs.

---

[9]https://www.gitbook.com/
[10]https://quarto.org/
[11]https://jupyterbook.org/

G

Glossary

absolute error: The absolute value of the difference between the observed and the correct value. Absolute error is usually less useful than **relative error**.

abstract base class: An **abstract class** from which the **class** in question is derived.

abstract class: A class that defines or requires methods it does not implement. An abstract class typically specifies the methods that **child classes** must have without providing default implementations.
See also: **concrete class**.

abstract method: In **object-oriented programming**, a **method** that is defined but not implemented. Programmers will define an abstract method in a **parent class** to specify operations that **child classes** must provide.

abstract syntax tree (AST): A deeply nested data structure, or **tree**, that represents the structure of a program. For example, the AST might have a **node** representing a while loop with one **child** representing the loop condition and another representing the loop body.

accidental complexity: The extra difficulty added to a problem because of poor notation, poor tooling, an unclear problem statement, distractions, etc. The term is used in contrast with **intrinsic complexity**.

accumulator: A variable that collects and/or combines many values. For example, if a program sums the values in an array by adding them all to a variable called result, then result is the accumulator.

actual result (of test): The value generated by running code in a test. If this matches the **expected result**, the test **passes**; if the two are different, the test **fails**.

affordance: An action that a thing can do: for example, a door can be opened or a document can be printed. Good user interfaces make affordances easy to discover.

alias: A second or subsequent reference to the same object. Aliases are useful, but increase the cognitive load on readers who have to remember that all these names refer to the same thing.

anonymous function: A function without a name. Languages like JavaScript make frequent use of anonymous functions; Python provides a limited form called a **lambda expression**.

ANSI character encoding: An extension of **ASCII** that standardized the characters represented by the codes 128 to 255.

append mode: An option for writing to a file in which new data is appended to existing data rather than replacing it.

Application Binary Interface (ABI): The low-level layout that a piece of software must have to work on a particular kind of machine.
See also: **Application Programming Interface**.

Application Programming Interface (API): A set of functions provided by a software library or web service that other software can call.
See also: **Application Binary Interface**.

argument: A value passed into a function or method call.
See also: **parameter**.

ASCII character encoding: A standard way to represent the characters commonly used in the Western European languages as 7-bit integers, now largely superceded by **Unicode**.
See also: **ANSI character encoding**.

assembler: A **compiler** that translates software written in **assembly code** into machine instructions.
See also: **disassembler**.

assembly code: A low-level programming language whose statements correspond closely to the actual **instruction set** of a particular kind of processor.

assertion: A **Boolean expression** that must be true at a certain point in a program. Assertions may be built into the language or provided as functions.

atomic operation: An operation that is guaranteed to complete, i.e., one that cannot be interrupted part-way through.

atomic value: A value that cannot be broken down into smaller parts, such as a **Boolean** or integer.

attention budget: The amount of time your activity is allowed to require of other people in an organization.

attribute: A name-value pair associated with an object, used to store **metadata** about the object such as an array's dimensions.

backward-compatible: A property of a system that enables interoperability with an older legacy system, or with input designed for such a system.

base class: In **object-oriented programming**, a **class** from which other classes are derived.
See also: **child class, derived class, parent class**.

batch processing: Executing a set of non-interactive tasks on a computer, such as backing up files or copying data from one database to another overnight.

benchmark: A program or set of programs used to measure the performance of a computer system.

big endian: A storage scheme in which the most significant part of a number is stored in the byte with the lowest address. For example, the 16-bit big-endian representation of 258 stores 0x01 in the lower byte and 0x02 in the higher byte.
See also: **little endian**.

big-oh notation: A way to express how the running time or memory requirements of an algorithm increase as the size of the problem increases.
See also: **space complexity**, **time complexity**.

binary mode: An option for reading or writing files in which each byte is transferred literally. The term is used in contrast with **text mode**.

bit mask: A pattern of bits used to set or clear bits in a byte or **word** in memory.

bit shifting: To move the bits in a byte or **word** left or right.

bitwise operation: An operation that manipulates individual bits in memory. Common bit-wise operations include and, or, not, and xor.

block (of memory): A region of memory of a fixed, constant size. Data is often divided into blocks to optimize input and output at the hardware level; software is then used to convert between blocks and **streams**.

block (on page): A rectangular region of a page that may contain text, images, and other visual elements along with other blocks.

body (of HTTP request or response): The "extra" data associated with an **HTTP request** or **response**, such as the file being uploaded or the page being returned for display.

Boolean expression: An **expression** that is either true or false, i.e., one that produces a **Boolean value**.

Boolean value: One of the two values "true" or "false". Named for George Boole, a 19th century mathematician.

boxed value: A value (such as an integer) that is embedded in a larger structure in memory that carries **metadata** about its type, how many structures are referring to it, and so on.

breakpoint: A point in a program where a debugger should halt execution in order to inter-act with a user.

bucket: A subset of values from a dataset, typically represented by a single bar in a his-togram.

buffer (in memory): A temporary storage area in memory.

buffer (of text): A data structure that stores text while it is being viewed or edited.

build manager: A program that keeps track of how files depend on one another and runs commands to update any files that are out-of-date. Build managers were invented to **compile** only those parts of programs that had changed but are now often used to implement workflows in which plots depend on results files, which in turn depend on raw data files or configuration files.

build recipe: The part of a **build rule** that describes how to update something that has fallen out-of-date.

build rule: A specification for a **build manager** that describes how some files depend on others and what to do if those files are out-of-date.

bytecode: A set of instructions designed to be executed efficiently by an **interpreter**.

cache: Something that stores copies of data so that future requests for it can be satisfied more quickly. The CPU in a computer uses a hardware cache to hold recently-accessed values; many programs rely on a software cache to reduce network traffic and latency. Figuring out when something in a cache is out-of-date and should be replaced is one of the **two hard problems in computer science**.

call stack: A data structure that stores information about the active subroutines executed.

catch (an exception): To handle an error or other unexpected event represented by an **exception**.

Chain of Responsibility pattern: A **design pattern** in which each **object** either handles a request or passes it on to another object.

character encoding: A way to represent characters as bytes. Common examples include **ASCII** and **UTF-8**.

child (in a tree): A **node** in a **tree** that is below another node (call the **parent**).

child class: In **object-oriented programming**, a **class** derived from another class (called the **parent class**).

circular dependency: A situation in which a **build target** depends on itself either directly or indirectly, i.e., a situation in which the **DAG** of **dependencies** contains a **cycle**.

class: In **object-oriented programming**, a structure that combines data and operations (called **methods**). The program then uses a **constructor** to create an **object** with those properties and methods. Programmers generally put generic or reusable behavior in **parent classes**, and more detailed or specific behavior in **child classes**.

class method: A function defined inside a class that takes the class object as an input rather than an instance of the class.
See also: **static method**.

clear (a breakpoint): To remove a **breakpoint** from a program.

client: A program such as a browser that sends requests to a server and does something with the response.

closing tag: The textual marker showing the end of an **element** in an HTML document, written `</tag>`.

closure: A record that stores a function and its **environment** so that variables that were in scope when the function was defined can still be accessed from within the function even if they are no longer visible to other parts of the program.

code point: A number that uniquely identifies a character in the **Unicode** standard.

cognitive load: The mental effort required to solve a problem.

collision (in hashing): A situation in which two or more values have the same **hash code**.

column-wise storage: To organize the memory of a two-dimensional table so that the values in each column are laid out in contiguous blocks.
See also: **row-wise storage**.

combinatorial explosion: The exponential growth in the size of a problem or the time required to solve it that arises when all possible combinations of a set of items must be searched.

Command pattern: A **design pattern** in which operations are represented as objects so that they can be stored and re-used.

compact (data or files): To pack data so as to remove wasted or unused space.

compile: To translate textual source into another form. Programs in **compiled languages** are translated into machine instructions for a computer to run, and **Markdown** is usually translated into **HTML** for display.

compiled language: Originally, a language such as C or Fortran that is translated into machine instructions for execution. Languages such as Java are also compiled before execution, but into **bytecode** instead of machine instructions, while **interpreted languages** like JavaScript are compiled to byte code on the fly.

compiler: An application that translates programs written in some languages into machine instructions or **bytecode**.

compression (of file): Any of several techniques for reducing the size required to store a file. Compression works by finding patterns and replacing them with shorter sequences of bits or bytes.

concrete class: A class that can actually be instantiated. The term is used in contrast with **abstract class**.

conditional breakpoint: A **breakpoint** at which the debugger should only halt if some user-specified condition is true.

conditional jump: An instruction that tells a processor to start executing somewhere other than at the next address if a condition is true. Conditional jumps are used to implement higher-level constructs like `if` statements and loops.

confirmation bias: The tendency for someone to look for evidence that they are right rather than searching for reasons why they might be wrong.

constructor: A function that creates an **object** of a particular **class**.

context manager: An object that automatically executes some operations at the start of a code block and some other operations at the end of the block.

continuation byte: The second or subsequent byte in a multi-byte **character encoding**.

control code: Originally a "character" that made a teletype perform some operation, such as moving to the next line or ringing the bell. Only a handful of control codes such as tab and newline are still in common use.

control flow: The order in which a program executes statements and expressions.

Coordinated Universal Time (UTC): The standard time against which all others are defined. UTC is the time at longitude 0° and is not adjusted for daylight savings. **Timestamps** are often reported in UTC so that they will be the same no matter what timezone the computer is in.

cross product: The set of all possible combinations of items from one or more sets.

cryptographic hash function: A **hash function** that produces an apparently-random value for any input.

CSV (comma-separated values): A text format for tabular data in which each **record** is one row and **fields** are separated by commas. There are many minor variations, particularly around quoting of **strings**.

cycle: A path through a **directed graph** that leads from a **node** back to itself.

data engineer: Someone responsible for designing, developing, and maintaining systems for collecting, storing, and analyzing data.

data migration: The act of moving data from one system or format to another.

dataframe: A two-dimensional data structure for storing tabular data in memory. Rows represent **records** and columns represent **fields**.

deadlock: A situation in which no one can proceed because everyone is blocked on someone else.

debugger: A program that enables its user to monitor and control another program, typically by **single-stepping** through its execution or setting **breakpoints**.

decorator: A function A that can be applied to another function B when function B is being defined to change its behavior in some way.

defensive programming: A set of programming practices that assumes mistakes will happen and either reports or corrects them, such as inserting **assertions** to report situations that are not ever supposed to occur.

delayed construction: The practice of constructing an object after something that needs it has been constructed rather than before.
See also: **lazy evaluation**.

dependency (in build): Something that a **build target** depends on.

derived class: In **object-oriented programming**, a class that is a direct or indirect extension of a **base class**.
See also: **child class**.

design by contract: A style of designing software in which functions specify the **pre-conditions** that must be true in order for them to run and the **post-conditions** they guarantee will be true when they return. A function can then be replaced by one with weaker pre-conditions (i.e., it accepts a wider set of input) and/or stronger post-conditions (i.e., it produces a smaller range of output) without breaking anything else.
See also: **Liskov Substitution Principle**.

design pattern: A recurring pattern in software design that is specific enough to be worth naming, but not so specific that a single best implementation can be provided by a **library**.
See also: **Iterator pattern**, **Singleton pattern**, **Template Method pattern**, **Visitor pattern**.

dictionary: A data structure that allows items to be looked up by value. Dictionaries are often implemented using **hash tables**.

dictionary comprehension: A single expression that constructs a dictionary by looping over key-value pairs.
See also: **list comprehension**.

directed acyclic graph (DAG): A **directed graph** which does not contain any **cycles** (i.e., it is not possible to reach a **node** from itself by following edges).

directed graph: A **graph** whose **edges** have directions.

disassemble: To convert machine instructions into **assembly code** or some higher-level language.

disassembler: A program that translates machine instructions into **assembly code** or some higher-level language.
See also: **assembler**.

docstring: A string at the start of a module, class, or function in Python that is not assigned to a variable, which is used to hold the documentation for that part of code.

DOM (DOM): A standard, in-memory representation of **HTML** and **XML**. Each **element** is stored as a **node** in a **DOM tree** with a set of named **attributes**; contained elements are **child nodes**.

DOM tree: The **tree** formed by a set of properly-nested **DOM nodes**.

Domain Name System (DNS): A decentralized naming system for computers that translates **hostnames** into the **IP address** of particular computers.

dry run: An execution of a program that doesn't change anything.

duck typing: A programming style in which the methods an object happens to have determines how it can be used, rather than what classes it inherits from.

dynamic dispatch: To find a function or a property of an **object** by name while a program is running. For example, instead of getting a specific property of an object using `obj.name`, a program might use `obj[someVariable]`, where `someVariable` could hold `"name"` or some other property name.

dynamic scoping: To find the value of a variable by looking at what is on the **call stack** at the moment the lookup is done. Almost all programming languages use **lexical scoping** instead, since it is more predictable.

dynamic typing: A system in which types are checked as the program is running. See also: **static typing**, **type hint**.

eager evaluation: Evaluating expressions before they are used. See also: **lazy evaluation**.

easy mode: A term borrowed from gaming meaning to do something with obstacles or difficulties simplified or removed, often for practice purposes.

edge: A connection between two **nodes** in a **graph**. An edge may have data associated with it, such as a name or distance.

element (in HTML): A named component in an **HTML** or **XML** document. Elements are usually written `<name>...</name>`, where "..." represents the content of the element. Elements often have **attributes**.

enumeration: A set of distinct named values defined in a program.

environment: The set of variables currently defined in a program.

error (result of test): Signalled when something goes wrong in a **unit test** itself rather than in the system being tested. In this case, we do not know anything about the correctness of the system.

error handling: What a program does to detect and correct for errors. Examples include printing a message and using a default configuration if the user-specified configuration cannot be found.

escape sequence: A series of two or more characters used to represent a character that otherwise couldn't be represented. For example, the escape sequence \" is used to represent a single " character inside a double-quoted string.

exception: An object that stores information about an error or other unusual event in a program. One part of a program will create and **raise an exception** to signal that something unexpected has happened; another part will **catch** it.

exclusive or: A logical (or bitwise) operator that is true (or 1) if its arguments have different values and false (or 0) if they are the same. Exclusive or implements "either/or" or "one or the other".

expected result (of test): The value that a piece of software is supposed to produce when tested in a certain way, or the state in which it is supposed to leave the system.

exponent: The portion of a floating-point number that controls placement of the decimal point.
See also: **mantissa**.

expression: A part of a program that produces a value, such as 1+2.
See also: **statement**.

extensibility: How easily new features can be added to a program or existing features can be changed.

Extract Parent Class refactoring: A **refactoring** in which some functionality of an existing class or set of classes is moved into a newly-created **parent class**.

factory method: A **method** whose only job is to construct an object of some type. Factory methods are typically created to make it easier for **child classes** to construct objects of other types.

failure (result of test): A test fails if the **actual result** does not match the **expected result**.

false negative: A report that something is missing when it is actually present.
See also: **false positive**.

false positive: A report that something is present when it is actually absent.
See also: **false negative**.

falsy: Refers to a value that is treated as false in Boolean expressions. In Python, this includes empty strings and lists and the number zero.
See also: **truthy**.

field: A component of a **record** containing a single value. Every record in a database **table** has the same fields.

file locking: The act of restricting updates to a file, or its deletion, so that operations on it appear **atomic**.

fixture: The thing on which a test is run, such as the **parameters** to the function being tested or the file being processed.

format string: A string that contains special markers showing how to format values. For example, the string `"{age:02d} years old"` specifies that the value of `age` is to be inserted at the front of the string and formatted as a 2-digit decimal number with a leading 0 (if necessary).

garbage collection: An automatic process in a program that finds and recycles memory that is no longer being used.

generic function: A collection of functions with similar purpose, each operating on a different class of data.

global: Referring to the top or outermost **scope** a program.
See also: **local**.

globbing: Matching filenames against patterns. The name comes from an early Unix utility called `glob` (short for "global"). Glob patterns are a subset of **regular expressions**.
See also: **regular expression**.

grammar: The rules that define a formal language recognized by a **parser**.

graph (data structure): A data structure in which **nodes** are connected to one another by **edges**.
See also: **tree**.

greedy matching: Matching as much as possible while still finding a valid match.
See also: **lazy matching**.

hash code: A value generated by a **hash function**. Good hash codes have the same properties as random numbers in order to reduce the frequency of **collisions**.

hash function: A function that turns arbitrary data into a bit array, or a **key**, of a fixed size. Hash functions are used to determine where data should be stored in a **hash table**.

hash table: A data structure that calculates a pseudo-random key (location) for each value passed to it and stores the value in that location. Hash tables enable fast lookup for arbitrary data. This occurs at the cost of extra memory because hash tables must always be larger than the amount of information they need to store, to avoid the possibility of data collisions, when the hash function returns the same key for two different values.

header (of HTTP request or response): A name-value pair at the start of an **HTTP request** or **response**. Headers are used to specify what data formats the sender can handle, the date and time the message was sent, and so on.

headless application: An application run without its usual graphical interface. Browsers, editors, and other applications are often run headless for testing purposes.

helper class: A **class** created to support another class that has no other purpose on its own.

helper function: A function created to support another function (or functions) that has no other use on its own.

helper method: A **method** designed to be used only by other methods in the same **class**. Helper methods are usually created to keep other methods short and readable.

heterogeneous: Containing mixed data types. For example, an array in Javascript can contain a mix of numbers, character strings, and values of other types.
See also: **homogeneous**.

hexadecimal: A base-16 numerical representation that uses the letters A-F (or a-f) to represent the values from 10 to 15.

homogeneous: Containing a single data type. For example, a **vector** must be homogeneous: its values must all be numeric, logical, etc.
See also: **heterogeneous**.

hostname: The human-readable name for a networked computer, such as `example.com`.

HTML (HyperText Markup Language): The standard **markup language** used for web pages. HTML is represented in memory using **DOM** (Digital Object Model).
See also: **XML**.

HTTP (HyperText Transfer Protocol): The protocol used to exchange information between browsers and websites, and more generally between other clients and servers. Communication consists of **requests** and **responses**.

HTTP method: The verb in an **HTTP request** that defines what the **client** wants to do. Common methods are `GET` (to get data) and `POST` (to submit data).

HTTP protocol version: Specifies the version of **HTTP** being used, which in turn defines what headers can appear, how they are to be interpreted, etc.

HTTP request: A precisely-formatted block of text sent from a **client** such as a browser to a **server** that specifies what resource is being requested, what data formats the client will accept, etc.

HTTP response: A precisely-formatted block of text sent from a **server** back to a **client** in reply to a **request**.

HTTP status code: A numerical code that indicates what happened when an **HTTP request** was processed, such as 200 (OK), 404 (not found), or 500 (internal server error).

immutable: Data that cannot be changed after being created. Immutable data is easier to think about, particularly if data structures are shared between several tasks, but may result in higher memory requirements.

index (a database): An auxiliary data structure in a database used to speed up search for some entries. An index increases memory and disk requirements but reduces search time.

infinite loop: A loop (usually a `while` loop) that never ends because its controlling condition is never false.
See also: **infinite recursion**.

infinite recursion: **Recursion** that never stops because it never reaches a case that doesn't require further evaluation; the recursive equivalent of an **infinite loop**.

infix notation: Writing expressions with operators between operands, as in `1 + 2` to add 1 and 2.
See also: **prefix notation, postfix notation**.

inheritance: The act of creating a new **class** from an existing class, typically by adding or changing its properties or **methods**.
See also: **multiple inheritance**.

instance: An **object** of a particular **class**.

instruction pointer: A special **register** in a processor that stores the address of the next instruction to execute.

instruction set: The basic operations that a particular processor can execute directly.

Internet Protocol (IP): A set of specifications for ways computers can communicate. **TCP/IP** is the most widely used.

interpreted language: A high-level language that is not executed directly by the computer, but instead is run by an **interpreter** that translates program instructions into machine commands on the fly.

interpreter: A program that runs programs written in a high-level **interpreted language**. Interpreters can run interactively but may also execute commands saved in a file.

intrinsic complexity: The inherent difficult of a problem. The term is used in contrast to **accidental complexity**.

introspection: See **reflection**.

IP address (IP): A four-part number that uniquely identifies a computer on a network.

ISO date format: An international standard for formatting dates. While the full standard is complex, the most common form is `YYYY-MM-DD`, i.e., a four-digit year, a two-digit month, and a two-digit day, separated by hyphens.

iterator: A function or object that produces each value from a collection in turn for processing.

Iterator pattern: A **design pattern** that uses **iterators** to hide the differences between different kinds of data structures so that everything can be processed using loops.
See also: **Visitor pattern**.

join (tables): An operation that combines two **tables**, typically by matching **keys** from one with keys from another.

JSON (JavaScript Object Notation): A way to represent data by combining basic values like numbers and character strings in **lists** and **key-value** structures. The acronym stands for "JavaScript Object Notation"; unlike better-defined standards like **XML**, it is unencumbered by a syntax for comments or ways to define a **schema**.

key: A **field** or combination of fields whose value(s) uniquely identify a **record** within a **table** or dataset. Keys are often used to select specific records and in **joins**.

key-value store: A simple form of database in which each **record** can only be accessed by a single **key**.

label (of address in memory): A human-readable name given to a particular location in memory when writing programs in **assembly code**.

lambda expression: An expression that takes zero or more parameters and produces a result. A lambda expression is sometimes called an **anonymous function**; the name comes from the mathematical symbol λ used to represent such expressions.

layout engine: A piece of software that decides where to place text, images, and other elements on a page.

lazy evaluation: Evaluating expressions only when absolutely necessary.
See also: **eager evaluation**.

lazy matching: Matching as little as possible while still finding a valid match.
See also: **greedy matching**.

lexical scoping: To look up the value associated with a name according to the textual structure of a program. Most programming languages use lexical scoping instead of **dynamic scoping** because the latter is less predictable.

library: An installable collection of software, also often called a **module** or **package**.

link (a program): To combine separately **compiled** modules into a single runnable program.

linter: A program that checks for common problems in software, such as violations of indentation rules or variable naming conventions. The name comes from the first tool of its kind, called `lint`.

Liskov Substitution Principle: A design rule stating that it should be possible to replace objects in a program with objects of derived classes without breaking the program. **Design by contract** is intended to enforce this rule.

list: A **vector** that can contain values of many different (**heterogeneous**) types.

list comprehension: A single expression that constructs a list by looping over its items.

literal (in parsing): A representation of a fixed value in a program, such as the digits 123 for the number 123 or the characters "abc" for the string containing those three letters.

little endian: A storage scheme in which the most significant part of a number is stored in the byte with the highest address. For example, the 16-bit big-endian representation of 258 stores 0x02 in the lower byte and 0x01 in the higher byte.
See also: **big endian**.

local: Referring to the current or innermost **scope** in a program.
See also: **global**.

log file: A file to which a program writes status or debugging information for later analysis.

log-structured database: A database to which data can only be appended, i.e., existing records cannot be overwritten.

manifest: A list of something's parts or components.

mantissa: The portion of a floating-point number that defines its specific value.
See also: **exponent**.

Markdown: A **markup language** with a simple syntax intended as a replacement for **HTML**.

markup language: A set of rules for annotating text to define its meaning or how it should be displayed. The markup is usually not displayed, but instead controls how the underlying text is interpreted or shown. **Markdown** and **HTML** are widely-used markup languages for web pages.
See also: **XML**.

metadata: Data about data, such as the time a dataset was archived.

method: An implementation of a **generic function** that handles objects of a specific class.

method injection: To add methods to an existing class after its definition.

mixin class: A class that is not meant to be instantiated itself but which contains methods to be added to other classes (typically via **multiple inheritance**).

mock object: A simplified replacement for part of a program whose behavior is easy to control and predict. Mock objects are used in **unit tests** to simulate databases, web services, and other complex systems.

model: A set of values for variables that satisfies a specific set of constraints.

module: A reusable software **package**, also often called a **library**.

monkey patching: To replace **methods** in a **class** or **object** at run-time without modifying the original code.

multiple inheritance: Inheriting from two or more classes when creating a new class.

name collision: A situation in which two or more things are trying to use the same name at the same time or in the same **scope**.

node: An element of a **graph** that is connected to other nodes by **edges**. Nodes typically have data associated with them, such as names or weights.

null byte: A byte with the value zero. Null bytes are used to mark the ends of strings in C and C++, and are sometimes used to fill unused space in fixed-size binary records.

Null Object pattern: A **design pattern** in which a placeholder object is used instead of None. The placeholder object has the methods of the object usually used, but those methods do nothing. This pattern saves other code from having to check repeatedly for None.

object: In **object-oriented programming**, a structure that contains the data for a specific instance of a **class**. The operations the object is capable of are defined by the class's **methods**.

object-oriented programming (OOP): A style of programming in which functions and data are bound together in **objects** that only interact with each other through well-defined interfaces.

off-by-one error: A common error in programming in which the program refers to element i of a structure when it should refer to element i-1 or i+1, or processes N elements when it should process N-1 or N+1.

online analytical processing (OLAP): Analyzing data in bulk. The term is used in contrast to **OLTP**.

online transaction processing (OLTP): Adding records to a database or querying individual records. The term is used in contrast to **OLAP**.

op code: The numerical operation code for an instruction that a processor can execute.

Open-Closed Principle: A design rule stating that software should be open for extension but closed for modification, i.e., it should be possible to extend functionality without having to rewrite existing code.

opening tag: The textual marker showing the start of an **element** in an HTML document, written <tag>. An opening tag may contain **attributes**.

operator overloading: Defining or redefining the implementation of built-in operators like +.

package: A collection of code, data, and documentation that can be distributed and reused. Also referred to in some languages as a **library** or **module**.

page: A fixed-size block of storage space. Most modern filesystems manage disks using 4K pages, and many other applications such as databases use the same page size to maximize efficiency.

parameter: The name that a function gives to one of the values passed to it when it is called.
See also: **argument**.

parameter sweeping: To execute a program multiple times with different parameters to find out how its behavior or performance depends on those parameters.

parent (in a tree): A **node** in a **tree** that is above another node (called a **child**). Every node in a tree except the **root node** has a single parent.

parent class: In **object-oriented programming**, the **class** from which a subclass (called the **child class**) is derived.

parser: A function or program that reads text formatted according to some **grammar** and converts it to a data structure in memory. Every programming language has a parser that reads programs written in that language; parsers also exist for various data formats.

pass (result of test): A test passes if the **actual result** matches the **expected result**.

patch: A single file containing a set of changes to a set of files, separated by markers that indicate where each individual change should be applied, or the **semantic versioning** identifier for such a file.

path resolution: The process of converting the filename portion of a **URL** into a specific file on disk.

persistence: The act of saving and restoring data, particularly **heterogeneous** data with irregular structure.

phony target: A **build recipe** that doesn't update any files. Phony targets are typically used to make tasks such as running tests reproducible.

pipe (in the Unix shell): The | used to make the output of one command the input of the next.

polymorphism: Having many different implementations of the same interface. If a set of functions or objects are polymorphic, they can be called interchangeably.

port: A logical endpoint for communication, like a phone number in an office building. Only one program on a computer may use a particular port on that computer at any time.

post-condition: Something that is guaranteed to be true after a function runs successfully. Post-conditions are often expressed as **assertions** that are guaranteed to be true of a function's results.
See also: **design by contract**, **pre-condition**.

postfix notation: Writing expressions with the operator after the operand, as in 2 3 + to add 2 and 3.
See also: **infix notation**, **prefix notation**.

pre-condition: Something that must be true before a function runs in order for it to work correctly. Pre-conditions are often expressed as **assertions** that must be true of a function's inputs in order for it to run successfully.
See also: **design by contract, post-condition**.

prefix notation: Writing expressions with the operator in front of the operand, as in + 3 4 to add 3 and 4.
See also: **infix notation, postfix notation**.

prerequisite: Something that a **build target** depends on.
See also: **dependency (in build)**.

pretty print: To format textual output in a way that makes it easier to read.

profiler: A tool that measures one or more aspects of a program's performance.

profiling: The act of measuring where a program spends its time, which operations consume memory or disk space, etc.
See also: **profiler**.

protocol: A set of rules that something promises to obey, i.e., the contract between that thing and its users.

Pythonic: Conforming to common Python programming style and practices.

query parameter: A key-value pair appended to the path portion of a **URL**.

race condition: A situation in which a result depends on the order in which two or more concurrent operations are carried out.

raise (an exception): To signal that something unexpected or unusual has happened in a program by creating an **exception** and handing it to the **error-handling** system, which then tries to find a point in the program that will **catch** it.
See also: **throw exception**.

record: A group of related values that are stored together. A record may be represented as a **tuple** or as a row in a **table**; in the latter case, every record in the table has the same **fields**.

recursion: To define something in terms of itself, or the act of a function invoking itself (directly or indirectly).

Recursive Enumeration pattern: A **design pattern** that generates the **cross product** of a set of items using recursive function calls. Each level of recursion adds items from one more set of possibilities to an **accumulator**.

refactor: To rewrite existing code in order to make it simpler or more efficient without changing its functionality.

reflection: To inspect the properties of a running program in a generic way. Reflection relies on the fact that a program is just another data structure.

register (in code): To add a function, class, or other object to a lookup table for later use.

register (in hardware): A small piece of memory (typically one **word** long) built into a processor that operations can refer to directly.

regular expression: A pattern for matching text, written as text itself. Regular expressions are sometimes called "regexp", "regex", or "RE", and are powerful tools for working with text.

relational database: A database that organizes information into **tables**, each of which has a fixed set of named **fields** (shown as columns) and a variable number of **records** (shown as rows).
See also: **SQL**.

relative error: The absolute value of the difference between the actual and correct value divided by the correct value. For example, if the actual value is 9 and the correct value is 10, the relative error is 0.1. Relative error is usually more useful than **absolute error**.

reverse lookup: To find the key associated with a particular value in a table.

root (in a tree): The **node** in a **tree** of which all other nodes are direct or indirect **children**, or equivalently the only node in the tree that has no **parent**.

row-wise storage: To organize the memory of a two-dimensional table so that the values in each row are laid out in contiguous blocks.
See also: **column-wise storage**.

runtime: A program that implements the basic operations used in a programming language.

sandbox: A space where code can execute safely.

schema: A specification of the format of a dataset, including the name, format, and content of each **table**.

scope: A region of a program in which names can be defined without colliding with definitions in other parts of the program. In Python, each **module** and function creates a new scope.

scoring function: A function that measures how good a solution to a problem is.

search space: The set of all possible solutions to a problem, i.e., the set of possibilities that an algorithm must search through to find an answer.

self-closing tag: A textual marker representing an **element** in an HTML document that has no content, written `<tag/>`. A self-closing tag may contain **attributes**.

semantic versioning: A standard for identifying software releases. In the version identifier `major.minor.patch`, `major` changes when a new version of software is incompatible with old versions, `minor` changes when new features are added to an existing version, and `patch` changes when small bugs are fixed.

server: A program that waits for requests from **clients** and sends them data in response.

SHA-256 (hash function): A **cryptographic hash function** that produces a 256-bit output.

sign and magnitude: A binary representation of integers in which one bit indicates whether the value is positive or negative and the remaining bits indicate its magnitude.
See also: **two's complement**.

signature: The ordered list of parameters and return values that specifies how a function must be called and what it returns.

single stepping: To step through a program one line or instruction at a time.

singleton: A set with only one element, or a **class** with only one **instance**.
See also: **Singleton pattern**.

Singleton pattern: A **design pattern** that creates a **singleton object** to manage some resource or service, such as a database or **cache**. In **object-oriented programming**, the pattern is usually implemented by hiding the **constructor** of the **class** in some way so that it can only be called once.

socket: A communication channel between two computers that provides an interface similar to reading and writing files.

space complexity: The way the memory required by an algorithm grows as a function of the problem size, usually expressed using **big-oh notation**.
See also: **time complexity**.

spread: To automatically match the values from a list or dictionary supplied by the caller to the parameters of a function.

SQL: The language used for writing queries for a **relational database**. The term was originally an acronym for Structured Query Language.

stable sort: A sorting algorithm that preserves the original order of items that are considered equal.

stack frame: A section of the **call stack** that records details of a single call to a specific function.

stale (in build): To be out-of-date compared to a **prerequisite**. A **build manager** finds and updates things that are stale.

standard error: A predefined communication channel typically used to report errors.
See also: **standard input, standard output**.

standard input: A predefined communication channel typically used to read input from the keyboard or from the previous process in a **pipe**.
See also: **standard error, standard output**.

standard output: A predefined communication channel typically used to send output to the screen or to the next process in a **pipe**.
See also: **standard error, standard input**.

statement: A part of a program that doesn't produce a value. `for` loops and `if` statements are statements in Python.
See also: **expression**.

static method: A function that is defined within a class but does not require either the class itself or an instance of the class as a parameter.
See also: **class method**.

static site generator (SSG): A software tool that creates HTML pages from templates and content.

static typing: A system in which the types of values are checked as code is being **compiled**.
See also: **dynamic typing, type hint**.

stream: A sequence of bytes or other data of variable length that can only be processed in sequential order.

streaming API: An **API** that processes data in chunks rather than needing to have all of it in memory at once. Streaming APIs usually require handlers for events such as "start of data", "next block", and "end of data".

string: A block of text in a program. The term is short for "character string".

successive refinement: See **top-down design**.

synthetic data: Made-up data that has the same significant characteristics as real data, typically created for testing.

table: A set of **records** in a **relational database** or **dataframe**.

tag (in HTML): The textual marker showing the start and/or end of an **element** in an HTML document.
See also: **closing tag, opening tag, self-closing tag**.

target (in build): The file(s) that a **build rule** will update if they are out-of-date compared to their **dependencies**.

technical debt: The work that will be required in the future because of limited quick-fix solutions or unaddressed complexity today.

Template Method pattern: A **design pattern** in which a **parent class** defines an overall sequence of operations by calling **abstract methods** that **child classes** must then implement. Each child class then behaves in the same general way, but implements the steps differently.

test fidelity: The degree to which a **mock object** or other replacement for part or all of a system mimics the behavior of that system for testing purposes.

test-driven development: The practice of writing tests before writing the code to be tested. Research shows that the order doesn't actually make a difference; what does is alternating in short bursts between testing and coding.

text mode: An option for reading or writing files in which bytes are translated to or from characters and end-of-line markers are normalized. The term is used in contrast with **binary mode**.

throw exception: Another term for **raising** an exception.

throw low, catch high: A widely-used pattern for managing **exceptions** whereby they are **raised** in many places at low levels of a program but **caught** in a few high-level places where corrective action can be taken.

time complexity: The way the running time of an algorithm grows as a function of the problem size, usually expressed using **big-oh notation**.
See also: **space complexity**.

time of check - time of use: A **race condition** in which a process checks the state of something and then operates on it, but some other process might alter that state between the check and the operation.

timestamp: A digital identifier showing the time at which something was created or accessed. Timestamps should use **ISO date format** for portability.

token: An indivisible unit of text for a parser, such as a variable name or a number. Exactly what constitutes a token depends on the language.

tokenizer: A piece of software that groups individual characters together into meaningful **tokens**.

top-down design: In software design, the practice of writing the more abstract or higher-level parts of the program first, then filling in the details layer by layer. In practice, programmers almost always modify the upper levels as they work on the lower levels, but high-level changes become less common as more of the details are filled in.
See also: **successive refinement**.

topological order: Any ordering of the **nodes** in a **graph** that respects the direction of its **edges**, i.e., if there is an edge from node A to node B, A comes before B in the ordering. There may be many topological orderings of a particular graph.

Transmission Control Protocol (TCP/IP): The most popular member of the **IP** family of protocols. TCP/IP tries to deliver messages reliably and in order so that programs can communicate as if they were reading and writing files.

tree: A **graph** in which every node except the **root** has exactly one **parent**.

truthy: Refers to a value that is treated as true in Boolean expressions. In Python, this includes non-empty strings and lists and numbers other than zero.
See also: **falsy**.

tuple: A value that has a fixed number of parts, such as the three color components of a red-green-blue color specification.

two hard problems in computer science: Refers to a quote by Phil Karlton: "There are only two hard problems in computer science—cache invalidation and naming things." Many variations add a third problem as a joke, such as **off-by-one errors**.

two's complement: A binary representation of integers that "rolls over" like an odometer to represent negative values.
See also: **sign and magnitude**.

type hint: Extra information added to a program to indicate what data type or types a variable is supposed to have. Type hints are a compromise between **static typing** and **dynamic typing**.

Unicode: A standard that defines numeric codes for many thousands of characters and symbols. Unicode does not define how those numbers are stored; that is done by standards like **UTF-8**.

unit test: A test that exercises one function or feature of a piece of software and produces **pass**, **fail**, or **error**.

Universal Resource Locator (URL): A multi-part identifier that specifies something on a computer network. A URL may contain a protocol (such as `http`), a **hostname** such as `example.com`, a **port** (such as 80), a path (such as `/homepage.html`), and various other things.

upcall: The act of explicitly invoking a method of a **parent class** from inside a **child class**. A method in a child class may upcall to the corresponding method in the parent class as part of extending that method.

UTF-32: A way to store the numeric codes representing **Unicode** characters in which every character is stored as a 32-bit integer.

UTF-8: A way to store the numeric codes representing **Unicode** characters that is **backward-compatible** with the older **ASCII** standard.

varargs: Short for "variable arguments", a mechanism that captures any "extra" arguments to a function or method.

variable capture: The process by which a **closure** "remembers" the variables that were in scope when it was created.

variable-length encoding: Any technique for representing data in which a single logical unit of data may be represented by a variable number of bits or bytes.

vector: A sequence of values, usually of **homogeneous** type.

version control system: A system for managing changes made to software during its development.

viewport: A **class** or other data structure whose purpose is to keep track of what can currently be seen by the user.

virtual machine: A program that pretends to be a computer. This may seem a bit redundant, but VMs are quick to create and start up, and changes made inside the virtual machine are contained within that VM so we can install new **packages** or run a completely different operating system without affecting the underlying computer.

Visitor pattern: A **design pattern** in which the operation to be done is taken to each element of a data structure in turn. It is usually implemented by having a generator "visitor" that knows how to reach the structure's elements, which is given a function or method to call for each in turn, and that carries out the specific operation.
See also: **Iterator pattern**.

watchpoint: A location or variable being monitored by a debugger. If the value at that location or in that variable changes, the debugger halts and gives the user a chance to inspect the program.

word (of memory): The unit of memory that a particular processor most naturally works with. While a byte is a fixed size (8 bits), a word may be 16, 32, or 64 bits long depending on the processor.

XML (Extensible Markup Language): A set of rules for defining **HTML**-like tags and using them to format documents (typically data). XML was popular in the early 2000s, but its complexity led many programmers to adopt **JSON**, instead.

YAML (YAML Ain't Markup Language): A way to represent nested data using indentation rather than the parentheses and commas of **JSON**. YAML is often used in configuration files and to define **parameters** for various flavors of **Markdown** documents.

z-buffering: A drawing method that keeps track of the depth of what lies "under" each pixel so that it displays whatever is nearest to the observer.

Index

absolute error, 282
abstract base class, 233, 237
abstract class, 99, 102, 104, 131
abstract method, 99, 102
abstract syntax tree, 35, 36, 111
accidental complexity, 119, 127
accumulator, 187, 191
actual result (of test), 43, 44
affordance, 177, 183, 226
alias, 7, 8, 150
anonymous function, 59, 60, 221
ANSI character encoding, 155, 157
append mode, 69, 79
Application Binary Interface, 243
Application Programming Interface, 99, 101
argument, 7, 11, 60, 70, 112
array (implementation of), 250
ASCII character encoding, 155, 157
assembler, 243, 247
assembly code, 243, 265
assertion, 43, 44
atomic operation, 81, 85
atomic value, 145, 146
attention budget, 271
attribute, 91, 99, 129

backward-compatible, 187, 188
base class, 81, 86, 133, 280
batch processing, 131, 137
benchmark, 131, 137
big endian, 283
big-oh notation, 17, 189
binary mode, 17, 18, 159, 214
bit mask, 155, 157
bit shifting, 155, 157
bitwise operation, 155, 156, 245
block, 72
block (of memory), 165, 171, 243
block (on page), 119
body (of HTTP request or response), 209, 210

Boolean expression, 99, 107
Boolean value, 187, 195
boxed value, 155, 159
Brand, Sy, 255
breakpoint, 255, 261
Brubeck, Matt, 119
bucket, 17, 20
buffer (in memory), 155, 162, 204
buffer (of text), 219, 226, 233
build manager, 177
build recipe, 177
build rule, 177, 178
bytecode, 243, 244

C, 178
cache, 7, 16, 121
call stack, 59, 61
Chain of Responsibility pattern, 25, 26
character encoding, 155, 157, 214
child, 120
child (in a tree), 91, 92
child class, 25, 30, 39, 87, 102, 183, 237, 263
circular dependency, 177, 180, 185, 199
class, 1, 7, 94, 145
class method, 7, 15
clear (a breakpoint), 255, 261
client, 201, 209
closing tag, 91, 107
closure, 59, 63, 73
code point, 155, 158
cognitive load, 1, 2, 8, 173
collision (in hashing), 17, 22, 82
column-wise storage, 131, 132
combinatorial explosion, 187, 189
Command pattern, 233, 237
compact (data or files), 165, 175
compiled language, 177, 178
compiler, 51, 247
Comprehensive TeX Archive Network, 187
compression (of file), 81, 87

Printed in the United States
by Baker & Taylor Publisher Services